Contents

KT-441-397

Plan of book

	Content Areas	Listening Skills	Grammar/ Vocabulary
Before you begin: Getting ready to listen and learn	Listening-preparation strategies	Identifying speakers' purposes Identifying previously known information	
Unit 1: What do you say first?	First impressions and conversation strategies	Identifying strategies for introductions Planning introduction routines	Introductory routines
Unit 2: Sights and sounds	Talking about sensory information	Inferring topics Following instructions	Imperatives Sense words
Unit 3: Pirates and such	Talking about historical events	Identifying incorrect information Identifying locations Understanding numbers	Past tenses: simple past and past progressive *Must* for strong possibility Large numbers
Unit 4: Dating	Talking about dating customs	Identifying reasons Understanding details Identifying opinions	Adverbs of frequency Past tenses: simple past and past progressive Descriptive adjectives
Unit 5: A broad view of health	Alternative health techniques	Making connections Identifying steps in a process	Imperatives Real conditionals Parts of the body and physical/medical problems
Unit 6: Advertising	Talking about advertising	Understanding details Understanding mistakes and problems	Passive *Should have*
Unit 7: Superstitions	Describing beliefs	Understanding specific information Understanding and adding to statements	Possible and unreal conditionals
Unit 8: Communication and culture	Discussing cultural behavior	Understanding cultural differences Understanding cultural information	*Should, must,* and *have to* for advice Simple past
Unit 9: People's best friends	Talking about cats and dogs	Making, confirming, and revising predictions Identifying reasons Understanding and enjoying stories	Past tenses: simple past and past perfect
Unit 10: Mind your manners!	Giving opinions about types of behavior	Inferring feelings Identifying examples and reasons	Present tenses: simple present and present progressive

MARC HELGESEN·STEVEN BROWN·DOROLYN SMITH

Active Listening

EXPANDING

Understanding Through Content

WITHDRAWN

Teacher's Edition 3

To our students, for making the project – and teaching – worthwhile,
To our colleagues, for their many helpful insights, and
To our families, especially Masumi, Kent, Renee, Peter, and Louise, for all their support.

PUBLISHED BY THE PRESS SYNDICATE OF THE UNIVERSITY OF CAMBRIDGE
The Pitt Building, Trumpington Street, Cambridge CB2 1RP, United Kingdom

CAMBRIDGE UNIVERSITY PRESS
The Edinburgh Building, Cambridge CB2 2RU, United Kingdom
40 West 20th Street, New York, NY 10011–4211, USA
10 Stamford Road, Oakleigh, Melbourne 3166, Australia

© Cambridge University Press 1997

First published 1997

Printed in the United States of America

Typeset in Gill Sans and New Baskerville

Library of Congress Cataloging-in-Publication Data

Helgesen, Marc.
Active listening : expanding understanding through content:
student's book 3 / Marc Helgesen and Steven Brown and Dorolyn Smith.
p.   cm.
ISBN 0-521-39883-5
1. Listening – Study and teaching.   2. Listening – Problems,
exercises, etc.   3. Active learning.   I. Brown, Steven.
II. Smith, Dorolyn.   III. Title.
LB1065.H44   1996
370.15'23 – dc20   96-38841
                                                      CIP

A catalogue record for this book is available from the British Library

ISBN 0 521 39886 X   Teacher's Edition
ISBN 0 521 39883 5   Student's Book
ISBN 0 521 39889 4   Cassettes

Book design: Six West Design
Art direction, layout, and design services: Anna Veltfort and Don Williams
Illustrators: Adventure House, Lloyd P. Birmingham, Edgar Blakeney, Blaine J. Graboyes, Susan Ferris Jones,
         Randy Jones, Patricia Ossowski, Janet Pietrobono, Anna Veltfort, and Sam Viviano
Photo research: Sylvia P. Bloch

	Content Areas	Listening Skills	Grammar/ Vocabulary
Unit 11: **Tales from the past**	Appreciating stories	Understanding and imagining a story Understanding details and questions	Past tenses: simple past and past progressive Question forms
Unit 12: **Decisions, decisions**	Deciding on schools and living situations	Understanding details Identifying key information Understanding reasons	*Wh-*questions
Unit 13: **Your type of personality**	Talking about personality types	Inferring personality characteristics Understanding and appreciating a cartoon Following instructions	Habitual present Imperatives Descriptive adjectives
Unit 14: **You've got to have art.**	Discussing examples of fine art	Following instructions Identifying supporting details	Imperatives Present tenses: simple present and present progressive
Unit 15: **I wonder how that works.**	Talking about how machines work	Identifying steps in processes	Simple present Sequence markers
Unit 16: **A matter of values**	Debating and explaining difficult decisions	Understanding and evaluating opinions Identifying problems and reasons	Future with *will* and *going to* Transition words for contrast
Unit 17: **Food for thought**	Explaining food trends and customs	Understanding topics Interpreting charts and graphs Identifying places Recognizing details	Simple present Food and health words
Unit 18: **We mean business.**	Talking about successful people and companies	Listening for specific information Understanding main ideas	Simple present Simple past Possible and unreal conditionals
Unit 19: **Everything we know is wrong.**	Explaining and challenging "common knowledge"	Understanding and evaluating information Following instructions Giving opinions	Comparative and superlative of adjectives
Unit 20: **Poetry**	Appreciating and creating poetry	Identifying poetry types Creating a poem/song	Verb + present participle Literary terms

Authors' acknowledgments

We would like to thank our **reviewers** for their helpful suggestions on *Active Listening: Expanding Understanding Through Content:* Julia Burks, Leann Howard, Chuck Sandy, Eric Strickland, and Peter Sturman.

We would like to acknowledge the **students** and **teachers** in the following schools and institutes who piloted components of the *Active Listening* series:

Alianza Cultural Uruguay-Estados Unidos, Montevideo, Uruguay; **Bae Centre,** Buenos Aires, Argentina; **Bunka Institute of Foreign Languages,** Tokyo, Japan; **Central Washington University,** Washington, USA; **Chin-Yi Institute of Technology,** Taichung City, Taiwan; **Drexel University,** Philadelphia, Pennsylvania, USA; **Educational Options,** Santa Clara, California, USA; **Fairmont State College,** Fairmont, West Virginia, USA; **Fu Jen University,** Taipei, Taiwan; **Gunma Prefectural Women's University,** Japan; **Impact English,** Santiago, Chile; **Instituto Cultural de Idiomas Ltda.,** Caxias do Sul, Brazil; **Kansai University of Foreign Studies,** Osaka, Japan; **Koyo Shoji Co. Ltd.,** Hitachi, Japan; **Kyoto YMCA (Central Branch),** Kyoto, Japan; **Miyagi Gakuin Women's College,** Sendai, Japan; **Miyagi Gakuin High School,** Sendai, Japan; **National Yunlin Polytechnic Institute,** Yunlin, Taiwan; **Osaka Institute of Technology,** Osaka, Japan; **Queen Alexandra Senior School,** Toronto, Canada; **Sendai YMCA English School,** Sendai, Japan; **Southern Illinois University,** Niigata, Japan; **Suzugamine Women's College,** Hiroshima City, Japan; **Technos International Academy,** Tokyo, Japan; **Tokyo Air Travel School,** Tokyo, Japan; **Tokyo Foreign Language College,** Tokyo, Japan; **Umeda Business College,** Osaka, Japan; **University of Iowa,** Iowa City, Iowa, USA; **University of Michigan English Language Institute,** Ann Arbor, Michigan, USA; **University of Pittsburgh English Language Institute,** Pittsburgh, Pennsylania, USA; **University of South Carolina,** Columbia, South Carolina, USA; **Wen Tzao Ursuline Junior College of Modern Languages,** Taiwan; **Youngstown State University,** Youngstown, Ohio, USA.

For their help on *Active Listening: Expanding Understanding Through Content*, thanks also go to Mei Hey Chang, Gerald Couzens, Betsy Davis, Marion Delarche, Carl Dusthimer, Yoko Futami, David Gilbey, Robin Guenzel, Yoko Hakuta, Brenda Hayashi, Patricia Hunt, Sean Lewis, Michael McLaughlin, Susanne McLaughlin, Lalitha Manuel, Lionel Menasche, Lisa Minetti, Hiroyuki Miyawaki, Christine O'Neill, Ruth Owen, Susan Ryan, John Smith, Serena Spenser, Noriko Suzuki, Kazue Takahashi, Brian Tomlinson, Paul Wadden, and Michiko Wako.

Many thanks to the following people at Cambridge University Press: Suzette André, Colin Bethell, Sylvia P. Bloch, Mary Carson, Riitta da Costa, Kyoko Fukunaga, Lisa Hutchins, Jinsook Kim, Stephanie Karras, Thares Keeree, Yuko Kidokoro, J.R. Kim, Gareth Knight, Emily Kuo, Koen Van Landeghem, Kathy Niemczyk, Molly Pike Riccardi, Helen Sandiford, Kumiko Sekioka, Mary Vaughn, and Janaka Williams.

Also, a special thanks to Karen Davy for countless hours and insights.

Finally, special thanks to our editor, Deborah Goldblatt, who has given direction to the entire *Active Listening* series. Thank you for the ideas, the challenges, and especially, thank you for listening.

Students' introduction

Welcome to *Active Listening: Expanding Understanding Through Content,* Student's Book 3. We hope this book will help you learn to listen to English more effectively. You'll practice listening to English. At the same time, you'll learn "how to listen." That is, you'll learn to make use of the English you already know. You'll also think about your reasons for listening. When you do that, listening and understanding become much easier. As you use the book, you'll be focusing on content. That means that instead of learning about English, you'll be learning information *in* English.

This book has twenty units. Each unit has five parts:

- **Warming Up** Warming Up activities will help you remember what you know about the unit topic. These activities are important. They help you get ready for listening.
- **Listening Task 1** You'll listen to people in many different situations. Sometimes you'll listen for specific information. Other times, you'll have to use what you hear to figure out things that aren't said directly.
- **Culture Corner** This is a short reading. It gives information about the unit topic.
- **Listening Task 2** Listening Task 2 is on the same theme as Listening Task 1, but it's a little more challenging.
- **Your Turn to Talk** This is a speaking activity. You'll use the language you have just heard. You'll do this task in pairs or small groups.

Listening tips

- Think about the reason you're listening. Ask yourself, "What do I need to know? What do I need to do?" You'll listen to many kinds of language and do many kinds of tasks. You'll need to listen in different ways. Each listening task in this book has a box at the top of the page. The box tells you the purpose of the activity. It reminds you of what you are listening for.
- The tapes that go with the book are very natural. You won't be able to understand every word you hear. That's OK. You don't need to. Listen for the general meaning.
- Don't worry about words you don't know. Many students look up every new word in their dictionaries. Here's an idea: When you hear a new word, just listen. When you hear it a second time, try to guess the meaning. When you hear it a third time and still don't understand, then look it up in your dictionary.

We hope you enjoy using this book and that you learn to be a better, more active listener.

Teacher's introduction

Active Listening: Expanding Understanding Through Content is a course for intermediate to high-intermediate students of North American English. As the name implies, the course recognizes that listening is a very active process. Learners bring knowledge to the class and perform a wide variety of interactive tasks. Throughout the book, the learners focus on content – often unusual information – rather than on language itself. *Active Listening* can be used as the main text for listening classes or as a supplement in speaking or integrated skills classes.

ABOUT THE BOOK

The book includes twenty units, each with a warming-up activity; two main listening tasks; Culture Corner, a reading passage that presents information related to the unit theme; and Your Turn to Talk, a short speaking activity done in pairs or small groups. In addition, there is an introductory unit called "Before You Begin." This unit introduces learning strategies and the idea of making use of previous knowledge.

The units can be taught in the order presented or out of sequence to follow the themes of the class or another book it is supplementing. In general, the tasks in the second half of the book are more challenging than those in the first.

Unit organization

Each unit begins with an activity called **Warming Up**. This activity, usually done in pairs, serves to remind learners of the language they already know. The tasks are designed to activate prior knowledge, or "schemata." In the process of doing the warm-up activity, students work from their knowledge and, at the same time, use vocabulary and structures that are connected with a particular function or grammar point. The exercise makes the listening tasks that it precedes easier because the learners are prepared.

Listening Task 1 and **Listening Task 2** are the major listening exercises. The tasks are balanced to include a variety of listening types and tasks. The purpose of each task is identified in a box in the top-right corner of each page. Because *Active Listening* features a task-based approach, learners should be doing the activities as they listen, rather than waiting until they have finished listening to a particular segment. To make this easier, writing is kept to a minimum. In most cases, students check boxes, number items, or write only words or short phrases.

Culture Corner is a short reading passage on the theme of the unit. In most cases, you'll want to use it as homework or as a break in classroom routine. Each Culture Corner ends with one or two discussion questions.

Your Turn to Talk, the final section of each unit, is a short, fluency-oriented speaking task done in pairs or small groups. In general, corrections are not appropriate during these activities. However, you may want to note common mistakes and, at the end of the period, write them on the board. Encourage learners to correct themselves.

Hints and techniques

■ Be sure to do the Warming Up section for each unit. This preview can foster a very healthy learning strategy. It teaches the students "how to listen." Also, it makes students more successful, which, in turn, motivates and encourages them.

■ In general, you'll only want to play a particular segment one or two times. If the learners are still having difficulty, try telling them the answers. Then play the tape again and let them experience understanding what they heard.

■ If some students find listening very difficult, have them do the task in pairs, helping each other as necessary. The Teacher's Edition contains additional ideas.

■ Some students may not be used to active learning. Those learners may be confused by instructions since they are used to a more passive role. Explaining activities is usually the least effective way to give instructions. It is better to demonstrate. For example, give the instructions as briefly as possible (e.g., "Listen. Number the pictures."). Then play the first part of the tape. Stop the tape and elicit the correct answer. Those students who weren't sure what to do will quickly understand. The same technique works for Warming Up and Your Turn to Talk. Lead one pair or group through the first step of the task and have the other learners watch. They will quickly see what they are supposed to do.

> *Active Listening: Expanding Understanding Through Content* is accompanied by a *Teacher's Edition* that contains a complete tapescript, step-by-step lesson plans, and expansion activities, as well as grammar and general notes.

FEATURES OF THE TEACHER'S EDITION

Each unit includes step-by-step lesson plans for Warming Up, Listening Task 1, Culture Corner, Listening Task 2, and Your Turn to Talk. You'll notice that the lesson plans include "how to say it" instructions printed in italics. These are provided to encourage teachers to use short, direct instructions in command form, since they are easiest for learners to understand. Most lessons also offer optional steps which may be included or left out, depending on the time available and the teacher's and learners' needs and interests.

In addition to detailed teaching procedures for each activity, every unit of the Teacher's Edition also includes Notes, Additional Support activities, a Strategy Exercise, and Optional (listening/speaking) Activities.

The **Notes** include cultural information. They define idiomatic usage and provide grammatical explanations where appropriate.

The **Additional Support** activities provide another chance to listen and another purpose for listening. They may be used with classes that have a difficult time with listening.

The **Strategy Exercise** is designed to help students become more aware of their own language-learning strategies and ways that they learn best. It will also make them aware that many different ways to learn exist. One important listening strategy is previewing to think about what one is likely to hear. In the Strategy Exercise in Unit 1 in this Teacher's Edition, students become aware of what they did in the Warming Up activity. This gives them a skill they can apply not only in class but anytime they listen in English. Strategies for learning a new language are not new. Good language learners have always used a variety of techniques to make progress. However, it is only recently that the field of English language teaching has begun to look at strategies in an organized way. Like any new aspect of teaching, strategies are promising, but they are not a magic key that will open any door.

We encourage you to look at the **Strategy Exercises** as you would any other language learning/awareness activity. Pick and choose. Select those you think would be of interest to your students. In general, encourage students to experiment with different ways to learn.

The **Optional Activities** are task-based listening/speaking activities that may be done anytime during or after the completion of a unit. They give students a chance to use the language they have been hearing. A unique feature of this Teacher's Edition is the inclusion of photocopiable **Activity Sheets** that are designed to be handed out to students. The activities appear on pages T41–T77. The activity instructions, marked EXPANSION , are included in their respective units.

HOW STUDENTS LEARN HOW TO LISTEN

Many students find listening to be one of the most difficult skills in English. The following explains some of the ideas incorporated into this book to make students more effective listeners. *Active Listening: Expanding Understanding Through Content* is designed to help students make real and rapid progress. Recent research into teaching listening and its related receptive skill, reading, has given insights into how successful students learn foreign/second languages.

Bottom-up vs. top-down processing, a brick-wall analogy*

To understand what our students are going through as they learn to listen or read, consider the "bottom-up vs. top-down processing" distinction. The distinction is based on the ways learners process and attempt to understand what they read or hear. With bottom-up processing, students start with the component parts: words, grammar, and the like. Top-down processing is the opposite. Students start from their background knowledge.

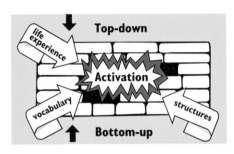

This might be better understood by means of a metaphor. Imagine a brick wall. If you're standing at the bottom looking at the wall brick by brick, you can easily see the details. It is difficult, however, to get an overall view of the wall. And, if you come to a missing brick (e.g., an unknown word or unfamiliar structure), you're stuck. If, on the other hand, you're sitting on the top of the wall, you can easily see the landscape. Of course, because of distance, you'll miss some details.

Students, particularly those with years of "classroom English" but little experience in really using the language, try to listen from the bottom up. They attempt to piece the meaning together, word by word. It is difficult for us, as native and advanced non-native English users, to experience what learners go through. However, try reading the following from right to left.

> ,now doing are you as ,time a at word one ,slowly English process you When
> very is it ,However .word individual each of meaning the catch to easy is it
> .passage the of meaning overall the understand to difficult

You were probably able to understand the paragraph:

> When you process English slowly, one word at a time, as you are doing now,
> it is easy to catch the meaning of each individual word. However, it is very
> difficult to understand the overall meaning of the passage.

While reading, however, it is likely that you felt the frustration of bottom-up processing; you had to get each individual part before you could make sense of it. This is similar to what our students experience – and they're having to wrestle with the meaning in a foreign language. Of course, this is an ineffective way to listen since it takes too long. While students are still trying to make sense of what has been said, the speaker keeps going. The students get lost.

The Warming Up activities in *Active Listening* help students integrate bottom-up and top-down

*Thanks to Brian Tomlinson for suggesting the brick-wall analogy to explain bottom-up/top-down processing. Our model for content-based instruction, while differing from one proposed by William Grabe, was influenced by his work.

processing by engaging them in active, meaningful prelistening tasks. In doing so, the learners "activate" their previous knowledge of the topic as well as relevant grammar and vocabulary.

What is content-based learning?

To a greater extent than the other books in the *Active Listening* series, *Expanding* teaches listening through content. This means that students learn information about the world as they are refining their listening skills. There are a number of reasons for intermediate and high-intermediate students to learn in this way. One is that many students at this level have clear ideas of how they want to use their English skills. Some are focused on academics, others on business or careers. Content instruction can provide topics and vocabulary valuable to these students. Also, students at this level have typically spent several years focused on learning the grammar and functions of English. A content focus, that is, "learning information through English," can be a useful and refreshing change of pace.

To be effective, content-based instruction needs to balance the language-learning needs of the students with data presented. To do so, the syllabus of this book is based on the *3-D A P* model: Diversity of tasks, Diversity of topics, Depth of learning, Activation and use of the learner's previous knowledge, and Progression of syllabus. The following introduces these elements. Examples from the *Active Listening: Expanding* Student's Book are indicated (in parentheses).

Diversity of tasks. Outside of the language classroom, learners need to listen in a variety of ways, depending on their purpose. At times, they need to listen for specific information (p. 13). In other cases, they need simply to catch the gist of a conversation (p. 17). At other times, students must infer meaning (p. 10), take notes (p. 25), follow instructions (p. 46), or give personal opinions/evaluations (p. 38). Instead of relying on a few activity types, the book is organized to include a wide range of tasks.

Diversity of topics. Very few educational programs have the luxury of being able to group students by interest. It is not possible to meet the specific content needs of all students in each unit. For that reason, we have attempted to provide a wide range of topics that are likely to interest most students. Even the most academically focused learner will, at times, need to use English outside of their majors or specialties. We have attempted to take different, even unusual, approaches to some topics to create interest. Some students may not be overly knowledgeable about or interested in, for example, science or art (Units 2 and 14) but are likely to be surprised by sensory afterimaging (p. 11) or surrealism (p. 47).

Depth of learning. Not only is there a great deal of information contained in the major listening tasks, but the units are structured so that learners receive or activate data about each topic several times. Each unit's Warming Up activity reminds learners of what they already know about the topic. The Culture Corner provides information about the topic as it relates to various places around the world. The Your Turn to Talk section expands the topic by asking the learners, in pairs or small groups, to speak about it, adding their own ideas. Additionally, the Teacher's Edition provides two related expansion activities for each unit. The above elements, combined with the major listening tasks, mean that each topic is dealt with at least seven times, each providing, activating, or generating new information and ideas.

Activation and use of the learner's previous knowledge. Learners come to class with a great deal of knowledge as well as natural curiosity to learn more. It's a mistake not to make specific use of that knowledge. The Warming Up tasks ask students to think about what they already know about the topic. Their answers come from their life-knowledge and are in the form of vocabulary and structures useful in discussing the topic (see the "top-down/bottom-up" metaphor above). Additionally, we often ask the learners to predict answers (p. 61) and to make evaluations (p. 44).

Progression of syllabus. It is not enough, of course, for the students to learn data about a topic. To achieve real student progress, there needs to be a flow from narrow activation/reception to more open, task-based outcomes:

activation	input	product
Schema activation (starting with known information and/or learner questions).	Input through listening tasks* with ascending difficulty. Included in identifying level of difficulty is (a) complexity of language in text, (b) task difficulty, and (c) how abstract/concrete the task is.	Goal (the completion of the listening tasks which lead to a production task such as Your Turn to Talk).

Our interest here is primarily in listening. However, it is important to recognize that skills don't exist in isolation. Input for a listening task might also include written information such as the instructions or the Culture Corner, spoken data, or small writing tasks.

These five elements – *3-D A P* – provide the foundation for the syllabus of this book and for effective task-based learning for the students. The combination teaches more than just the content itself. It uses the content to expand the learners' skills. They become active listeners.

LISTENING TRAINING TIPS

These are techniques you can use with your students so they become better listeners.

■ **Listen in pairs.** People usually think of listening as a solo skill – students do it alone even if they are in a room with lots of other learners. If a listening is challenging, try doing the task in pairs. Each pair uses only one book. That way, learners help each other by pointing out what they did understand rather than worrying about what they missed.

■ **Do something physical.** If a particular listening segment is very difficult, pick a specific item (colors, place names, dates, etc.) that occurs four to eight times. Students close their book. Play the tape. Students do a physical action, such as tapping their desks or raising their hands each time they hear the target item. The task is focused enough that most learners can accomplish it. The physical action gives immediate feedback/support to learners who missed it on the tape.

■ **Choose an appropriate level of support.** After students have heard a segment, check it as a group. Write the answers on the board. Then play the tape again. Learners choose their own level of support. Those who basically understood close their eyes and imagine the conversations. Those who understood some look at their books and try to hear the items mentioned. Those who found it quite challenging should watch you. As you play the tape, point to the information on the board just before it is mentioned.

■ **Listen a month later.** If your students found a particular segment very challenging, go back after a month or two and play it again. They will usually find it much easier than when they heard it the first time. It helps students see their own progress.

■ **Do not look at the tapescript.** Generally, don't give students the tapescript. It reinforces word and sentence level (bottom-up) processing and reinforces the myth that learners can't understand meaning without catching everything they hear.

Marc Helgesen
Steven Brown
Dorolyn Smith

Content references

Before you begin
Ellis, G. and Sinclair, B. 1989. *Learning to Learn English: A Course in Learner Training.* Cambridge University Press.
O'Malley, J. M. and Chamot, A. U. 1990. *Learning Strategies in Second Language Acquisition.* Cambridge University Press.

Unit 1
Wenden, A. and Rubin, J. (eds.). 1987. *Learner Strategies in Language Learning.* Prentice Hall.

Unit 2
Ackerman, D. 1990. *A Natural History of the Senses.* Vintage Books.
Flatow, I. 1988. *Rainbows, Curve Balls and Other Wonders of the Natural World Explained.* Harper & Row.

Unit 3
Cousteau, J-Y. and Doilé, P. 1971. *Diving for Sunken Treasure.* Doubleday.
Rieseberg, H. E. 1962. *Treasure of the Buccaneer Sea.* The Naylor Company.

Unit 4
Krantz, L. 1993. *America by the Numbers: Facts & Figures from the Weighty to the Way-Out.* Houghton Mifflin.
Stories based on personal interviews.

Unit 5
Shibata, M. 1995. *Ashi tsubo kenko hô.* Tokyo: Shufu to seikatsu-sha.

Unit 6
Blake, G. and Blake-Bohne, N. 1992. *Crafting the Perfect Name: The Art and Science of Naming a Company or Product.* Probus Publishing Co.
Ricks, D. 1983. *Big Business Blunders: Mistakes in Multinational Marketing.* Dow Jones-Irwin.

Unit 7
Opie, I. and Tatem, M. 1982. *A Dictionary of Superstitions.* Oxford University Press.
Choe Sang-su. 1983. *Annual Customs of Korea.* Seoul: Seomun-dang.
Harrison, P. 1983. *Behaving Brazilian.* Newbury House (HarperCollins).
Also, personal interviews and correspondence.

Unit 8
California Department of Education Staff. 1992. *Handbook for Teaching Korean-American Students.* California Department of Education.
Smith, D., Brown, S., and Kaylani, C. 1994. *Cross Cultural Communication* (a videotape on the interaction styles of three different cultures). University of Pittsburgh English Language Institute.
Also, personal interviews and correspondence.

Unit 9
Squire, A. 1988. *101 Questions and Answers About Pets and People.* Macmillan.

Unit 10
Wallenchinsky, D. and Wallace, A. 1993. *The Book of Lists – the 90's Edition.* Little, Brown.

Unit 11
Suzuki, D. T. 1959. *Zen and Japanese Culture.* Tokyo: Tuttle.

Unit 12
Information provided by the respective schools and based on the authors' experience there.

Unit 13
Saphir, A. Dec. 1994. "Ketsueki-gata: Japan's answer to 'What's your Sign?'" *Mangajin,* No. 41, 14–19, 50, 87.

Unit 14
Surrealism: Revolution by Night. 1993. Canberra: National Gallery of Australia.
Dali, S. and Halsman, P. (1954, 1982, 1994) *Dali's Mustache.* Paris: Flammarion.

Unit 15
Flatow, I. 1988. *Rainbows, Curve Balls and Other Wonders of the Natural World Explained.* Harper & Row.
Macaulay, D. 1988. *The Way Things Work.* Houghton Mifflin Company.

Unit 16
Boniface, P. and Fowler, P. 1993. *Heritage and Tourism in the Global Village.* London: Routledge.

Unit 17
Steenhuysen, J. "Consumers Overcome Their Food Guilt." *Advertising Age.* 5/2/94.
Levin, D. P. "Fat Times Are Over for Premium Ice Cream Makers." *The New York Times.* 7/31/94.
Michels, A. J. "Hot Sales for Mexican Sauces." *Fortune.* 10/7/91.
Schwabe, C. W. 1979. *Unmentionable Cuisine.* University Press of Virginia.

Unit 18
Walton, S. with Huey, J. 1992. *Sam Walton, Made in America: My Story.* Bantam.
Kroc, R. with Anderson, R. 1977. *Grinding It Out: The Making of McDonald's.* St. Martin's Press.
Bryson, B. 1994. *Made in America.* London: Minerva.
Crystal, D. (ed.). 1994. *Cambridge Biographical Encyclopedia.* Cambridge University Press.
Matthews, P. (ed.). 1995. *The Guinness Book of Records 1995.* Bantam.

Unit 19
Burnam, T. 1986. *The Dictionary of Misinformation.* Perennial.
Bishop, G. "Who's the most deadly?" *Ranger Rick.* 12/94.
Also, "scientific proofs" suggested by Augustana Flat Earth Society.

Unit 20
Kovacs, E. 1994. *Writing Across Cultures: A Handbook on Writing Poetry & Lyrical Prose.* Blue Heron Publishing, Inc.

Getting ready to listen and learn

From the People Who Wrote This Book

Dear students:

You've learned a lot of English so far. We hope this book will help you learn even more. We also hope that you enjoy learning it.

Before you begin, we would like to give you some hints about learning how to listen. First of all, it is important to think about your task. <u>Why</u> are you listening? What do you need to know?

Work with a partner.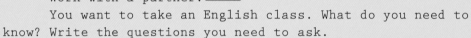
You want to take an English class. What do you need to know? Write the questions you need to ask.

☐ *What time are the classes?*

☐ *What kind of class is it?*

☐ *How many students are there?*   SAMPLE
                                      ANSWERS
☐ *Where are the classes?*

What is the most important question for you? Check (✔) it.

You also need to think about your knowledge. What do you already know? To help you answer this question, each of the units in this book begins with a Warming Up activity. This helps you think about the words and ideas you will hear. It makes listening and understanding easier.

We hope you will be <u>active</u> when you listen. Sometimes you will work in pairs or small groups. Help your partners. Listen to their ideas. When you don't understand something, ask your teacher or another student.

Good luck with learning English. You can do it!

Sincerely,

Marc Helgesen
Steven Brown
Dorolyn Smith

Getting ready to listen and learn

> **Content area:** Listening-preparation strategies, including identifying purpose and previous knowledge
> **Listening skills:** Identifying speakers' purposes (Listening Task 1); identifying previous knowledge and predicting (Listening Task 2)

Note: Throughout this *Teacher's Edition,* the symbol "T:" followed by *italic* type indicates the teacher's script.

From the people who wrote this book

1. Hold your book so that students can see page 2. T: *Look at page 2. This is a letter from the people who wrote this book. It will help you understand how to listen – and learn – more effectively. It suggests things to do before and while you listen.*

2. Read the letter (or play the tape) as the students read along silently.

3. Stop reading (or pause the tape) after the sentence: *Write the questions you need to ask.* Divide the class into pairs. Encourage students to write at least three more questions. Then read the next line: *What is the most important question for you? Check it.*

4. Have students work in pairs to compare questions or have students call out all their questions. Write the ideas on the board. (Sample answers appear in blue on the opposite page.) Point out that the questions are based on the listening task and students' own knowledge of the kind of information they need.

5. Read (or play) the rest of the letter.

6. (Optional) After students have read and listened to the letter, have them work in pairs to identify the most important ideas in the letter. (Answers:

• Think about your task. Why are you listening? What do you need to know?
• Think about your knowledge. What do you already know?
• Be active when you listen.
• Help your partners. Listen to their ideas.
• When you don't understand, ask.)

NOTES

• The idea of "learning how to listen" may be new to some students. Although practice is an important part of listening development, strategies such as those introduced in this book are also essential. As you go through this unit, allow time for students to think through the ideas and suggestions. Encourage learners to connect the ideas to real situations in which they listen to English.

• In the earlier levels of *Active Listening,* the Before You Begin unit focuses on types of listening, such as for specific information or gist and understanding inferences. While those remain essential, and activities to practice them all appear in this book, we find that students at this level already understand listening types (or perhaps the opposite is sadly true: students who don't understand listening in different ways for different purposes and continue to try to understand every word never make it to this level).

Strategy exercise

Each unit of this *Teacher's Edition* introduces a language-learning strategy designed to build students' awareness and control over their own learning. However, since the Before You Begin unit is entirely about listening strategies, an additional strategy is not recommended at this time.

The main strategies in this unit are (a) identification of the purpose of listening, (b) prediction, and (c) awareness of previous knowledge/information.

Listening Task 1
What do you need to know?

> **Listening skill:** Identifying speakers' purposes

Note: The tapescript for Before You Begin starts on page T1.

1. T: *Look at page 3.*

2. (Optional) Read the title: *"What do you need to know?"* Ask: *What do you think this will be about?* Elicit answers. (Answer: information speakers and listeners need)

3. Play the first set of instructions: *Work with a partner. Look at the ad. What questions might people ask about this apartment? Why? Write your answers.* Allow time for students to work.

4. (Optional) If your students will find this task very difficult, do the Additional Support procedure.

5. Check responses by having several pairs say their questions and reasons.

6. Play the instructions and the main task on the tape. Gesture for students to write their answers. **(Optional)** To make sure students understand what to do, stop after the first item and read the answers. Stop again after the second item. Ask two or three students: *What was the most important question? Why was it important?* (Answers: Where is the apartment? The caller wants a place near the university.) Then play the rest of Listening Task 1.

7. If necessary, play Listening Task 1 a second time.

8. Check by eliciting answers. Write them on the board. (Answers appear in blue on the opposite page.)

ADDITIONAL SUPPORT Students close their books. Play the main task on the tape. After each item, stop the tape and have students work in pairs to talk about what they heard and to write one or two words to indicate the main topic. Note that it is better to have the students decide among themselves rather than calling out answers because if they do, the fastest group will reveal the answers.

NOTE

• When you rent an apartment in the U.S., you are usually required to pay a deposit worth one-month's rent. This will be returned when you move out unless there is damage to the apartment. If there is some damage, the landlord will keep some of the deposit to pay for repairs. Pets, especially dogs, are usually not allowed in apartments. Some landlords will allow cats; most will allow fish and other small animals, such as hamsters and guinea pigs. Most landlords also require that you sign a lease, a contract (usually for one year) that says how much the rent is, when it is due, and what the responsibilities of the landlord and tenant are.

Optional activity

(For use anytime during or after the unit.)

• *Listening – what, how, and why?* In pairs or groups of three, students list all the types of listening they have already done today. For example, many woke up to an alarm clock; they may have had a conversation with a family member or roommate; they may have turned on the radio or TV; the ring of a toaster may have indicated breakfast was ready; and they may have heard bus or train announcements. After students have identified at least 15 items, have them talk about "how" and "why" they listened to each: carefully, to catch specific information; as background sound; or "in and out" (general listening, with periods of focused attention such as with news or weather reports). You may want to have students categorize their listening items to identify those that were similar. This activity helps students think about the different ways in which they listen.

What do you need to know?

We listen for different reasons.

Apartment for rent
Call 555-2938

❏ Work with a partner.
Look at the ad. What questions might people ask about this apartment?
Why? Write your answers.

SAMPLE
ANSWERS

How big is the apartment? (The family has 3 children.)
Where is the apartment? (The person wants to live downtown.)
How much is the rent? (The person doesn't have much money.)

❏ Listen. People are calling about the apartment.
What's the most important question for each person?
Why do you think it's important? Write your answers.

1. Are pets OK?
(She has a cat.)

2. Where is it?
(He wants to be close to
the university.)

3. How big is it?
(She needs 2 bedrooms.)

4. Can I share with a
roommate? (His brother
lives with him.)

5. When can I move in?
(She wants to move as
soon as possible.)

LISTENING TASK 2

What do you already know?

Before you listen, you need to think
about what you already know.

❑ Read the message below.

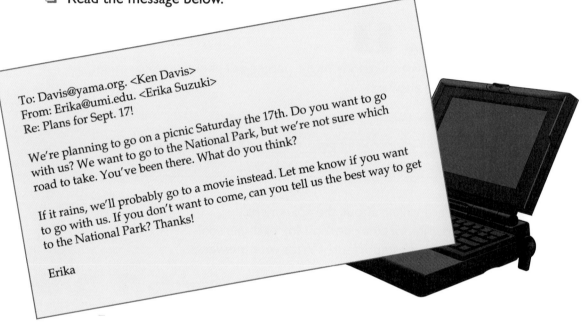

To: Davis@yama.org. <Ken Davis>
From: Erika@umi.edu. <Erika Suzuki>
Re: Plans for Sept. 17!

We're planning to go on a picnic Saturday the 17th. Do you want to go
with us? We want to go to the National Park, but we're not sure which
road to take. You've been there. What do you think?

If it rains, we'll probably go to a movie instead. Let me know if you want
to go with us. If you don't want to come, can you tell us the best way to get
to the National Park? Thanks!

Erika

❑ Look at these things. What do you think Ken will tell Erika?

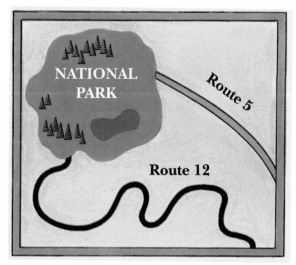

Listening Task 2
What do you already know?

Listening skills: Identifying previous knowledge, predicting

1. T: *Look at pages 4 and 5.*

2. (Optional) Read the title: *"What do you already know?"* Ask: *What do you think this will be about?* Elicit answers. (Answer: making use of previous knowledge)

3. Read or play the instructions: *Before you listen, you need to think about what you already know. Read the message below.* You may wish to read the message aloud as students follow along silently.

4. T: *Look at these things. What do you think Ken will tell Erika?* **Note:** You may want students to do this step in pairs.

5. (Optional) If your students find Step 4 very difficult, do the Additional Support procedure.

6. (Optional) Elicit answers from a few students.

7. T: *Now look at page 5. Ken is talking to Erika. Look at Erika's questions. If you know Ken's answers, check them.* **Note:** You may want students to do this step in pairs.

8. Check by reading each question and asking several students for their predictions. If students don't know an answer, they should say, "I don't know." **Note:** Students should know the answers to questions 2, 3, 4, and 5.

9. T: *Now listen. Check the answers you didn't know.*

10. Check by reading questions 1 and 6 and eliciting answers. (Answers appear in blue on Student's Book page 5.)

11. (Optional) You may want to play the tape again for students to confirm answers.

ADDITIONAL SUPPORT If learners have difficulty imagining what Ken will say to Erika, have them look at the map and the tickets. They should write at least two sentences about each. (*Examples:* Route 5 is straight. Route 12 is not straight. The tickets are for a concert by Cosmos. The concert is on September 17.)

NOTES

• This task helps students notice that they usually already know at least some information about topics they hear about. In most natural listening situations, we have background information. Even in a situation such as a classroom lesson on an unfamiliar topic, there are often illustrations in the book that provide information. Unfortunately, many students, when listening in a foreign language, focus only on the language without making use of the knowledge they possess, either from outside sources such as the book or from background information. To help students realize how much they do know, see the optional activity called *But I don't know anything about that!* on the next page.

• Some of the lesson plans in this *Teacher's Edition* start by suggesting that you read the title and ask, "What do you think this will be about?" This is not simply a way to start off the lesson. It is a technique to get students to notice titles, pictures, and topics and to think about what they already know as well as what they think they are about to hear. This is an important skill that learners should apply whenever they listen to English.

• We included the "teacher script" in the lesson plans in this manual for two reasons. First, we wanted to keep the instructions very short since it is easy to confuse learners with needlessly complex explanations. Second, all teachers, from time to time, get caught teaching a lesson with less preparation than they would like. We want you to be able to open the manual and teach the lesson immediately when necessary.

T

Listening Task 2 (cont.)

See page 4 for the procedure for the listening activities on this page.

Optional activities

(For use anytime during or after the unit.)

• *But I don't know anything about that!*
Students sometimes panic at new topics, thinking they know nothing about them. This activity points out that there really are very few topics that learners don't know at least a little about. Divide the class into groups of six. Each group then divides itself into three pairs of two students each. Tell students that you will call out a topic. Each pair thinks of as many things about it as they can in one minute. They write their ideas, but don't need to use full sentences. You may want to use two or three of the following as topics. The topics are in *italics* (possible information the students will write follows).

> *Norway* (northern Europe, skiing, Vikings, fishing)
> *Kangaroos* (Australia, brown or gray, jump high, strong tails, pouch [bag] for baby [joey])
> *Superheroes* (Superman, Batman, very strong, not real, comic books, movies)
> *Flamingos* (large, pink, beautiful, Florida, Africa, eat shrimp)

Once students notice that they actually do know something about these "not so common" topics, they play a game in their groups of six. One pair suggests a topic they think will be "challenging." The other pairs race to say as many things as they can in one minute. They get one point for each detail. Then another pair suggests a topic. Each time, the pair with the most points suggests the next topic.

Variation: Have students think of as many questions (things they would like to know) as possible about the topic.

EXPANSION *Clarification phrases.* Students at this level probably know how to clarify things they don't understand. However, many forget to do so in English, especially when talking to another student.

Before class, make copies of the Before You Begin Activity Sheet on page T41. You will need one copy for every ten students. Cut the copies into strips. In class, give one strip to each student. Have students copy the sentence from their strip onto the inside cover of their books. Tell the students that there are ten sentences and they need to collect them all. You may need to pre-teach the word "blank," which is used in place of an unknown word. (*Example:* The answer is *blank* .) Learners then stand and circulate. They dictate their sentences to each other.

After students have done the activity, the phrases are always conveniently available. When students should use one of the phrases but forget, simply flip the book open to the inside cover and silently gesture for them to use English to clarify.

❑ Ken is talking to Erika. Look at Erika's questions. If you
   know Ken's answers, check (✔) them.

❑ Now listen. Check (✔) the answers you didn't know.

1. What are you doing today, Ken?
   - ✔ I'm going to work soon.
   - ☐ I have class this afternoon.

2. You've been to the National Park, right?
   - ✔ Yes. I went last summer.
   - ☐ No. I've never been there before.

3. What's the best way to get to the
   National Park?
   - ☐ Take Route 12.
   - ✔ Take Route 5.

4. Would you like to go with us on
   the 17th?
   - ☐ I'd love to.
   - ✔ I'd really like to, but I can't.

5. What are you going to do that day?
   - ☐ I have to work.
   - ✔ I'm going to a concert.

6. How about the weekend after that?
   - ✔ That sounds good.
   - ☐ Sorry. I'm busy then, too.

Erika

Ken

What do you say first?

❏ Work with a partner.
Complete the chart.

**How many ways do you know to introduce yourself in English?
Write as many as you can.**

Hi. I'm (your name).

I don't think we've met. My name's _____.

Hello. My name is _____. I'm from _____.

_____

**What topics do you talk about when you first meet someone?
Write at least five.**

school/jobs	sports
hometown	hobbies
family	

**What topics DON'T you talk about?
Write at least three.**

salary	
politics	
religion	

❏ Now join another pair. Compare answers.

U N I T 1
What do you say first?

Content area: First impressions and
   conversation strategies
Listening skills: Identifying strategies for
   introductions (Listening Task 1);
   planning introduction routines
   (Listening Task 2)
Grammar/vocabulary: Introductory
   routines

Warming Up

1. Hold your book so that students can see
page 6. T: *Look at page 6.*

2. Divide the class into pairs. Read the
instructions. Pause when you see the
symbol ♦ to give students time to answer
the questions.

> *Work with a partner. Complete the chart. How
>   many ways do you know to introduce
>   yourself in English? Write as many as you
>   can.* ♦
> *What topics do you talk about when you first
>   meet someone? Write at least five.* ♦
> *What topics DON'T you talk about? Write at
>   least three.* ♦

3. As students work, circulate and help
pairs having difficulty.

4. Read the rest of the instructions: *Now
join another pair. Compare answers.*

5. Check responses by having students call
out answers to the questions.

NOTES

• To introduce a gamelike element of
competition, have learners earn points in
Step 4 of the lesson plan. Students get one
point each time they listed an item their
partners didn't list.

• When meeting someone for the first
time, people in the U.S. and Canada
generally talk about jobs, school,
hometown, family (occupations and
number of siblings), sports, special
interests/hobbies. It is generally
considered impolite to talk about money
(salary or cost of personal belongings),
politics, or religion.

Strategy exercise: Recognizing and using common patterns

Every language is full of set phrases and
common patterns, or routines. One way to
become a better listener is to learn to
anticipate and recognize these patterns. If
a listening activity is about introductions
and meeting people, we expect to hear,
"Hello, I'm Sue. I'm from New York." and
"John, this is Mary. Mary, John. Mary is in
my English class." Learning to anticipate
these set phrases can decrease the effort
necessary when listening. Knowing which
phrases are likely to be used allows students
to get ready for the information they need.

   To get this point across, before students
do Listening Task 1, tell them they are
going to hear people introducing
themselves. Ask students what people
usually say to introduce themselves in
English and in their language(s). Write the
ideas on the board. As the students listen
to Listening Task 1, have them raise their
hands when they hear a phrase that is
written on the board.

Optional activity

(For use anytime during or after the unit.)

EXPANSION   ***It's a match.*** Before class, make
   copies of the Unit 1 Activity
Sheet on page T43. You will need one copy
for each student. In class, give one activity
sheet to each learner. Have students first
write their own answers in the white boxes.
Students then stand and circulate. They ask
classmates the questions. When they find
someone with the same answer as theirs,
they write that person's name in the gray
box. They continue until their sheet is full.

Listening Task 1
A good first impression

Listening skill: Identifying strategies for introductions

Note: The tapescript for Unit 1 begins on page T3.

1. T: *Look at page 7.*

2. (Optional) Read the title: *"A good first impression."* Ask: *What do you think this will be about?* Elicit answers. (Answer: ways [strategies] for creating a good impression when you meet someone for the first time)

3. Read or play the introduction: *"First impressions" are what you think when you meet someone for the first time. Your opinion is based on what the person says and does.*

4. Read or play the instructions: *Listen. People are meeting for the first time. What do they say? Write the missing words. What do the people do to make a good first impression? Write their strategies.*

5. (Optional) If your students will find this task very difficult, do the Additional Support procedure.

6. Play Listening Task 1 on the tape. Gesture for students to write their answers. **(Optional)** To make sure students understand what to do, stop after the first item. Ask: *What word goes after ". . . join me"?* (Answer: Sue) *What is her strategy?* (Answer: Try to remember people's names by using them.) Then play the rest of Listening Task 1.

7. If necessary, play Listening Task 1 a second time.

8. Check by having students call out their answers. (Answers appear in blue on the opposite page.)

ADDITIONAL SUPPORT Have students do Step 6 in pairs. Stop the tape after each conversation and after the commentator's part. Give the pair members time to share the information they understood. Note that students working in pairs will often focus on what they did understand rather than worrying about what they missed.

NOTES

• In the first item, the speaker starts with a tag question: *You're new here, aren't you?* A tag question is a kind of yes-no question – it begins with a statement but ends with a short question. We use tag questions when we think we might know the answer.

• The second conversation has a reference to great jazz trumpeters Miles Davis and Wynton Marsalis.

• Be sure students understand that the strategy in the last item is NOT to memorize a self-introduction. However, it can be useful to think of a few things one wants to say. These things can – and should – include questions to ask to get the conversation started.

Culture corner

Culture Corner is a short reading passage that appears at the bottom of each Listening Task 1 page. An optional activity for using the Culture Corner appears in each unit of this *Teacher's Edition*.

1. After students have read the Culture Corner, have them work in pairs or small groups to answer this question: *What do you say to end a conversation in your country?*

2. (Optional) Before students read the Culture Corner, write the first letter of each word in the sample sentences on the board. Include the punctuation. For example, the first sentence (*I'm sorry, but I have to go.*) is written as: I s , b I h t g .
Do this for each example. Tell students they will hear ways to end a conversation. They should guess what the words will be and write down their sentences. Then one student in each group looks at the book. That student gives hints while the others try to correct their sentences. This activity encourages learners to predict based on the topic.

LISTENING TASK 1

A good first impression

"First impressions" are what you think when you meet someone
for the first time. Your opinion is based on what the person
says and does.

❏ Listen. People are meeting for the first time.
What do they say? Write the missing words.
What do the people do to make a good first impression?
Write their strategies.

1.

It's nice to meet
you, *Sue* .
Would you like to
join me, *Sue* ?

Strategy:
Try to remember *people's*
names by using them
                            .

2.

Yes. I really like
jazz .

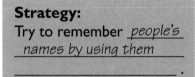

Strategy:
Try to add *information* .
Don't just say
yes or no   .

3.

Have you ever taken
a *class* with
this *teacher*
before?

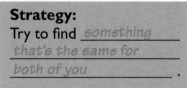

Strategy:
Try to find *something*
that's the same for
both of you   .

4.

Before I meet someone,
I sometimes *think*
about what I want
to say   .

Strategy:
Think about *what you*
want to say
                            .

CULTURE CORNER

The ways we start and end a conversation can depend on culture. In English,
if you are the person who is ending the conversation, it's usually a good idea to
give a reason. Here are some examples:

• I'm sorry, but I have to go. It was nice talking to you.
• You'll have to excuse me. I need to talk to someone over there.
• It's late. I need to be going. I'll see you tomorrow.

What do you say to end a conversation in your country?

7

Keeping the conversation going

What do you say when you meet people?
When English-speaking people meet, they
often follow a pattern.

❏ Listen. What do the people talk about?
Number the items (1–3).

When people meet, they usually

3	ask questions.
1	talk about something they have in common.
2	say their names.

❏ Listen. You're going to get ready to have a conversation.
Follow the instructions.

SAMPLE
ANSWERS

Situation 1: In class

1. *This class is great.*
2. *By the way, I'm _____.*
3. *How many classes are you taking?*

Situation 2: At a party

1. *Nice party.*
2. *I'm _____. Don and I work together.*
3. *How do you know Don?*

YOUR TURN TO TALK

Now you're going to have your own conversations. Stand up. Go up to a classmate
you don't know. Start a conversation, using these steps:
- Talk about something you both have in common.
- Say your name and find out your partner's name.
- Ask a question.

Keep the conversation going for as long as possible. Then end your conversation.
("Excuse me. I need to talk to someone over there. It was nice meeting you.")
After you end the conversation, find a new partner and start a new conversation.
Meet as many classmates as possible.

Listening Task 2
Keeping the conversation going

1. T: *Look at page 8.*

2. (Optional) Read the title: *"Keeping the conversation going."* Ask: *What do you think this will be about?* Elicit answers. (Answer: specific ways/techniques/strategies for keeping a conversation going)

3. Play the introduction and instructions: *What do you say when you meet people? When English-speaking people meet, they often follow a pattern. Listen. What do the people talk about? Number the items (1–3).*

4. Play the first part of Listening Task 2. Gesture for students to write their answers. (See the variations on this step in the first teaching Note below.)

5. Check by asking: *What's number one? Number two? Number three?*

6. Read the instructions to Step Two: *Listen. You're going to get ready to have a conversation. Follow the instructions.* Play Situation One on the tape. You may want to stop after the first one or two questions and elicit ideas from some students.

7. (Optional) If your students find this task very difficult, do the Additional Support procedure.

8. Check answers in Situation One by having learners call out their ideas. Encourage several answers for each step. (Sample answers appear in blue on the opposite page.)

9. Do Situation Two in the same way.

10. It isn't necessary to formally check students' answers because simply completing the task makes learners able to do Your Turn to Talk as a follow-up. However, you may want to have students compare their answers in small groups or call out possible answers as in Step 8 above.

ADDITIONAL SUPPORT Do the "conversation preparation" steps (Situations One and Two) either in small groups or as a full class. Stop the tape after each step and have two or three students suggest answers.

NOTES

• During Step 4, you may want to stop the tape after each topic (the weather, names, the question) and have learners number the items based only on the conversation. OR you may want to pause between the conversation and the commentator's explanation.

• Students may be surprised that saying names isn't always the first step of a conversation. Of course, names sometimes come first, but the steps outlined here are – in most situations – a more natural, relaxed model. Knowing the steps can help learners avoid some of the abruptness often associated with non-native speakers.

Your turn to talk

1. Read the instructions: *Now you're going to have your own conversations. Stand up. Go up to a classmate you don't know. Start a conversation, using these steps:*

• *Talk about something you both have in common.*
• *Say your name and find out your partner's name.*
• *Ask a question.*

2. (after a few minutes) T: *Keep the conversation going for as long as possible. Then end your conversation.* ("Excuse me. I need to talk to someone over there. It was nice meeting you.") *Find a new partner and start a new conversation. Meet as many classmates as possible.*

3. Allow time for students to circulate and meet several partners.

NOTE

• If all the students know one another, you might have them take on imaginary roles as famous people.

Sights and sounds

Content area: Talking about sensory
information
Listening skills: Inferring topics (Listening
Task 1); following instructions (Listening
Task 2)
Grammar/vocabulary: Imperatives, sense
words

Warming Up

1. Hold your book so that students can see
page 9. T: *Look at page 9.*

2. Read the instructions. Pause when you
see the symbol ♦ to give students time to
answer the questions. (For an alternate
introduction, see the Note below.)

> *Think of something you did recently that you
> enjoyed. What did you do? Write it in the
> green box.* ♦
> *What did you see, hear, feel, smell, and taste?
> Write the things you remember. Write in at
> least eight boxes.* ♦

3. As students work, circulate and help. If
several students are having difficulty, ask
specific questions as in the Note below.

4. (after a few minutes) T: *Work with a
partner. Tell about your experience. Include as
many details as you can.*

5. You may want partners to ask two or three
follow-up questions. OR Have pairs that
finish early change partners and continue.

NOTE

• It is very important that students really
focus on a specific event. One good way to
help them "recreate" the event in their
minds is by having them close their eyes.
They sit quietly for 15 to 30 seconds. Then
slowly read the instructions (leaving out the
part about writing). You may want to add to
the instructions. For example, the first part
could become: *Think about something you did
recently that you enjoyed. You really had a good*
*time. What were you doing? Imagine it. Get a
clear picture in your mind. Where were you? Who
were you with? Now, think carefully. What did
you see? Look at the place. Look at the things.
Notice the colors.*, etc. Then have students
write short notes in the spaces in the book.

Strategy exercise: *Semantic mapping*

This unit's Warming Up introduces a
strategy called "semantic mapping." It
helps students think about the words they
are likely to hear in a listening passage; it
also helps them associate new words with
old ones so that the words are better
remembered. One way to get students to
practice this strategy is to have them work
in pairs or small groups. Set a time limit
(usually 3 to 5 minutes). Groups see how
many words they can list in the given time
period. You can also practice this
technique with color words.

Optional activity

(For use anytime during or after the unit.)

EXPANSION **What's your experience?** Before
class, make copies of the Unit 2
Activity Sheet on page T45. You will need
one copy for every three students. In class,
write the names of the five senses on the
board. Learners work in groups of three.
Each group gets one sheet. They should
cut the cards apart. Each partner receives a
"Your idea" card. On it, they write the word
or phrase of a person, place, or situation.
Partners then shuffle all 12 cards and place
them facedown on a desk. One player picks
a card and reads it aloud. Everyone tries to
think of as many senses as possible
connected to the word or phrase on the
card. (*Examples:* A baby – [sight] baby
sleeping, smiling; [hearing] crying,
"Mama"; [touch] soft skin) Then they go
on to the next card. Give one point for
each example, with students competing
within their groups or with groups
competing against one another.

Sights and sounds

❑ Think of something you did recently that you enjoyed.
What did you do? Write it in the green box.

❑ What did you see, hear, feel, smell, and taste?
Write the things you remember.
Write in at least eight boxes.

SAMPLE
ANSWERS

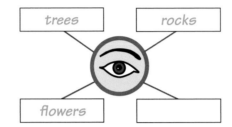

trees   rocks

flowers

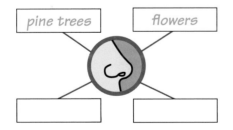

birds   a stream

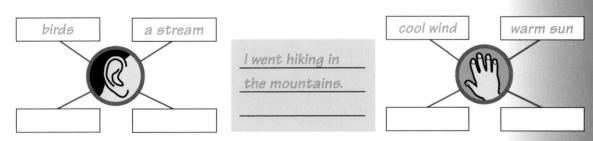

I went hiking in
the mountains.

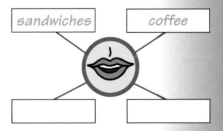

cool wind   warm sun

pine trees   flowers

sandwiches   coffee

❑ Work with a partner.
Tell about your experience. Include as many
details as you can.

Example
It was last summer. It was really hot. I was sitting
outside, alone. I was watching the moon and the
stars. Suddenly, I heard …

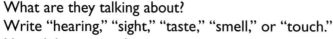

LISTENING TASK 1

The five senses

❏ Listen. People are talking about the senses.
What are they talking about?
Write "hearing," "sight," "taste," "smell," or "touch."
How did you guess?
Write at least one thing for each sense.

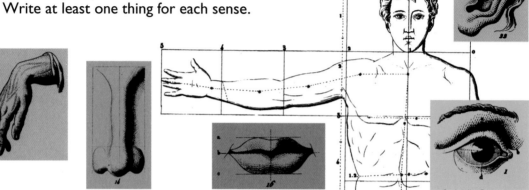

1. Sense: _touch_

How I guessed:

wool

blind people

2. Sense: _smell_

How I guessed:

difficult to describe

baby

3. Sense: _sight_

How I guessed:

painters

shapes

4. Sense: _taste_

How I guessed:

chocolate

pasta

CULTURE CORNER

Sight is one of our strongest senses. Of course, color is an important part of what we see. However, things we associate with different colors can depend on the cultures we are from. For example, in the United States and Canada, red can mean "anger." The Chinese, on the other hand, think of red as a symbol of good luck.

In many countries, white is a sign of pure things. That's why brides wear white at weddings. In traditional Arab cultures, white is the color of death and mourning. People wear white to funerals. In the United States and Japan, people associate black with funerals and death.

What colors have special meanings in your country? Can you imagine why?

Listening Task 1
The five senses

Note: The tapescript for Unit 2 begins on page T4.

1. T: *Look at page 10. The five senses.*

2. Play the instructions: *Listen. People are talking about the senses. What are they talking about? Write "hearing," "sight," "taste," "smell," or "touch." How did you guess? Write at least one thing for each sense.*

3. (Optional) If your students will find this listening very difficult, do the Additional Support procedure.

4. Play Listening Task 1 on the tape. Gesture for students to write their answers. Stop after the first item to point out that the speaker never says the word "touch." However, other words on the tape like "wool" and "blind people" give clues. Then play the rest of Listening Task 1.

5. If necessary, play Listening Task 1 a second time.

6. Check by having students volunteer answers. (Answers appear in blue on the opposite page.)

ADDITIONAL SUPPORT Write the names of the five senses on the board (*sight, hearing, touch, smell, taste*). Students work in groups of three or four. First, they see how many English words they can think of that are associated with each sense – for example, sight: "eye," "see," "vision," "glasses." Then they imagine problems they would have if they did not have this sense and things they would do to get around those problems.

NOTE

• Although all five senses are listed, only four are answers. This is to require students to pay attention through the end of the task, instead of just filling in the unused

word for the last item. The irony, of course, is that the missing item is "hearing" – the main sense they are using during the task.

Culture corner

1. Have students read the Culture Corner and answer the follow-up questions alone or in small groups: *What colors have special meanings in your country? Can you imagine why?*

2. (Optional) After reading the Culture Corner, students work in groups of three. Two learners have their books closed; the other reads the passage aloud. The two partners with their books closed raise their hands each time they hear the name of a color. Then a different partner reads. The other two raise their hands when they hear a country mentioned. Finally, the third partner reads. The others raise their hands when they hear any word that begins with the letter "c." This activity encourages selective listening.

Optional activity

(For use anytime during or after the unit.)

• *Vacation.* On the board, draw this:

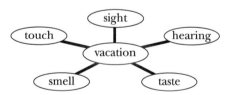

Students think about a vacation they have taken. They think of one thing from each sense that the vacation reminds them of. They may want to copy the drawing and write the items on it. Then they work in pairs. Student **A** describes the vacation in detail to **B. A** can speak for 90 seconds. **B** asks at least one question. Then **B** speaks for 90 seconds as **A** listens. Then **A** asks questions. Finally, students change partners. They continue, but this time they can speak for only 75 seconds. They try to say the same amount in the shorter time.

Listening Task 2
Colors and sight

Listening skill: Following instructions

1. T: *Look at page 11.*

2. (Optional) Read the title: *"Colors and sight."* Ask: *What do you think this will be about?* Elicit answers. (Answer: how vision affects the colors we see)

3. Play the introduction and instructions: *A scientist is talking on television. He's talking about color vision, the way we see colors. Listen. Try the experiment.*

4. Play the first part of Listening Task 2. As you do, gesture for students to stare at the green box. Then, when the tape indicates, make sure they look at the white box.

5. Read the instructions to the next part: *Work with a partner. Describe what you saw. Did you and your partner have the same experience? Check your answer.* Allow time for students to compare their experiences.

6. Read the instructions to Step Three: *At night, we really see black and white like this picture. Why? Listen. Check the answer.* Play the next segment of the tape. **Note:** If at all possible, turn out the lights in the room. Encourage students to really look at the book cover. You may want to stop the tape to give everyone's eyes time to adjust to the darkness.

7. If necessary, play Listening Task 2 a second time. Before replaying the tape, you may want to have students compare answers: *Work with a partner. Look at your partner's answers. Are they the same as yours?*

8. Check by asking: *Why do we see black and white at night?* and having students answer. (Answer: Rods see light but not color.)

9. Once learners have done the entire task, you may want to play the tape again. Have them repeat the experiments, this time focusing entirely on the sensations rather than checking the answer boxes.

NOTES

• Some people don't see afterimages right away, so you may want to do Step 4 of the lesson plan more than once.

• Other colors will work for seeing afterimages. The afterimage color is that which is opposite on a color wheel:

red / purple / orange / blue / yellow / green

• This task is an example of "learning by doing." Rather than simply overhearing conversations or lectures, the students are directed through the tasks by the tape. Since the unit theme is the five senses, we thought it was particularly important that the learners experience the information, rather than just collect data.

• We usually use the simple present or simple past – but not the progressive – to talk about sense experiences. In English, verbs of perception are considered "states" that do not change. Thus, we say, "I'*m touching* the cloth." but "It *feels* soft." Remind students that they should not use the progressive to describe their experiences in Your Turn to Talk.

Your turn to talk

1. Divide the class into pairs. T: *Think about a time you experienced a sense very strongly. For example, it could be something you saw that you will never forget, or it might be a smell – good or bad – that you remember clearly.*

2. Give students a few minutes to think about their experience. Then continue with the instructions: *Tell your partner about your experience. How long can you keep speaking? Your partner will listen and keep time. Your turn is over when you stop for five seconds or when you say a word that isn't English. When you finish, your partner will ask at least two questions. After you answer the questions, it's your partner's turn to speak.*

3. Have students do the activity. You may want pairs that finish quickly to change partners and try again.

Colors and sight

A scientist is talking on television. He's talking about color vision, the way we see colors.

❑ Listen. Try the experiment.

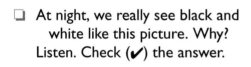

❑ Work with a partner.
Describe what you saw.
Did you and your partner have the same experience?
Check (✔) your answer.   yes ☐   no ☐

❑ At night, we really see black and white like this picture. Why?
Listen. Check (✔) the answer.

We see with "cones" and "rods."

☐ Cones see light but not color.
☑ Rods see light but not color.
☐ Rods see color but not light.

YOUR TURN TO TALK

Think about a time you experienced a sense very strongly. For example, it could be something you saw that you will never forget, or it might be a smell – good or bad – that you remember clearly.

Work with a partner. Tell your partner about your experience. How long can you keep speaking? Your partner will listen and keep time. Your turn is over when you stop for five seconds or when you say a word that isn't English. When you finish, your partner will ask at least two questions. After you answer the questions, it's your partner's turn to speak. Start like this:

I'll never forget the time …

11

Pirates and such

Many countries have "heroes" who were really not good people. Even though they were "bad guys," they represent adventure or a romantic lifestyle.

❑ Work with a partner.
How many "bad guys" (male or female) can you think of?
Write their names.

_____   _____

_____   _____

_____   _____

❑ Choose one "bad guy." What else do you know about him or her? Where was the person from? When did he or she live? What did he or she really do?
Write as much information as you can.

_____

_____

_____

_____

❑ Now join another pair.
Tell them what you wrote.
Listen to what they wrote.

U N I T   3
Pirates and such

> **Content area:** Talking about historical events
> **Listening skills:** Identifying incorrect information (Listening Task 1); identifying locations, understanding numbers (Listening Task 2)
> **Grammar/vocabulary:** Past tenses: simple past and past progressive, *must* for strong possibility, large numbers

Warming Up

1. Hold your book so that students can see page 12. T: *Look at page 12.*

2. Read the introduction: *Many countries have "heroes" who were really not good people. Even though they were "bad guys," they represent adventure or a romantic lifestyle.*

3. Read the instructions to Step One: *Work with a partner. How many "bad guys" (male or female) can you think of? Write their names.* As students work, circulate and help pairs having difficulty. If possible, help by asking questions leading to "bad guy heroes" for the students' culture(s) – for example, *Who's the bank robber who gave money to poor people?*

4. (Optional) Have students call out their ideas and write the names on the board. This will give all the learners more choices for the next step.

5. T: *Choose one "bad guy." What else do you know about him or her? Where was the person from? When did he or she live? What did he or she really do? Write as much information as you can.* Allow time for students to work.

6. T: *Now join another pair. Tell them what you wrote. Listen to what they wrote.*

NOTES

• Note that students do not need to name the "bad guys" shown on the page. The pictures are there to provide context. In most cases, students will name people from their own culture or from literature or movies.

The people in the pictures are the English pirate Blackbeard (Edward Teach, d.1718), American Bandit Queen and horse thief Belle Starr (1848–1889), Mexican outlaw Joaquín Murieta (d.1853), bank robbers Bonnie Parker (1911–1934) and Clyde Barrow (1909–1934), and Japanese criminal Rat Thief Jirokichi (1796[?]–1832).

• "Guy" has traditionally been an informal term for "man." However, the plural "guys" can include both men and women, especially in American and Australian English.

Strategy exercise: *Listening for explanation and clarification*

Listening Task 1 presents words that students are not likely to know (pirate, buccaneer, boucan, piece of eight). Point out that a listener sometimes has to be patient and wait for the speaker to give a definition of an uncommon term. Speakers do not, of course, always do this, and if they do not, it is the responsibility of the listener to ask for clarification. To get this point across, put students into pairs and have them select an everyday object. They should make up a new name (a nonsense word) for the object and write a set of clues for it. For example, they may rename a cassette tape a "glorp." They would then write clues like: "I use a *glorp* when I study English." "Sometimes I listen to music on a *glorp*." "A *glorp* is about 10 x 6 centimeters (4 x 2.5 inches)." After students have written the clues, they work with another pair and see if that pair can guess their object from the context clues.

Listening Task 1
Pirates of the Caribbean

Note: The tapescript for Unit 3 begins on
page T6.

1. T: *Look at page 13.*

2. (Optional) Read the title: *"Pirates of the
Caribbean."* Ask: *What do you know about the
Caribbean Sea? Where is it? What countries are
there? Do you know anything about pirates
there?*

3. T: *Read this passage.* **Note:** If new
vocabulary makes reading difficult, see the
Strategy Exercise on page 12.

4. Play the instructions: *Now listen. Some
information is wrong. The tape is correct. Find
the mistakes. Write the correct information.*

5. (Optional) If your students will find this
task very difficult, do the Additional
Support procedure.

6. Play Listening Task 1 on the tape.
Gesture for students to write their
corrections. **(Optional)** To make sure
students understand what to do, stop after
one or two sentences. Read the sentences.
Students raise their hands or call out
corrections when they hear "mistakes."
Then play the rest of Listening Task 1.

7. If necessary, play Listening Task 1 a
second time.

8. Check as in Step 6 above. (Answers
appear in blue on the opposite page.)

ADDITIONAL SUPPORT Demonstrate by
reading the first sentence, making several
"mistakes" (underlined): *The word "pirates"
makes us think of workers who attacked ships in
the Atlantic Ocean during the 19th and 20th
centuries.* Have students identify your
"mistakes." Then have students work in
pairs. Student **A** uses the first paragraph,
and Student **B** uses the second paragraph.

Each plans three or four "mistakes." They
then read their paragraph to their partner,
who tries to find the "mistakes."

Culture corner

1. Have students read the Culture Corner
and then answer the questions: *Are "bad guy
heroes" remembered in your country? How?*
Remind students that over time, images
can change. Someone who was really a
vicious murderer may now be remembered
as a brave warrior.

2. (Optional) Before students read the
Culture Corner, draw simple pictures of the
following on the board: a fish, a football, a
hotel, a baseball, a flag (either with no
picture or a "skull and crossbones" [see the
picture in the Culture Corner]). Have
learners copy the pictures. As they read,
they write a name next to each picture.
This activity helps learners associate written
and visual information.

Optional activity

(For use anytime after Listening Task 1.)

EXPANSION *Pirates today.* Before class,
make copies of the Unit 3
Activity Sheet on page T47. You will need
one copy for every two students. Cut each
copy into two parts: **A** and **B**. In class,
divide students into pairs. First, they do a
peer dictation: Each Student **A** reads the
first **A** sentence (*When people talk about
pirates . . .*), and **B** writes the missing words.
Then **B** reads and **A** writes. Students
continue until both partners of every pair
have a complete story. Finally, they answer
the questions.

- What magazine reported pirate
  attacks? (Answer: *Yachting World*)
- Where are pirate attacks taking place?
  (Answer: in the South China Sea, off
  the east coast of Africa, and off the
  northeast coast of South America)
- What do some pirates look like?
  (Answer: government officials)

LISTENING TASK 1

Pirates of the Caribbean

❏ Read this passage.

❏ Now listen. Some information is wrong. The tape is correct. Find the mistakes. Write the correct information.

The word "pirates" makes us think of ~~soldiers~~ *sailors* who attacked ships in the Caribbean Sea during the 16th and 17th centuries. Most pirates were English, ~~Italian~~ *French*, or Dutch. They mainly attacked Spanish ships that were carrying gold to Spain from colonies in ~~North~~ *South* America and Mexico. Sometimes pirates attacked towns where the gold and silver were stored before it was taken to Spain. When pirates attacked a town, they stole the riches that were hidden there, robbed important *rich* families' houses, and then burned the town down.

There were other adventurers living on the Caribbean islands. These men were hunters. They learned to make smoked ~~fish~~ *meat*, called "boucan," from the Tupi Indians in the Caribbean. "Boucan" was the Indian word for smoked ~~fish~~ *meat*; the hunters became known as buccaneers. Until the end of the *At beginning* 1600s, buccaneers were only hunters and adventurers who sold boucan and other food to pirates. However, by ~~1750~~ *1650*, they had become pirates too and began attacking ships for the gold. The gold that pirates and buccaneers stole was usually in the form of a coin called a piece of eight. The symbol for a piece of eight was the ~~word~~ *number* "eight" written on top of the letter P. This symbol eventually became abbreviated to the letter S with a vertical line through it, and this became the symbol for ~~money~~ *the American dollar*.

CULTURE CORNER

Pirates and buccaneers are popular symbols in the United States today. You can see these symbols in different places:
- sports teams: the Pittsburgh Pirates (baseball)
  the Tampa Bay Buccaneers (football)
- seafood restaurants: Long John Silver's (a famous pirate)
- beach hotels: the Jolly Roger (the pirates' flag)
  the Treasure Chest

Are "bad guy heroes" remembered in your country? How?

Sunken treasure

Since the 1500s, many ships carrying valuable cargo have sunk in the ocean.
These ships were carrying gold and silver when they sank.

❏ Listen. Where did these ships sink? Write the numbers in the circles.

1. the *Egypt*

2. the ships at Vigo

3. the *Nuestra Señora de la Concepción*

4. the *Lutine*

❏ Now listen to some more information. What was the total value of the cargo?
How much is still at the bottom of the ocean? Write the numbers.

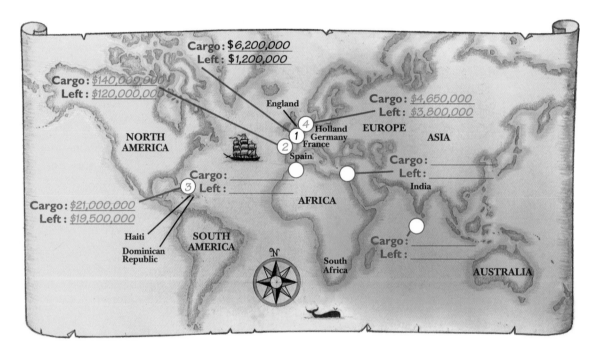

Cargo: $6,200,000
Left: $1,200,000

Cargo: $140,000,000
Left: $120,000,000

England

Cargo: $4,650,000
Left: $3,800,000

NORTH
AMERICA

4 Holland   EUROPE
1 Germany   ASIA
2 France
Spain

Cargo: _____
Left: _____
India

Cargo: _____
3 Left: _____

AFRICA

Cargo: $21,000,000
Left: $19,500,000

Haiti

Dominican
Republic

SOUTH
AMERICA

South
Africa

Cargo: _____
Left: _____

AUSTRALIA

❏ Now you will hear a question. Write your answer. <u>$144,500,000</u>

YOUR
TURN TO
TALK

In the 1920s, a family in Florida was digging a hole on their property when they hit
something metal. It was a chest filled with 3,700 Spanish coins from the 1740s to the
1760s. The coins were worth around $150,000.

If you found $150,000, what would you spend it on? Work in groups of three. Make a
list of five ways to spend the money. Explain why you chose each way.

Now stand up and talk to other students. Find groups that spent the money in
similar ways.

Listening Task 2
Sunken treasure

> **Listening skills:** Identifying locations, understanding numbers

1. T: *Look at page 14.*

2. (Optional) Read the title: *"Sunken treasure."* Ask: *What do you think this will be about?* Elicit answers. (Answer: the location and value of treasure under the sea)

3. Play the introduction and instructions to Step One: *Since the 1500s, many ships carrying valuable cargo have sunk in the ocean. These ships were carrying gold and silver when they sank. Listen. Where did these ships sink? Write the numbers in the circles.*

4. (Optional) If your students will find this task very difficult, do the Additional Support procedure.

5. Play Step One of Listening Task 2 on the tape. Gesture for students to write their answers. You may want to stop after each item to check by having students call out their answers. OR Have students compare answers with a partner before checking as a class. (Answers appear in blue on the opposite page.)

6. Read the instructions for the next step: *Now listen to some more information. What was the total value of the cargo? How much is still at the bottom of the ocean? Write the numbers.* Play the next segment on the tape. You may want to check answers as in Step 5 above.

7. T: *Now you will hear a question. Write your answer.* Play the final tape segment.

8. Check by having students call out answers.

ADDITIONAL SUPPORT Have students close their books. Tell them to raise their hand each time they hear the name of a country or a number (either a date or an amount of money). Play the tape for Listening Task 2. The hand-raising gives a cue to learners who missed the item.

NOTES

- Remind students to read large numbers in groups of threes and to add the place name after each group. For example, 3,450,625 is read "3 (three) million, 450 (four hundred fifty) thousand, 625 (six hundred twenty-five)."

- Students have probably learned that the modal *must* indicates obligation or necessity. It can also indicate strong possibility or deduction. Several of the items end with "There *must* be around . . . ," which means "We can assume, given what we already know, that there is . . . ."

Your turn to talk

1. Divide the class into groups of three. Read the first paragraph aloud. Then: *If you found $150,000, what would you spend it on? Make a list of five ways to spend the money. Explain why you chose each way.*

2. (after about 10 minutes) T: *Now stand up and talk to other students. Find groups that spent the money in similar ways.*

Optional activity

(For use anytime after Listening Task 2.)

- ***Treasure hunt.*** Students work in pairs. They imagine they are pirates who have landed on an island! They have to hide the treasure they have taken from a ship. They want to be able to find the treasure later when they return to the island. On a piece of paper, they write "Our treasure." They think of a place somewhere in the school to hide the treasure. (Pairs take turns leaving the classroom to hide their "treasure.") Then they design a set of directions to the treasure – for example: Go through the classroom door. Take four steps to the right. Then turn to the left. Go six steps. Walk down the stairs. Find the picture of the school president. From the picture, walk six steps to the left.

When all the pairs have finished, they trade directions with another pair. The new pairs try to find the treasure. The pair who finds treasure first is the winner.

Dating

Content area: Talking about dating customs

Listening skills: Identifying reasons (Listening Task 1); understanding details, identifying opinions (Listening Task 2)

Grammar/vocabulary: Adverbs of frequency, past tenses: simple past and past progressive, descriptive adjectives

Warming Up

1. T: *Look at page 15.*

2. T: *How do people in your country meet and begin dating? Draw lines to show your answers.*

3. (after a few minutes) T: *What are some other ways?* Have students write at least one extra way on the last line.

4. T: *Work with a partner. Answer these questions. Listen to your partner's answers. 1. What do you think is the best way to meet someone? Why? 2. What ways don't you like? Why not?* Encourage several students to say their choices and reasons.

NOTES

• You may want to have each pair think of at least one good and one bad thing about each way listed before they go on to the discussion questions in Step 4 above. For example, a good thing about meeting someone at work or school is that you have a common interest. A bad thing is that, if the relationship doesn't last, work or school might become uncomfortable for both partners.

• The frequency adverbs are listed in order. It is sometimes tempting to assign a percentage to each. This, however, is usually not very helpful since frequency is relative. For example, people who watch TV only once a week may say that is "not very often." On the other hand, someone who goes to a movie once a month may identify that as "often."

• Remind students of the placement of frequency adverbs: before the main verb in simple past or present tenses and in all other cases after the verb *be* or the first auxiliary verb (We have *often* walked . . .).

Strategy exercise: Associating

People learn by associating new information with old. Often, students are not as successful as they could be because they see English as a random collection of rules and words. Divide students into groups of four or five. Give all the groups the same word and a time limit. One student in each group is the secretary. The groups race against each other to list as many associated words as they can. The group with the most associations wins. You may want to choose the word "date" or one of the places where people may go on a date as the word to begin with.

Optional activity

(For use anytime during or after the unit.)

• *Dating service.* Set up a dating service. First, in groups of five or six, students decide the most important qualities for a partner. Then the whole class designs a questionnaire to find out about these qualities.

Choose three to four students to be counselors. (The number of counselors depends on the class size – there should be one counselor for every five to six people.) Each counselor interviews five people, asking them about themselves and what characteristics they are looking for in a partner, based on the class questionnaire. While some students are being interviewed, the others are making small talk in the waiting room. When the counselors finish all their interviews, they meet to compare their information and match the people.

Dating

 ❏ How do people in your country meet and begin dating?
Draw lines to show your answers.

often   **sometimes**   **not very often**   **never**

They meet at work or school.

Friends introduce them.

They meet through a matchmaker.

Parents or other relatives introduce them.

They meet through a common interest (a club or free-time activity).

They meet through personal ads in a newspaper or magazine.

Other _____

❏ Work with a partner.
Answer these questions. Listen to your partner's answers.

1. What do you think is the best way to meet someone? Why?

2. What ways don't you like? Why not?

Which way is best?

❏ Listen. Some students are talking about ways people
meet and begin dating or get married.
What is an advantage and a disadvantage of each way?
Complete the chart.

WAY TO MEET	ADVANTAGE (+)	DISADVANTAGE (-)
1. formal introduction (a matchmaker)	*They know each other's background.*	*They might not <u>fall in love</u>* .
2. being introduced by <u>*friends*</u> or <u>*someone in family*</u>	*Everybody knows who everyone is. They know your interests.*	*There's pressure.*
3. meeting by chance	*You just fall in love.*	*You might never meet the right person.*

There are many ways for young people to meet and start dating. This is how
single people in the United States and Canada most often meet.

	Men	Women
Through friends	30%	36%
At social gatherings	22	18
At clubs/discos	24	18
At "singles" functions	14	18
At work	10	9
Through newspaper ads	1	1

Where do people go on dates? Movies, restaurants, sports events, concerts, and
dance clubs are all popular.

How do people in your country meet? What are the most common places for dates?

Listening Task 1
Which way is best?

Listening skill: Identifying reasons

Note: The tapescript for Unit 4 begins on page T8.

1. T: *Look at page 16.*

2. (Optional) Read the title: *"Which way is best?"* Ask: *What do you think this will be about?* Elicit answers. (Answer: the best way(s) to meet someone to date or marry)

3. Play the instructions: *Listen. Some students are talking about ways people meet and begin dating or get married. What is an advantage and a disadvantage of each way? Complete the chart.*

4. (Optional) If your students will find this task very difficult, do the Additional Support procedure.

5. Play Listening Task 1 on the tape. Gesture for students to write their answers. **(Optional)** To make sure students understand what to do, stop after the speakers finish talking about matchmakers. Ask two or three students: *What are the advantages and disadvantages of a matchmaker?* Then play the rest of Listening Task 1.

6. If necessary, play Listening Task 1 a second time.

7. Check by having students call out their answers. (Answers appear in blue on the opposite page.) You may want to have students compare answers first: *Work with a partner. Look at your partner's answers. How many were the same as yours?*

ADDITIONAL SUPPORT In pairs or small groups, have students do the activity suggested in the first Note on page 15. You may want them to do the discussion in their native language, but their list of advantages and disadvantages should be in English. If time doesn't permit discussion of all the items, have students guess who will do the introducing for item 2 on this page. They then guess the other information for the chart. When they listen, they check (✓) any ideas they wrote that match the information on the tape.

Culture corner

1. Have students read the Culture Corner and, alone or in small groups, answer the follow-up questions: *How do people in your country meet? What are the most common places for dates?* If you have students from different countries or who know something about dating customs elsewhere, have them work together.

2. (Optional) Before students read the Culture Corner, have them suggest ways young people meet and start dating. Then have them work in pairs. One student looks at the percentages for men. That student says the number and pantomimes each way that young men meet people in the U.S. and Canada. The partner guesses. After they are finished, the first student closes the book. The second student reads out the numbers for young women – but in the wrong order. The first student must try to remember the ways of meeting and guess which way each number represents. This activity encourages guessing and memory practice.

Optional activity

(For use anytime during or after the unit.)

EXPANSION *How did they meet?* Before class, make copies of the Unit 4 Activity Sheet on page T49. You will need one copy for each student. In class, give a copy to each learner. As an out-of-class activity, students should ask five people how they met their spouse, boyfriend, or girlfriend. They fill in the information on the chart. During the next class, they work in pairs or small groups. They combine all their answers to determine the most common method of meeting someone.

Listening Task 2
How did they meet?

> **Listening skills:** Understanding details, identifying opinions

1. T: *Look at page 17. How did they meet?*

2. Play the instructions: *Listen. First, you will hear people talking about how their parents met. Write the correct letter in the boxes. Next, write the parents' first impressions of each other. Do they still think the same thing? Circle "yes" or "no."*

3. (Optional) If your students will find this task very difficult, do the Additional Support procedure.

4. Play Listening Task 2 on the tape. Gesture for students to write their answers. **(Optional)** To make sure students understand what to do, stop after the second item and check by having students say their answers. Then play the rest of Listening Task 2.

5. If necessary, play Listening Task 2 a second time. Before replaying the tape, you may want to have students compare answers: *Work with a partner. Look at your partner's answers. How many were the same as yours?*

6. Check by having students say their answers. (Answers appear in blue on the opposite page.)

ADDITIONAL SUPPORT Have students work in pairs. Write the following on the board and have each pair make one copy: *Can I help?, boats, class, clever, college, nervous, dentist, funny, humor, relaxed, jokes, knew a lot, movie, restaurant, sailing, disaster, shy, teacher.*

Students close their books. Play the tape once. Students look at the words they copied and point to each one as they hear it.

NOTES

- You may prefer to check after each segment rather than waiting until students have heard all four items.

- *Met* is often followed by a prepositional phrase explaining where or how two people met. The preposition used depends on the noun that follows.
How?: met *by* chance, *through* a friend/a matchmaker, *on* a blind date
Where?: *at* work/school/the hospital, *in* Las Vegas/college

Your turn to talk

1. Divide the class into groups of three. T: *Think about dating. Where do people go on dates? What do they do? Design a "perfect" date. Answer these questions.* Refer students to the list of questions and encourage them to answer them all as part of their plans.

2. As students work, circulate. If students are listing only "regular" dating activities, encourage them to imagine a "wonderful, once-in-a-lifetime" date.

3. (after about 10 minutes) T: *Now imagine a date where you can spend very little money. Design the date.*

4. T: *Finally, join another group. Describe your plans. Listen to theirs. Decide on one word that describes each date, using words like* exciting, romantic, fun, cheap, expensive.

Optional activity

(For use anytime during or after the unit.)

- **The way they met was . . .** Students work in groups of four or five. They think about how a couple they know met. It could be parents, friends, themselves, or anyone else. Learners tell their stories. Partners each ask one question about each story. As in Your Turn to Talk, they must agree on one adjective to describe each story, such as *unusual, funny, sweet.*

LISTENING TASK 2

How did they meet?

❑ Listen. First, you will hear people talking
about how their parents met.
Write the correct letter in the boxes.

A. through a matchmaker
B. by chance
C. a "blind date" arranged by a friend
D. through the young woman's mother
E. in high school

Next, write the parents' first impressions
of each other. Do they still think the
same thing? Circle "yes" or "no."

Mom & Dad's wedding day

Mom & Dad – 40 years later!

1. How they met: C
First impression:
She was really funny .

Does he still think so? (yes) no

2. How they met: E
First impression:
He was quiet and shy .

Does she still think so? yes (no)

3. How they met: D
First impression:
She was a wonderful sailor .

Does he still think so? (yes) no

4. How they first met: A
First impression:
He was nervous .

Does she still think so? yes (no)

YOUR TURN TO TALK

Think about dating. Where do people go on dates? What do they do?
Work in groups of three. Design a "perfect" date. Answer these questions:

- Where will you go first? Where will you go next?
- How will you get there?
- How much will the date cost?
- If you go to the movies, which movie will you see?
- If you eat out, which restaurant will you go to? What will you order?

Now imagine a date where you can spend very little money. Design the date.

Finally, join another group. Describe your plans. Listen to theirs. Decide on one word
that describes each date, using words like *exciting, romantic, fun, cheap, expensive.*

A broad view of health

People have many different ways of
taking care of their bodies and minds.

❏ Work with a partner.
How many body parts can you name in English?
Write the words on the lines. Then write the
numbers on the picture.
How many health problems can you name?
Write them next to the words.

*SAMPLE
ANSWERS*

1. *shoulder (sore shoulder)*
2. *stomach (stomachache)*
3. *toes (blisters)*
4. *head (headache)*
5. *tooth (cavity)*
6. *wrist (sprained wrist)*
7. *ankle (twisted ankle)*
8. *eye (infection)*
9. *nose (stuffy nose)*
10. *back (pulled muscle)*
11. *heart (heart attack)*
12. *knee (dislocated knee)*
13. *foot (athlete's foot)*
14. *elbow (tennis elbow)*
15. *finger (broken finger)*
16. *lip (cold sore)*
17. *thigh (pulled hamstring)*
18. *ear (earache)*

❏ Now choose two or more problems. What would you do
if you had the problems? Write your answers.

I would take an aspirin if I had a headache.

I would go to the dentist if I had a cavity.

A broad view of health

Content area: Alternative health
techniques
Listening skills: Making connections
(Listening Task 1); identifying steps in a
process (Listening Task 2)
Grammar/vocabulary: Imperatives, real
conditionals, parts of the body and
physical/medical problems

Warming Up

1. Hold your book so that students can see
page 18. T: *Look at page 18. A broad view of
health.* **(Optional)** *What do you think this will
be about?* Elicit answers. (Answer:
alternative health techniques)

2. Read the introduction and instructions.
Pause when you see the symbol ♦ to give
students time to answer the questions.

> *People have many different ways of taking
> care of their bodies and minds. Work with
> a partner. How many body parts can you
> name in English? Write the words on the
> lines. Then write the numbers on the
> picture.* ♦ *How many health problems can
> you name? Write them next to the words.*

3. As students work, circulate and help
pairs having difficulty. Encourage students
to go beyond the basic-level vocabulary
(*head, arm, leg*) to be more specific
(*forehead, elbow, knee*).

4. Check by drawing simple stick figures
on the board and having students call out
body parts and health problems. Label
them on the picture. OR Have each pair
label a certain number of parts/problems
on the picture.

5. Read the last set of instructions: *Now
choose two or more problems. What would you do
if you had the problems? Write your answers.*
Note: A cold makes a good example for

this task since most students will know
several different remedies.

NOTES

• Encourage students to use dictionaries
to find out the names of body parts and
health problems they want to be able to say
in English.

• There are, of course, some body parts
and medical problems that some students
(and teachers) are not comfortable talking
about. We designed this Warming Up task
to allow students to go into as much or as
little depth as they want.

Strategy exercise: *Visualizing*

Having students visualize themselves doing
an action in a specific situation can help
them remember related vocabulary. After
students do Listening Task 2, have them
close their eyes and try to remember the
steps in the relaxation technique. They
should imagine themselves sitting in a
comfortable chair and then go through the
steps of the technique.

An alternative is for students to pair the
body parts and medical problems they
brainstormed in Warming Up. They should
imagine themselves trying to go to school
with a sore shoulder, a stomachache, etc.

Optional activity

(For use anytime during or after the unit.)

EXPANSION *Take care of yourself.* Before
class, make copies of the Unit
5 Activity Sheet on page T51. You will need
one copy for each student. In class,
distribute the sheets and have students
think about the various health problems
and write a solution for each. Then
students work in groups of three. They
compare answers. Students get one point
each time they gave an answer that no one
else gave.

Listening Task I
Reflexology

Listening skill: Making connections

Note: The tapescript for Unit 5 begins on page T10.

1. T: *Look at page 19.*

2. (Optional) Read the title: *"Reflexology."* Ask: *What do you think this will be about?* Elicit answers. (Answer: foot massage)

3. Play the introduction: *Reflexology is foot massage. It comes from ideas of traditional Chinese medicine. Reflexology believes that rubbing parts of the foot can help other parts of the body.*

4. Play the instructions: *Listen. What body parts go with these areas of the foot? Write the body parts in the boxes. There are two extra boxes.*

5. (Optional) If your students will find this task very difficult, do the Additional Support procedure.

6. Play Listening Task 1 on the tape. Gesture for students to write their answers. **(Optional)** To make sure students understand what to do, stop after the second item and have students say their answers. Then play the rest of Listening Task 1.

7. If necessary, play Listening Task 1 a second time.

8. Check by drawing the foot diagram on the board. Have students tell you what to label. (Answers appear in blue on the opposite page.)

9. You may want to play the tape a final time. See the first Note below.

ADDITIONAL SUPPORT Have students work in pairs. Together they describe the location of each space on the illustration. For example, the box labeled "brain" could be described as "a round space on the big(gest) toe, in the middle." The one

directly below it is "a long space that goes along the inside edge of the foot."

NOTES

• When testing this lesson before publication, we gave our classes the option of listening once more. They could, if they wanted, take their shoes off and, rather than looking at their books, actually give themselves a quick foot massage. This might seem like a strange in-class activity, but most of the students wanted to try it. Those that didn't (most of whom happened to be wearing tall, lace-up boots that would have taken awhile to get off) simply followed in their books one more time. The students enjoyed it, got to try something new, and listened once more with a new task!

• As with most practices that grew out of a folk tradition, there are different versions of reflexology. All agree on the basic theory of energy and meridians (see the Culture Corner), but some disagree on the number of meridians and the exact location of the "pressure points" on the feet and other parts of the body.

Culture corner

1. Have students read the Culture Corner and, alone or in groups, answer the questions: *What alternative medical practices are used in your country? Do you know people who have tried them? Did the techniques help?*

2. (Optional) Before students read the Culture Corner, write the following on the board: *relax muscles, meridians (lines), pains, problems, whole body, spirit, energy, balance.* Students copy the words. Tell the students that each word is connected with Western or Asian medicine. As they read, they write "A" (for "Asian") or "W" (for "Western") next to each. This activity encourages reorganizing information, a high-level comprehension skill.

LISTENING TASK 1

Reflexology

Reflexology is foot massage. It comes from ideas of traditional Chinese medicine. Reflexology believes that rubbing parts of the foot can help other parts of the body.

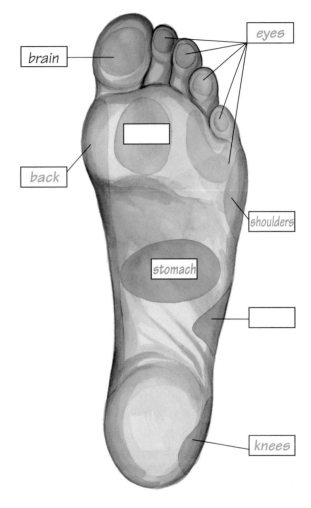

brain

eyes

back

shoulders

stomach

knees

❏ Listen. What body parts go with these areas of the foot?
Write the body parts in the boxes.
There are two extra boxes.

CULTURE CORNER

Reflexology is based on Chinese medicine, but similar techniques are used in Korean, Thai, and Japanese massage. Asian massage has a different philosophy and purpose from Western massage. In Western massage, the point is to relax the muscles. In Asian massage, it is believed that there are lines – called meridians – that go through the body. Massage is believed to heal the whole body.

Western and Chinese medicine also have different philosophies. In Asia, natural techniques are used to balance a person's spirit or energy (called *ki*). Western medicine looks more at specific pains or problems.

What alternative medical practices are used in your country? Do you know people who have tried them? Did the techniques help?

Relax!

There are many ways to relax. Some people play sports. Others read or watch TV.

❑ Listen. This is an alternative relaxation technique. What are the steps? Complete the sentences.

1. Sit in _a comfortable chair_ .
2. _Close your eyes_
   and take _a deep breath_ .
3. Think of _a word_ . It should be a _word with no special meaning_ _____
4. In your mind, _repeat_ the _word slowly_ .
5. When you think of other thoughts, just _go back_ to the _word_ .
6. Continue for _about 20 minutes_ _____ .
   Then slowly _open your eyes and take a deep breath_ .

Would you like to try this technique? Check (✔) your answer. ☐ yes ☐ no Why or why not?

YOUR TURN TO TALK

Work in groups of five. One person is the leader. The others work in two teams. Only the leader has the book open. The leader calls out the following topics one by one:

1. Healthy foods

2. Alternative health techniques

3. Ways to relax and get rid of stress

4. New health techniques

5. Ways to lose weight

6. Medical problems that doctors don't know how to cure yet

The teams try to give as many examples as they can in one minute each. The leader keeps score. Teams get one point for each answer.

Listening Task 2
Relax!

1. T: *Look at page 20.*

2. (Optional) Read the title: *"Relax!"* Ask: *What do you think this will be about?* Elicit answers. (Answer: a relaxation technique)

3. Play the introduction and instructions: *There are many ways to relax. Some people play sports. Others read or watch TV. Listen. This is an alternative relaxation technique. What are the steps? Complete the sentences.*

4. (Optional) If your students find the task very difficult, do the Additional Support procedure.

5. Play Listening Task 2 on the tape. Gesture for students to write their answers.

6. (Optional) To make sure students understand what to do, stop after a few sentences and have students say what they wrote. Then play the rest of Listening Task 2.

7. If necessary, play Listening Task 2 a second time. Before replaying the tape, you may want to have students compare answers: *Work with a partner. Look at your partner's sentences. How many were the same as yours?*

8. Check by having students read their sentences. (Answers appear in blue on the opposite page.) Have students talk about the follow-up question: *Would you like to try this technique?* in pairs or small groups.

9. You may want to play the tape again and let those who want to try the technique close their books and follow the instructions. Those who don't want to try it can just read along in the book.

ADDITIONAL SUPPORT Have students listen twice. The first time, they shouldn't write anything. They just listen and try to follow the general ideas. The second time, stop the tape after each step to give students time to think and write.

Your turn to talk

1. Divide the class into groups of five. T: *One person is the leader. The others work in two teams. Only the leader has the book open. The leader calls out the topics, one by one. Try to give as many examples as you can in one minute. The leader keeps score. Your team gets one point for each answer.*

2. (Optional) To help students get started, you may want to do one item as an example. Use this extra topic: Places in this town (or area) that are good for exercising.

3. At the end, have learners say some of their more interesting ideas.

Optional activity

(For use anytime during or after the unit.)

• *Your exercise routine.* An exercise routine is a common way to stay healthy. As a class, brainstorm names for exercises (sit-ups, push-ups, running in place, etc.). Then students work in pairs. They create an exercise routine that includes at least five exercises. It must be possible to do the exercises in the classroom in about two or three minutes. Instead of using the name of the particular exercise, they must describe what to do. For example, instead of saying, "Do five sit-ups," they say, "Lie on your back. Bend your knees. Lift your head and shoulders. Do this five times." After creating their routines, if space and the class atmosphere permit, have students take turns directing classmates through their sequences. Students work in groups of six to eight. Appoint two leaders for each group. The leaders call out the steps as the others do the exercises. Then they change roles, and a new pair of leaders calls out their routine.

U N I T 6
Advertising

Content area: Talking about advertising
Listening skills: Understanding details (Listening Task 1); understanding mistakes and problems (Listening Task 2)
Grammar/vocabulary: Passive, *should have*

Warming Up

1. T: *Look at page 21.*

2. Read the instructions. Pause when you see the symbol ♦ to give students time to answer the questions.

> *Work with a partner. Look at these advertisements. What products are the ads for? Write your answers in the boxes. ♦ What do you think of when you look at the ads? Write two adjectives for each ad.*

As students work, circulate and help pairs having difficulty.

3. T: *With your partner, think about advertisements you have seen. Write the name of a company or product for each type of ad below.*

4. (after about 10 minutes) T: *Now compare answers with another pair.*

5. (Optional) You may want students to share their ideas with the whole class.

NOTES

• "Ad" is the shortened form of "advertisement." A commercial is an advertisement on TV or radio.

• The Guardian is an automobile security device. It is locked on the steering wheel of a car, making the car impossible to drive.

Strategy exercise: *Contrasting languages*

Teachers sometimes worry whether or not to let their students use what they know in their own language(s). While we do not want to encourage translation, there is a place for contrasting languages. Students might want to share some humorous business names or commercials in their own language(s).

Optional activities

(For use anytime during or after the unit.)

• *From our country.* Students work in groups of two or three. They think of a product from their country that they think would not be common in most other countries. They create an ad introducing the product. If they have seen ads for the product, they can think of reasons the ads would or wouldn't make sense in another place. Finally, each group joins another group. They explain their ads. **Note:** If students are from different countries, have them reverse the process. They think of something available where they are that is not common in their native countries.

EXPANSION *What is it?* Before class, make copies of the Unit 6 Activity Sheet on page T53. You will need one copy for every nine students. In class, divide students into groups of nine. Those groups then divide themselves into three teams of three players each. Give each group a copy of the activity sheet. Students cut their sheet into separate cards. They shuffle the cards and place them facedown on a desk. Each team chooses one card. They have two minutes to think of an advertising slogan for their item (the slogan should not include the name of the item). They say their slogan. The other teams race to guess what the product is. If no one can guess, the team either gives more hints or describes the product. The first team to guess gets a point. They continue with all the cards. The team with the most points wins.

Advertising

WARMING **UP**

❏ Work with a partner.
Look at these advertisements. What products are the ads for? Write your answers in the boxes. What do you think of when you look at the ads? Write two adjectives for each ad.

athletic shoes

1. active, strong

laundry detergent

2. funny, dirty

perfume

3. pretty, expensive

car anti-theft device

4. frightening, dangerous

SAMPLE ANSWERS

❏ With your partner, think about advertisements you have seen. Write the name of a company or product for each type of ad below.

• a very funny ad _____

• a beautiful ad _____

• a surprising or shocking ad _____

• an ad with a slogan that's easy to remember _____

_____

• an ad you don't like _____

❏ Now compare answers with another pair.

LISTENING TASK 1 *What's in a name?*

Have you heard of these companies?

A.

B.

C.

D.

E.

❏ The companies used to have different names.
Can you match their names with the old names below?
Write your guesses (A–E) on the lines. There is one extra name.

❏ Now listen. Correct your answers.
Why did the companies change their names? Check (✔) the reasons.

1. Bank Americard ➔ _D_
The company …
☑ wanted to become international.
☐ began to offer passport services.

2. Consolidated Foods Corporation ➔ _A_
The company …
☐ began to make baked goods.
☑ wanted a well-known name.

3. Standard Oil ➔ _E_
The company wanted a name that …
☑ didn't exist in any language.
☐ was different, so they chose a word from the Maltese language.

4. Minnesota Valley Canning Company ➔ _B_
The company was named for …
☑ a type of green pea.
☐ the Prince of Wales, who was a large man.

CULTURE CORNER

Some companies choose names that are jokes. Do these company names seem funny to you?

- Fall in Coffee: A coffee shop in Korea where young people go to fall in love
- Curl Up and Dye: A hair salon in the United States
- Sleeping Giant: A large bedroom-furniture store in Australia
- Make-a-Date: A calendar company in Canada

Do you know any interesting company names from your country?
What ways do businesses that you know about choose their names?

Listening Task 1
What's in a name?

Listening skill: Understanding details

Note: The tapescript for Unit 6 begins on page T11.

1. T: *Look at page 22.*

2. (Optional) Read the title: *"What's in a name?"* Ask: *What do you think this will be about?* Elicit answers. (Answer: why companies choose and change their names)

3. Play the instructions: *The companies used to have different names. Can you match their names with the old names below? Write your guesses (A–E) on the lines. There is one extra name.* Allow time for students to work.

4. T: *Now listen. Correct your answers. Why did the companies change their names? Check the reasons.*

5. (Optional) If your students will find these tasks very difficult, do the Additional Support procedure.

6. Play Listening Task 1 on the tape. Gesture for students to write their answers. **(Optional)** To make sure students understand what to do, stop after the second item and say: *Consolidated Foods Corporation is now called . . . what?* Have students call out the answer. Then ask: *Why did it change its name?* Encourage answers. Finally, play the rest of Listening Task 1.

7. If necessary, play Listening Task 1 a second time.

8. Check by having students say their answers. (Answers appear in blue on the opposite page.)

ADDITIONAL SUPPORT Students work in pairs or groups of three. First, they look at the company logos and write down anything they know about the companies. Then tell students that all the companies changed their names. The students read the options. They guess what the

companies' new names are and the reasons they changed. Finally, they listen to the tape to check and correct their answers. Note that there is no reason students should know the answers, but the act of guessing will make them more familiar with the choices. Also, having made a guess, students are often more focused on finding out whether or not they were right.

NOTE

• You may prefer to check answers after each segment rather than waiting until students have heard all four items.

Culture corner

1. Have students read the Culture Corner. They work in pairs to figure out why the names are supposed to be funny (see the Note below). Then they go on to the follow-up questions: *Do you know any interesting company names from your country? What ways do businesses that you know about choose their names?*

2. (Optional) After reading the Culture Corner, students work in pairs. They list different ways businesses are named and an example of each. (*Examples:* For the person who started the business [McDonald's], the store's hours [7–11], a place [Kentucky Fried Chicken]) After about five minutes, they join another group and compare lists. This activity encourages students to expand what they read by relating it to known information.

NOTE

• *Fall in Coffee* is a play on words with the expression "to fall in love." *Curl Up and Dye* is a pun on the phrase "to curl up and die," used to express shame or embarrassment: "I was so embarrassed, I wanted to just curl up and die." *Sleeping Giant* refers to a character in a fairy tale, but here it means "a large store with beds, etc., for sleeping." *Make a Date* usually means "make an appointment," but here it means "get calendars made."

Listening Task 2
Lost in the translation

Listening skill: Understanding mistakes and problems

1. T: *Look at page 23.*

2. (Optional) Read the title: *"Lost in the translation."* Ask: *What do you think this will be about?* Elicit answers. (Answer: ads that had changes in meaning because of translation problems)

3. Play the introduction and instructions: *Some advertisements are effective in one language or country but not in another. This can be because of cultural differences or translation problems. Listen. These companies had advertising problems. What was the problem? What should they have done? Complete the sentences.*

4. (Optional) If your students will find this task very difficult, do the Additional Support procedure.

5. Play Listening Task 2 on the tape. Gesture for students to write their answers. **(Optional)** To make sure students understand what to do, stop after the second item to check. Then play the rest of Listening Task 2.

6. If necessary, play Listening Task 2 a second time.

7. Check by having students call out their answers. (Answers appear in blue on the opposite page.)

ADDITIONAL SUPPORT Write the following on the board:

___ Mexico	gasoline
___ China	soap
___ Brazil	shirts
___ Japan	cars
___ the Middle East	Pepsi

Students close their books and copy the lists. Play the tape once. Have students number the places and then match each place to the product being talked about. There is one extra in each group.

NOTES

• The passive form of a verb is used either when we don't know who did the action, it's not important who did it, or it's obvious who did it. The passive is formed with the verb *be* in the appropriate tense plus the past participle of the verb – for example, "It was translated . . . (by translators, of course)."

• The past form of the modal *should* is *should have* + past participle. We use this form to describe an action we did not do but later wish we had done (or an action we did do but later wish we had not done) – for example, "They *should have changed* the order of the pictures."

Your turn to talk

1. Divide the class into pairs. T: *Think of a product you have with you right now. For example, choose a bag, a piece of clothing, your notebook, even this book. Make a list of the good features of the product. Why is it useful? How is it better than similar products? Write a 30-second radio or television commercial. Then practice your commercial.*

2. (after about 10 or 15 minutes) T: *Now change partners. Present your commercial. Listen to your new partner's commercial. Then change partners again.* Students continue for as long as they seem interested.

Optional activity

(For use anytime during or after the unit.)

• *That wouldn't work.* Collect English-language magazines with a lot of ads. You will need at least one magazine for every two students. In pairs, students go through the magazines, looking at the ads. For each ad, they think of one or two adjectives. They then note which features of the product would or would not be good in their own culture if the ad were translated. Finally, pairs merge into groups of about eight. Each pair presents the ad they think would be the least appropriate for their country and explains why.

Lost in the translation

Some advertisements are effective in one language or country but not in another. This can be because of cultural differences or translation problems.

❏ Listen. These companies had advertising problems. What was the problem? What should they have done? Complete the sentences.

1. China
The slogan was " _Come alive_ !"
It was translated as " _Pepsi brings your_
ancestors back from the dead ."

2. the Middle East
The advertisement had dirty clothes
on the left .
They should have been _on the right_

_____ .

3. Mexico
The slogan was translated as " _Until_
I wore this shirt, I felt good."
The first word should have been
When .

4. Japan
The gas station's name was _Enco_ .
In Japanese, that word means
" _engine stop_ "

YOUR TURN TO TALK

Work in pairs. Think of a product you have with you right now. For example, choose a bag, a piece of clothing, your notebook, even this book. Make a list of the good features of the product. Why is it useful? How is it better than similar products?

Write a 30-second radio or television commercial. (Look at page 21 for different types of advertisements.) Then practice your commercial.

Now change partners. Present your commercial. Listen to your new partner's commercial. Then change partners again.

UNIT 7

Superstitions

su·per·sti·tion /ˌsupərˈstɪʃən/ n [C,U] (a) belief that is not based on human reason or scientific knowledge, but is connected with old ideas about magic, etc. Even in modern times, people cling to *superstitions* handed down through the centuries. [C] According to *superstition*, walking under a ladder brings you bad luck. [U]

Superstitions are beliefs. They're based on old ideas, not on science or facts. Superstitions are often about things that bring good luck or bad luck.

❏ Work with a partner.
These are things some people are superstitious about. What superstitions do you know? Write them below.

SAMPLE ANSWERS

Throwing salt over your left shoulder *brings good luck.*

A black cat that walks in front of you brings bad luck.

Thirteen is an unlucky number.

Garlic keeps away vampires or bad luck.

Sleeping in moonlight brings danger.

Breaking a mirror will bring 7 years' bad luck.

U N I T   7

Superstitions

> **Content area:** Describing beliefs
> **Listening skills:** Understanding specific information (Listening Task 1); understanding and adding to statements (Listening Task 2)
> **Grammar/vocabulary:** Possible and unreal conditionals

Warming Up

1. T: *Look at page 24. Superstitions.* Read the dictionary definition aloud and have students read along.

2. Read the introduction and instructions: *Superstitions are beliefs. They're based on old ideas, not on science or facts. Superstitions are often about things that bring good luck or bad luck. Work with a partner. These are things some people are superstitious about. What superstitions do you know? Write them below.* As students work, circulate. If students are having difficulty getting started, ask: *What do people do to bring good luck?*

3. Combine pairs and have them share their ideas. OR Work as a class and see how many different beliefs students listed.

NOTES

• Note that these do not need to be superstitions that the learners believe, just things some people believe. Also, learners are not limited to the items illustrated.

• Some students may say that their own culture has no superstitions. Be aware that this belief may be based on the students' own religion(s). Some religions say that superstitions are evil and against God. In this case, present this unit as a look at beliefs in other places, rather than encouraging the students to come up with their own superstitions.

• These are possible superstitions associated with the other objects in the illustration.

> Throw rice at a couple after the wedding ceremony for good luck.
> Seven is a lucky number.
> The ace of spades means death.

Strategy exercise: Getting ideas quickly

Listening Task 1 presents two different tasks. Students first listen for the meaning of each superstition and then listen to why it might be true. Remind students that they almost always listen for a specific purpose; point out that they should use the directions or the situation to help them decide why they are listening. This will focus students' attention, and they will understand more quickly than they could by trying to get all the information.

Optional activity

(For use anytime during or after the unit.)

• *How many different ones?* Students work in groups of two or three. Have students write (in English) as many superstitions or beliefs from their own culture(s) as possible. After about five minutes, combine groups. Have them compare lists. If students are from different cultural and/or language backgrounds, have them note any superstitions that are similar to ones in their own cultures. If the students are from the same background, have them note any the other group wrote that they didn't. **Variation:** If you have students from many different cultures, have them stand, circulate, and collect superstitions from as many cultures as possible in ten to fifteen minutes.

Listening Task I
The real meaning

Note: The tapescript for Unit 7 begins on page T13.

1. T: *Look at page 25.*

2. Play the instructions to Step One: *Listen. What do these superstitions mean? Check your answers.* Gesture for students to write their answers.

3. (Optional) If your students will find this task very difficult, do the Additional Support procedure.

4. Check answers by reading the first part of each item and having students say the ending.

5. T: *Now listen to the explanations. What do the superstitions really mean? Complete the sentences.* Play the rest of Listening Task 1 on the tape. **(Optional)** To introduce the idea of superstitions being based on fact, see the first Note below.

6. If necessary, play Listening Task 1 a second time.

7. Check by having students say their answers. (Answers appear in blue on the opposite page.)

ADDITIONAL SUPPORT Have students do the task in pairs. Stop after each item and let the students talk about what they think they understood. Because they are working together, learners will often focus on what they did understand rather than panic about what they missed.

NOTES

• To help students understand the task, you may want to use the example of "Walking under a ladder brings you bad luck." (See the dictionary definition on page 24.) Since someone is likely to be at the top of a ladder and something could

drop, it is easy for most students to see how this superstition might be based on fact.

• *"Kaminari"* is the Japanese word for thunder and lightning.

Culture corner

1. Have students read the Culture Corner and discuss the follow-up questions in pairs or small groups: *Does your culture have good luck/bad luck beliefs? What are they?*

2. (Optional) Before students read the Culture Corner, have them work in groups of three. Each student reads one of the examples from the Culture Corner. That student pantomimes the meaning. Partners guess. The first student to guess gets one point. Any student who can add a related belief from his or her own country also gets a point. This activity encourages guessing and personalization.

Optional activity

(For use anytime during or after the unit.)

 Superstition Concentration, Part 1. There are two ways to play this game.

Version 1 (If students are unfamiliar with American superstitions): Before class, make copies of the Unit 7 Activity Sheet on page T55 and the answer key on page 26 of this *Teacher's Edition.* You will need one copy for every three students. In class, divide the students into groups of three: **A, B,** and the Quizmaster. The Quizmaster has the answer key. Have the learners cut apart all the squares on the activity sheet. They put them faceup on a table. One student begins by taking a beginning phrase (on a white card) and matching it to the ending phrase (on a gray card). The Quizmaster checks to see if the guess is correct. If it is, that player keeps the squares and gets one point. If it is wrong, both squares go back on the table. Partners take turns, continuing until all the matches are completed.
THIS ACTIVITY CONTINUES ON THE NEXT PAGE.

LISTENING TASK 1

The real meaning

❏ Listen. What do these superstitions mean? Check (✔) your answers.
❏ Now listen to the explanations. What do the superstitions really mean? Complete the sentences.

1. In Mexico, when scorpions come down from the mountain, the mountain god is angry and soon …

☐ someone will die. ✔ it will rain.

Scorpions can feel _the wind before_ _people_ .

The wind blows _before the rainy_ _season_ .

2. An old British superstition says, "Never lend milk to anyone. The person might be a witch who will …

✔ put a magic spell on your cow."

☐ steal your cow."

This means: Don't _lend anything_ _to anyone_ .

3. Many years ago in Brazil, land owners told fruit pickers not to eat mangoes. If they did, they would …

✔ get sick.

☐ lose their jobs.

They said this so the fruit pickers wouldn't _eat the fruit they picked_ .

4. If Japanese children don't cover their stomachs during a storm, the thunder god will …

✔ steal their belly-buttons. ☐ steal the children.

During a storm, the temperature _goes down_ .
They cover themselves to _keep warm_ .

CULTURE CORNER

Many cultures have interesting beliefs about good and bad luck.

• the United States: It is bad luck to say "Good luck!" to an actor. Instead, people say "Break a leg!"
• Japan: Before a match, sumo wrestlers throw salt around the ring to purify it.
• Brazil: Wear a necklace or bracelet with a thumb pointing up for good luck.

Does your culture have good luck/bad luck beliefs? What are they?

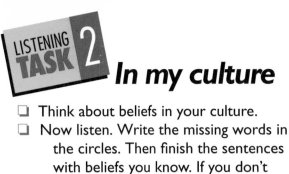

LISTENING TASK 2 *In my culture*

❑ Think about beliefs in your culture.
❑ Now listen. Write the missing words in the circles. Then finish the sentences with beliefs you know. If you don't know a belief, cross out the sentence.

True?

1. To have ⟨ *good luck* ⟩, you should _*carry a rabbit's foot*_ .   yes no

2. Don't __*break a mirror*__ , or you'll have ⟨ *bad luck* ⟩ .   yes no

3. In my culture, _7_ is a ⟨ *lucky number* ⟩ .   yes no

4. Some people say ⟨ *the number* ⟩ _13_ is unlucky .   yes no

5. If you ⟨ *get sick* ⟩, you should _*eat chicken soup*_ .   yes no

6. Be ⟨ *careful* ⟩ if you see _*a black cat cross your path*_ .   yes no

❑ Do you think the beliefs are true? Circle "yes" or "no."

YOUR TURN TO TALK

Work in groups of three. Read your sentences above. You get one point each time one other person in your group had the same answer. You get two points if all three of you had the same answer.

Now think about all the answers. Which might be based on fact? Try to give reasons for at least three beliefs.

Example: To have good luck, you should _____ . That might be because …

26

Listening Task 2 In my culture

1. T: *Look at page 26.*

2. Play the instructions: *Think about beliefs in your culture. Now listen. Write the missing words in the circles. Then finish the sentences with beliefs you know. If you don't know a belief, cross out the sentence.*

3. **(Optional)** If your students find this task very difficult, do the Additional Support procedure.

4. To encourage variety, you may want to stop after the first item and have several students suggest different answers. Then play the rest of Listening Task 2.

5. If necessary, play Listening Task 2 a second time. Before replaying the tape, you may want to have students compare their answers in pairs. Students need to compare only the dictated part of their answers, not the ideas they add themselves.

6. It isn't necessary to check the beliefs since students will do that in Your Turn to Talk. You may want to write the dictated parts of the sentences on the board. (Answers to the dictated parts and sample answers for the beliefs appear in blue on the opposite page.)

ADDITIONAL SUPPORT Do the activity as two separate steps. First, students listen and do only the dictation. When students finish, they go back and finish the sentences with beliefs they know.

NOTE

• See the second Note on page 24 about superstitions and religion. Students who believe superstitions are wrong should do this activity about their own beliefs.

Your turn to talk

1. Divide the class into groups of three. T: *Read your sentences above. You get one point*

each time one other person in your group had the same answer. You get two points if all three of you had the same answer.

2. To make sure everyone understands the scoring system, demonstrate with one group while the others watch.

3. T: *Now think about all the answers. Which might be based on fact? Try to give reasons for at least three beliefs.*

Optional activity

EXPANSION *Superstition Concentration, Part 2.* (See Part 1 of this activity on page 25.)

Version 2 (If students already know many American superstitions): Before class, make copies of the Unit 7 Activity Sheet on page T55. You will need one copy for every two students. In class, divide the students into pairs. Learners cut apart all the squares on the activity sheet. They put them facedown on a desk. Each student gets one turn to turn over two cards. If the cards make one complete superstition, the student keeps the match. If the halves do not match, the student turns them upside-down in their original place. Then it is the other partner's turn. Continue until all the cards are gone. (Answers:

If you break a mirror, you will have 7 years' bad luck.

Throw salt over your left shoulder to keep away bad luck.

If you walk under a ladder, you will have bad luck.

If you find a penny [a 1-cent coin] and pick it up, you will have good luck.

If you stand a broom upside-down behind a door, your visitors will go away.

If you step on a crack on the sidewalk, you will break your mother's back.

When the sky is red at night, tomorrow's weather will be good.

Throw rice at the couple after their wedding ceremony so they will have good luck.)

UNIT 8
Communication and culture

Content area: Discussing cultural behavior
Listening skills: Understanding cultural
  differences (Listening Task 1);
  understanding cultural information
  (Listening Task 2)
Grammar/vocabulary: *Should, must,* and
  have to for advice, simple past

Warming Up

1. T: *Look at page 27.*

2. Read the first set of instructions: *Every culture has its own communication style. Think about your culture. Check your answers. When people have conversations, do they . . . interrupt each other?* Read all the items, allowing time for students to answer after each question.

3. T: *Work with a partner. Compare answers. Which are the same? Which are different? When your answers are different, explain your reasons. Try to give examples.* As students work, circulate and help pairs having difficulty. If some pairs are giving only very short answers, encourage more interaction by having them think of times when people don't follow the "standard" behavior.

NOTES

• In any culture, there will be examples of people doing things that do not fit the cultural standards. On this page, learners should check what "most people do most of the time." If that is difficult, they can answer with things they personally do most of the time.

• If you have students from more than one culture, have them do Step 2 above with someone from their own country and Step 3 with a partner from somewhere else.

• This unit introduces students to the idea of culture – not the easy-to-see aspects of culture, such as holidays and wedding customs, but the subtle aspects, such as

nonverbal communication, conversational style, and ideas of friendship and hospitality. A difficulty in intercultural communication is that the same behavior can have different meanings in different cultures.

• Before finishing the Warming Up activities, you may want to see the Variation in the Culture Corner on the next page.

Strategy exercise: Using the body as well as the mind

One way to learn about new situations is to act them out. The motion is another clue to remembering. Divide students into an even number of groups. Each group selects a daily situation. One group acts out the situation for another group while the second group tries to guess the situation. In a monocultural class, have the students guess the participants (Is it an older person greeting a younger one?) and tell how they knew. In a multicultural class, groups from one culture may work together. In either case, the focus should be on the ways the body gives clues to the situation.

Optional activity

(For use anytime during or after the unit.)

EXPANSION **Gestures.** Before class, make copies of the Unit 8 Activity Sheet on page T57. You will need one copy for every 16 students. Cut the items apart and give one to each student. Have the learners take out a piece of paper and number from 1 to 17. Tell them that you will show them gesture Number 1. They should say the meaning and write it. Nod your head to indicate "Yes." After students guess that Number 1 is "Yes," have them stand and circulate. They gesture the item you gave them. They try to guess and write all 17 gestures. **Note:** If you don't have the right number of students, you can leave out a few items or give some students two items.

Communication and culture

❑ Every culture has its own communication style.
Think about your culture. Check (✔) your answers.

When people have conversations, do they ...

	Often	Sometimes	Not very often
interrupt each other?	☐	☐	☐
disagree directly?	☐	☐	☐
touch the other person when talking?	☐	☐	☐
say "no" directly?	☐	☐	☐

Do students call out answers in class?
☐ Yes, often. ☐ Yes, sometimes. ☐ No, not very often.

Someone invites you to a party that starts at 8:00. When should you arrive?
☐ Exactly on time. ☐ A little early. ☐ A little late.

When someone offers you something, what should you do?
☐ Take it right away. ☐ Say "no" the first time it is offered.

❑ Work with a partner.
Compare answers.
Which are the same? Which are different?
When your answers are different, explain
your reasons. Try to give examples.

LISTENING TASK 1
It's our style.

❑ Listen. People are describing conversation styles in three cultures.

Which things are OK to do?
Check (✔) the boxes.

Which are not OK?
Put an ✗ in the boxes.

	Latin America	Korea	Saudi Arabia
1. touching the other person while speaking	✔	✔	✔
2. interrupting someone	✔	✗	✔
3. saying "no" directly	✔	✗	✗
4. disagreeing with someone	✔	✗	✔
5. calling out answers in class	✔	✔	✔

 CULTURE CORNER

Cultures have different ideas about "personal space" – how close people generally like to sit or stand from each other. People in the Middle East stand the closest. Each of the other groups below stands a little farther away. People in East Asia stand the farthest away.

Middle East   **Southern Europe**   **Latin America**   **United States and Canada**   **Northern Europe**   **East Asia**

How close to other people do you like to stand? Work with a partner. First, stand up and face each other. Stand at arm's length. Then slowly move closer. What is the closest you can stand and still feel comfortable?

Listening Task 1
It's our style.

> **Listening skill:** Understanding cultural differences

Note: The tapescript for Unit 8 begins on page T14.

1. T: *Look at page 28.*

2. Play the instructions: *Listen. People are describing conversation styles in three cultures. Which things are OK to do? Check the boxes. Which are not OK? Put an X in the boxes.*

3. (Optional) If your students will find this task very difficult, do the Additional Support procedure.

4. Play Listening Task 1 on the tape. Gesture for students to write their answers. **(Optional)** To make sure students understand what to do, stop after the first part (about the time the teacher asks the Korean student the questions). Ask a few students: *What did Luis say about touching?* (Answer: Latin Americans do it often.) *Interrupting?* (Answer: It's OK.) Then play the rest of Listening Task 1.

5. If necessary, play Listening Task 1 a second time. You may want to pause the tape after each answer to give students time to think about what the speakers said.

6. Check by having students call out their answers. (Answers appear in blue on the opposite page.)

ADDITIONAL SUPPORT Write the following on the board:

1. touch	4. disagree
2. interrupt	5. answer
3. say "no"	

Learners close their books. Play the tape. Each time students hear one of the words or phrases, they hold up the number of fingers (one finger for "touch," two for "interrupt," etc.).

NOTE

- If you have learners from many countries, you might want to follow up by having them work in mixed cultural groups and do a similar type of interview. Encourage learners to go beyond simply answering the questions. They should give reasons, examples, etc.

Culture corner

1. Have students read the Culture Corner. **Variation:** During the Warming Up, have about half the students read the Culture Corner. Have students work in pairs. Each pair should consist of one member who has read the Culture Corner and one who has not. Secretly tell the members who have read it to "break the rules" by standing slightly too close. Assign a short listening/speaking task – for example: *Find three things you both did last weekend. Find three things your partner did that you didn't do.* Have students stand and face each other. They do the task. Afterwards, they talk about what happened. Did the other speaker move backwards? Feel uncomfortable? Then students all read the Culture Corner.

2. (Optional) After reading, have students do the experiment described at the bottom of the Culture Corner. Have them talk about an easy-to-discuss topic such as what they did the previous weekend. As they speak, they slowly move toward each other. At some point, they will feel uncomfortable with the closeness. This is because they feel their "personal space" has been invaded. They note about how far they were standing. Have them do this with at least five partners, add up the distances, and divide by the number of partners. This average is their personal distance zone. This activity encourages personalization and physical activity.

Listening Task 2
I didn't know that.

1. T: *Look at page 29.*

2. Play the introduction and instructions: *Many universities have an International Students' Association. This ISA is having a party. Students from several countries are getting to know one another. They're talking about mistakes they made when they were living abroad. Listen. Write the information.*

3. (Optional) If your students will find this task very difficult, do the Additional Support procedure.

4. Play Listening Task 1 on the tape. Gesture for students to write their answers. To make sure students understand what to do, stop after John finishes telling his story. Ask: *Where did John go?* (Answer: Peru) Then play the rest of Listening Task 2.

5. If necessary, play Listening Task 2 a second time.

6. Check by having students say their answers. (Answers appear in blue on the opposite page.)

ADDITIONAL SUPPORT Copy the answers on the board in a scrambled order, along with the following distractors: *Canada, Mexico, went the wrong day, didn't offer food again.* Play the tape and have students match the items to the people. Then play the tape again. Those students who basically understood the conversation should close their eyes and imagine it. Those who understood some but missed a lot should follow along in their books. Those who didn't understand much at all should listen and watch you. As you play the tape this time, point to the words and phrases on the board just before they are said.

Your turn to talk

1. Divide the class into groups of three. Read the instructions aloud. Have students decide on at least ten cultural rules. They should also give ways to explain the rules.

2. To help students get started, introduce a few rules that you know, either from the students' culture or from your own. Note that the rules don't need to be "major cultural beliefs." Small rules about eye contact, touching, smiling, etc., work fine.

3. (Optional) As a follow-up, have each group choose one situation and act it out twice: First, with someone as the "foreigner" making a mistake; then with the "foreigner" not making a mistake.

NOTE

• English uses several modals to give advice: *should/shouldn't, must* or *have to, must not, don't have to, had better/had better not. Must* is stronger than *should*: If we don't follow a *must* advice, we commit a serious error; if we don't follow a *should* advice, the error and thus the consequences are less serious. *Must not* and *don't have to* mean completely different things. *Must not* means "it is forbidden to," but *don't have to* means "it is not necessary to." *Had better (not)* is usually used by people with "more power" speaking to someone with "less power": doctor to patient, police officer to driver, etc. Students should be careful about using *had better*; it is easy to sound overbearing, even rude.

Optional activity

(For use anytime during or after the unit.)

• *My mistake!* Students work in pairs. They think of a time when they made a mistake either in a foreign country or when talking to a foreigner (or when a foreigner didn't understand one of their customs). They describe the situation, what happened, and how (or if) the situation was resolved.

I didn't know that.

Many universities have an International Students' Association. This ISA is having a party. Students from several countries are getting to know one another. They're talking about mistakes they made when they were living abroad.

❏ Listen. Write the information.

1. John, Ana, and Ken

John

from: *the U.S.*

went to: *Peru*

mistake: *He went to ...*
a party early.

Ana

from: *Peru*

went to: *the U.S.*

mistake: *She went*
to dinner late.

2. Karen and Hakan

Ken

from: *Japan*

went to: *the U.S.*

mistake: *He went*
to a party early.

Karen

from: *the U.S.*

went to: *Turkey*

mistake: *She didn't*
refuse food.

Hakan

from: *Turkey*

went to: *the U.S.*

mistake: *He said*
"no" to be polite.

YOUR TURN TO TALK

Work in groups of three. What customs in your own country do foreigners find surprising? Make a list of at least ten.

People from other cultures sometimes "break the rules" simply because they don't know the customs. Decide which customs are very serious (many people will think it's very bad if someone doesn't follow the customs). How would you explain each custom to someone who doesn't know it? Can you give a reason for the custom?

You shouldn't _____ because ...

People's best friends

Dogs and cats are popular pets in
    many countries.
What are the differences between the two animals?

❑ Work with a partner.
    Draw lines to match the words and phrases
        with the animals. Some describe both dogs and cats!

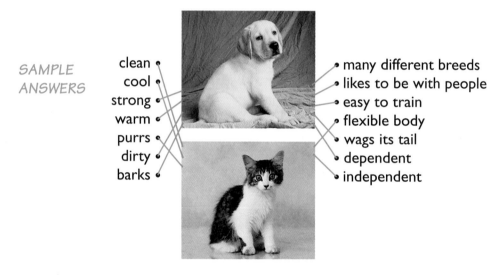

*SAMPLE
ANSWERS*

clean
cool
strong
warm
purrs
dirty
barks

many different breeds
likes to be with people
easy to train
flexible body
wags its tail
dependent
independent

❑ Do you know a dog or cat?
    Do the above words and phrases describe it?
    How? Give examples.

❑ What other words and phrases can you think of to describe
    dogs and cats? Write them on the lines.

*SAMPLE
ANSWERS*

soft	*friendly*	*mean*
lazy	*meows*	*growls*

❑ Are dogs and cats popular in your culture?
    What other animals are popular? List as many as you can.

birds	*fish*	*hamsters*
guinea pigs	*snakes*	*rabbits*

❑ Why do (or don't) people keep pets?
    Think of as many reasons as you can.

People's best friends

Content area: Talking about cats and dogs
Listening skills: Confirming and revising predictions, identifying reasons (Listening Task 1); understanding and enjoying stories, making predictions (Listening Task 2)
Grammar/vocabulary: Past tenses: simple past and past perfect

Warming Up

1. T: *Look at page 30.*

2. Read the introduction and instructions: *Dogs and cats are popular pets in many countries. What are the differences between the two animals? Work with a partner. Draw lines to match the words and phrases with the animals. Some describe both dogs and cats!* (**Optional**) You may want to do the first one or two items as a full class to help learners get started. Call out the words and have students say "dogs," "cats," or "both" and give reasons.

3. As students work, circulate and help pairs having difficulty by asking if they have ever known a dog or a cat (or even seen a movie about one). They can use that animal as an example.

4. Read the remaining questions. Have pairs discuss and write their answers.

5. You may want to go over answers as a full class or have pairs merge into groups of six or eight.

NOTES

• Make sure students know the meanings of the words in the lists. *Cool* can mean "emotionally distant" (the emotional equivalent of the temperature); it can also mean "fashionable." Students can think about this word whichever way they want.

• In the U.S., dogs are considered to be people's best friend – loyal, trustworthy, friendly, and good companions. However, on the negative side (especially from the point of view of cat-lovers), dogs are considered sloppy, loud, and not very intelligent. Cats are seen as intelligent, aloof, independent, and free spirits. On the negative side, as many dog-lovers are happy to point out, cats are unfriendly, snobbish, sly, and untrustworthy.

Strategy exercise: *Self-monitoring*

The most successful language learners monitor their own mistakes but also know when they are monitoring too much. As they near the mid-point of the course, students, individually or collectively, should think about their next step in language learning (the things they need to work on). They should then decide which things are important and which are not.

Optional activity

(For use anytime during or after the unit.)

EXPANSION **Describing dogs and cats.** Before class, make copies of the Unit 9 Activity Sheet on page T59. You will need one copy for every two students. Cut each copy into two parts: **A** and **B**. In class, divide students into pairs. Each student is either **A** or **B**. **A** holds the sheet so **B** can't see the pictures. **A** describes the dogs' pictures in a scrambled order. The description of each dog can include size, shape, appearance, etc., and what **A** imagines the animal's character to be like – but not the dog's breed (dachshund, boxer, etc.). **B** listens and takes notes. When **A** has described all the dogs, **B** looks at the pictures and says the order the pictures were described in and the clues that made it possible to guess. Then **B** describes the cats in the same way, and **A** takes notes.

Listening Task 1
Your dog/cat IQ

Listening skills: Confirming and revising predictions, identifying reasons

Note: The tapescript for Unit 9 begins on page T16.

1. T: *Look at page 31.*

2. (Optional) Read the title: *"Your dog/cat IQ."* Ask: *What do you think this will be about?* Elicit answers. (Answer: a quiz about dogs and cats)

3. Play the instructions: *How much do you know about dogs and cats? Read the statements. Do you think they're true or false? Check your answers.* Allow time for students to work. You might want them to do this step in pairs.

4. (Optional) If your students will find this task very difficult, do the Additional Support procedure.

5. Play Listening Task 1 on the tape. Gesture for students to write their answers. **(Optional)** To make sure students understand what to do, stop after the second item and ask: *True or false? Cats wag their tails when they're happy.* (Answer: false) When someone answers, ask: *Why?* (Answer: They move their tails when annoyed or angry.) Then play the rest of Listening Task 1.

6. If necessary, play Listening Task 1 a second time.

7. Check by reading the questions and having students volunteer answers. (Answers appear in blue on the opposite page.)

ADDITIONAL SUPPORT Before students listen, have them work in pairs. Together they read the questions. Then, as you play the tape, stop after each item. Allow time for students to discuss and write their answers.

Culture corner

1. Have students read the Culture Corner. Then, alone or in pairs, they answer the questions: *What beliefs do you know about animals? Do you think they're true?*

2. (Optional) Before class, make a copy of the Culture Corner. On the copy, block out all the verbs. Then make copies – one copy for every two students. In class, give a copy to each pair. Have students read the text and try to guess the missing words. They should think about the verbs and their correct tenses. Then they read in their books to check. If they wrote a verb with the same or a similar meaning to the one in the book, they should consider their choice correct. This activity encourages students to make use of what they already know to understand things that are new.

Optional activity

(For use anytime during or after the unit.)

- *Dog people/cat people.* Students work in pairs. Present this information: *Some people think of themselves as a "dog person" or a "cat person." A dog person likes dogs better than cats. Dog people think they have some of the positive characteristics of dogs, such as being loyal, friendly, and open. Cat people are proud of being independent, graceful, clean, etc.*

  Are you a dog person or a cat person? Or some other animal? Work with a partner. You and your partner each choose an animal that you think you resemble. Write down four characteristics that you and that animal have in common. Then write down four characteristics that you think your partner has in common with an animal.

  Then partners compare what they wrote and see if they agree.

Your dog/cat IQ

❏ How much do you know about dogs and cats?
Read the statements. Do you think they're true or false?
Check (✔) your answers.

❏ Now listen. Correct your answers. Write a reason for each.

1. Dogs can make themselves sick by eating too much.
✔ true ☐ false
Reason: *They hunted in groups and had to eat fast.*

2. Cats wag their tails when they're happy.
☐ true ✔ false
Reason: *They move their tails when annoyed or angry.*

3. Cats can be trained to do many different tasks.
☐ true ✔ false
Reason: *They aren't used to working with other animals.*

4. There are many different breeds of dogs but only a few breeds of cats.
✔ true ☐ false
Reason: *Humans have bred dogs to do many different jobs.*

5. Cats can fall from high places and land on their feet without getting hurt.
✔ true ☐ false
Reason: *Their backs and legs turn easily.*

6. Dogs cause more allergies in people than cats do.
☐ true ✔ false
Reason: *People are allergic to cats' saliva, not hair.*

CULTURE CORNER

The ancient Egyptians believed in the cat-goddess *Bast. Bast* had the body of a woman and the head of a cat. She also had nine lives. In Europe and North America, many people still say that a cat has nine lives.

In Ghana, in western Africa, some people believe that when someone dies, his or her spirit passes into the body of a cat. In England, people used to think that a hair from a cat's tail could cure a sore eye.

What beliefs do you know about animals? Do you think they're true?

LISTENING TASK 2 — True stories

Pets sometimes do amazing things.

❏ Listen. You will hear two stories from the newspaper.
Follow the instructions.

1.

2.

> He was walking toward the fire, but the
> dog stopped him.

> Hero was lying on top of a little girl.

❏ How are the two stories similar? Write your answer.

Both the dog and the cat saved a child.

YOUR TURN TO **TALK**

Work in groups of three. Choose one of these topics:

• An animal you know
• An animal that scared you
• An animal that you would like to be
• The strangest animal you've ever seen

Talk about the topic. Your partners will ask as many different questions as they can.

Example: I have a pet snake named …

Listening Task 2
True stories

Listening skills: Understanding and enjoying stories, making predictions

1. T: *Look at page 32.* **(Optional)** Read the title: *"True stories."* Ask: *What do you think this will be about?* Elicit answers. (Answer: true, surprising stories about animals)

2. Play the introduction and instructions: *Pets sometimes do amazing things. Listen. You will hear two stories from the newspaper. Follow the instructions.* Play Listening Task 2 on the tape, up through "Write or draw what you think she saw." Allow time for students to write/draw their predictions.

3. (Optional) If your students will find this task very difficult, do the Additional Support procedure.

4. T: *What really happened? Listen.* Play the rest of the first segment.

5. (Optional) You may want students to explain their story endings in pairs or small groups before going on.

6. (Optional) T: *Was the ending the same as what you drew (or wrote)? How?* OR Have learners change their pictures (or stories) to show what really happened.

7. Do the second item in the same way.

ADDITIONAL SUPPORT T: *This story is about a dog. Her name is Lucky. Lucky is a quiet dog. She doesn't usually bark.* Then have students close their eyes. Play the first part of the tape, up through "What do you think the mother saw?" Do this twice before having students draw or write their answers. Follow the same procedure with the second story: *Hero is a cat. Hero's owner is a seven-year-old girl named Lisa. This story happens on a cold winter day.*

NOTE

• Adding art to a task is a good way to encourage students to add an "affective"

(feeling) element to the task. However, some students worry that their art isn't good enough. It often helps if the teacher draws very simple, unsophisticated pictures on the board. Here are some ways to speed up student drawing time:

   • Remind the learners that they are studying English, not art.
   • Don't allow erasers. Once a line is drawn, it stays drawn.
   • Set a time limit (1 or 2 minutes) for each picture.

Your turn to talk

1. Divide the class into groups of three. T: *Choose one of these topics:*

   • *An animal you know*
   • *An animal that scared you*
   • *An animal that you would like to be*
   • *The strangest animal you've ever seen*

Talk about the topic. Your partners will ask as many different questions as they can.

2. (Optional) Demonstrate with a student who is a fairly good speaker. Have the student start to tell the story. Ask many, many questions – for example: *What color was it? How big was it? When did you see it? Where were you? Were you alone? Was it alone?*

Optional activity

(For use anytime during or after the unit.)

• *Your favorite pet.* (If all but a few students have had pets, you can still do the activity by having those without a pet talk about the kind of animal they would buy if they were to get one and why.) Students work in pairs. For as long as possible, they tell about a pet they have or had. The partner listens and keeps track of the time. When a speaker pauses for more than ten seconds, that person's turn is over. When both speakers have had a turn, they change partners and begin again.

Mind your manners!

Content area: Giving opinions about types of behavior
Listening skills: Inferring feelings (Listening Task 1); identifying examples and reasons (Listening Task 2)
Grammar/vocabulary: Present tenses: simple present and present progressive

Warming Up

1. T: *Look at page 33.*

2. Read the instructions. Pause when you see the symbol ♦ to give students time to answer the questions.

> *Think about things that make you angry.* ♦
> *How angry do these things make you? Draw lines.*
> *1. A friend is a half-hour late meeting you.* ♦
> *2. You're waiting in line at a public phone. Someone is talking for a long time.* ♦

3. (Optional) Draw two "anger meters" on the board. Write numbers 1–5 under each of them (1 = It doesn't bother me at all. 5 = It drives me crazy!). Read the items again and have students raise their hands to show their feelings.

4. Divide the class into pairs. T: *Work with a partner. Think of three more "rude behaviors." Write them below. How strongly do you feel about them? Draw lines.* As students work, circulate and help pairs having difficulty by pointing out some behaviors that drive you crazy. Ask students how they feel about those behaviors.

5. (after about 5 minutes) T: *Now join another pair. Ask how strongly they feel about your items.*

Variation: Instead of having the students work with another pair for the last step, have them conduct a poll. Students stand. Each partner asks five other students about the three items they wrote. Partners then combine their information. You may want to give students large pieces of paper and markers and have them prepare graphs showing the results.

NOTES

• In most cultures, "being late" depends on the situation. For example, in some situations, such as going to a party, most Americans think being late is acceptable. However, being late to class or an appointment is considered rude.

Some people believe there are generally two types of people: those who are always on time (and think that people who arrive late are irresponsible) and those who are always late (and think that people who are always on time are neurotic).

• *Mind* can mean "take care of" or "be careful about." *Business* sometimes means "personal affairs." Here are some expressions with *mind* and *business:*

> • Mind your manners. = Be careful to act appropriately.
> • Mind your own business. = Do not interfere with other people's lives.
> • It's none of your business. = It is not your concern.

Strategy exercise: *Using the emotions in learning*

Emotions are important in language learning. Students may be feeling restless with the school term and in need of encouragement. They should think of one positive thing they have accomplished or one activity they really enjoyed or did well. They may prefer not to say what it is. It is adequate to have them think about it or write it down. Stress the positive and the importance of not getting discouraged in language learning.

Mind your manners!

WARMING UP

❏ Think about things that make you angry.

❏ How angry do these things make you?
Draw lines.

It doesn't
bother me
at all.

It drives
me crazy!

1. A friend is a half-hour late meeting you.

2. You're waiting in line at a public phone. Someone is talking for a long time.

❏ Work with a partner.
Think of three more "rude behaviors."
Write them below.
How strongly do you feel about them?
Draw lines.

_____

_____

❏ Now join another pair.
Ask how strongly they feel about your items.

LISTENING TASK 1 · *It drives me crazy!*

Inferring feelings

❏ Listen. People are talking about rude
   behavior and how strongly they feel about it.
   Draw lines.
   How did you know their feelings?
   Write a few words.

1. Chatting on a public telephone

bothers me

talking and talking

2. Using a mobile phone in a public place

wasn't terrible

should have gone outside

3. Double-parking

just cannot stand

drives me nuts

4. Not giving up a seat on the train or bus

bothers me

really inconsiderate

5. Friends who are late

nice guy

not that big a deal

6. Students who are late for class

don't like

rude

CULTURE CORNER

What are polite topics of conversation? What topics are impolite? In some
countries, it is impolite to talk about money, politics, or religion. You probably
aren't surprised by that. In England, Spain, and other parts of Europe, it is
unusual in social situations to talk about work. In the Middle East, people who
do business together don't usually talk about their families. In most places,
sports, travel, and free-time activities are good things to talk about with someone
you don't know very well.

What things do strangers talk about in your country? What topics are impolite?

Listening Task 1
It drives me crazy!

Note: The tapescript for Unit 10 begins on page T18.

1. T: *Look at page 34.* **(Optional)** Read the title: *"It drives me crazy!"* Ask: *What do you think this will be about?* Elicit answers. (Answer: how people feel about certain behaviors)

2. Play the instructions: *Listen. People are talking about rude behavior and how strongly they feel about it. Draw lines. How did you know their feelings? Write a few words.*

3. **(Optional)** If your students will find this task very difficult, do the Additional Support procedure.

4. Play Listening Task 1 on the tape. Gesture for students to mark their answers and write two or three "clue" words. **(Optional)** To make sure students understand what to do, stop after the second item. Have students show where they drew the line and what words they wrote. Then play the rest of Listening Task 1.

5. If necessary, play Listening Task 1 a second time.

6. Check by having students say their answers. To check the meters, have students use their arms to represent a needle on a meter. The farther to their right they move their arm, the more anger they show. (Answers appear in blue on the opposite page.)

ADDITIONAL SUPPORT Draw an "anger meter" on the board. Also write: *I really don't like that.* Point to different points on the meter and have students practice saying the sentence, "I really don't like that." with different levels of emotion. Then students work in pairs. They ask their partners about the items. Partners answer using only the sentence, "I really don't like that." The first partner must figure out how angry the other student is.

NOTES

• Point out that this is an inference activity. Students need to listen to the way things are said as well as to the words.

• In item 3, the second speaker says, "Chill out." This is an informal expression meaning, "Relax. Calm down."

Culture corner

1. Have students read the Culture Corner. Alone or in small groups, they answer the follow-up questions.

2. **(Optional)** Before students read the Culture Corner, they work in groups of three or four. If possible, give each group a large piece of paper and a marker. While learners have their books closed, read the Culture Corner aloud twice. Read at a natural speed, but pause between each sentence. Students listen but do not take notes. After you have read the paragraph twice, students work to try to "re-create" it. They write the paragraph as correctly as possible. After a few minutes, have students pass their paper to another group. The new group corrects the paragraph. Finally, each group gets their paper back and compares it to the book. This activity builds memory and encourages discussion of form and meaning.

Optional activity

(For use anytime during or after the unit.)

• *Pet peeves race.* Divide the class into groups of ten. Then each group divides itself into two teams of five people each. Each team sits facing the other team. Explain that they are going to talk about pet peeves (little things that bother them). One team begins by a person saying a pet peeve. Then a person on the other team says a pet peeve. Continue. If there is a pause of more than 10 seconds, the other team scores a point.

Listening Task 2
Ask Miss Manners

Listening skill: Identifying examples and reasons

1. T: *Look at page 35.* **(Optional)** Read the title: *"Ask Miss Manners."* Ask: *What do you think this will be about?* Elicit answers. (Answer: a newspaper column about manners)

2. Play the introduction and instructions: *Miss Manners is a newspaper columnist. She gives advice about manners and relationships. Read her list of the five worst behavior "mistakes." The list is surprising. At first, the things on the list look good. Now listen. Why does Miss Manners think the things can be bad? Write examples and reasons.* Play Listening Task 2 on the tape. Gesture for students to write their answers.

3. (Optional) If your students will find this task very difficult, do the Additional Support procedure.

4. If necessary, play Listening Task 2 a second time. Before replaying the tape, you may want to have students compare answers.

5. Check by having students call out their answers. OR Have ten students go to the board. Each writes one answer. The other students read the answer to see if they agree or want to add other ideas. Have students, as a full class or in small groups, compare their answers to the final questions on the tape.

ADDITIONAL SUPPORT Before students listen, have them read the words and make sure they know the meaning of each. Then have them listen twice. The first time, they only try to catch the example. The second time, they try to understand the reason the behavior is bad.

NOTES

• You may want to stop the tape just before the final questions to check the main answers before the personalization step.

• Many students think of English as a very direct language. If asked, most native English speakers would probably say that being direct is a good way to be and act with other people. In reality, while English speakers may be more direct than people from other cultures, there are many times when being direct would be impolite. Thus, most Americans would say that although all five values listed are good, what Miss Manners says about them is true.

• *Miss Manners* is syndicated in many newspapers around the world. The column, written by Judith Martin, is known for its witty approach to manners.

Your turn to talk

1. Divide the class into groups of six. T: *Each person writes one rude behavior on a piece of paper. Then mix up the papers.* Allow time for students to work.

2. T: *Now work in pairs. Each pair chooses one behavior. What would you say to someone doing it? What do you think Miss Manners would say? Write your answers.* Circulate, help, and encourage. If some pairs finish early, have them choose another behavior and continue.

3. (after about 5 minutes) T: *When everyone finishes, take turns reading your answers. Do the other pairs agree? Can they offer other ideas?*

Optional activity

(For use anytime during or after the unit.)

• *Advice columns.* From English-language newspapers, collect copies of advice columns.

Activity 1: Separate the problems from the answers. Have students read the problems and match them to the correct answers.

Activity 2: Students, alone or in pairs, select problems. They read them and write their own letters of advice.

LISTENING TASK 2 Ask Miss Manners

Miss Manners is a
   newspaper columnist.
She gives advice about
   manners and relationships.

❏ Read her list of the five
   worst behavior "mistakes."
   The list is surprising. At first,
   the things on the list
   look good.

❏ Now listen. Why does
   Miss Manners think the
   things can be bad?
   Write examples and reasons.

❏ Now listen to some questions.
   Follow the instructions.

JUDITH MARTIN
MISS MANNERS

The Five Worst Behavior Mistakes

1. **Honesty**

   Example: _Telling someone his/her clothes_
   don't look good

   Reason: _It's not OK to hurt people's feelings._

2. **Helpfulness**

   Example: _Telling someone who to date_

   Reason: _Mind your own business._

3. **Health-consciousness**

   Example: _Telling someone what to eat_

   Reason: _Don't spoil other people's dinner._

4. **Idealism**

   Example: _Giving advice about a dog_

   Reason: _Don't criticize things that aren't_
   your concern.

5. **Being true to your own feelings**

   Example: _Not going to a play_

   Reason: _Do what you've promised – even if_
   you don't want to.

YOUR TURN TO TALK

Work in groups of six. Each person writes one rude behavior on a piece of paper. Then mix up the papers.

Now work in pairs. Each pair chooses one behavior. What would you say to someone doing it? What do you think Miss Manners would say? Write your answers. (If you finish before the other pairs, choose another behavior and continue.)

When everyone finishes, take turns reading your answers. Do the other pairs agree? Can they offer other ideas?

Tales from the past

❏ Work in a group of four to six people.
Think about stories you know.
They can be old stories, like folk tales or fairy tales.
Or they can be new stories from books, movies, or TV.

❏ How many stories can you think of with the things below?
Write the names of the stories. Write as many as you can.

SAMPLE
ANSWERS

• a special gift
  Snow White

• magic
  Aladdin
  Beauty and the Beast

• someone breaking a rule
  Pinocchio

• someone with unusual clothes
  The Emperor's New Clothes

• bad weather or a storm
  The Wizard of Oz

• an animal
  Lassie

• a religious person
  (any story from any religion)

• a moral (a lesson)
  (any Aesop story, e.g., The Tortoise and the Hare)

U N I T 1 1
Tales from the past

Content area: Appreciating stories
Listening skills: Understanding a story,
  understanding details (Listening Task 1);
  imagining a story, understanding
  questions (Listening Task 2)
Grammar/vocabulary: Past tenses: simple
  past and past progressive, question forms

Warming Up

1. Hold your book so that students can see
page 36. T: *Look at page 36.*

2. Divide the class into groups of four to
six. Read the instructions: *Work in a group of
four to six people. Think about stories you know.
They can be old stories, like folk tales or fairy
tales. Or they can be new stories from books,
movies, or TV. How many stories can you think
of with the things below? Write the names of the
stories. Write as many as you can.* To help
students get started, you might want to
have a group brainstorm. (Examples of
each story type appear in blue on the
opposite page.)

3. As students work, circulate and help
groups having difficulty. If a group can't
think of a story for a particular item, give a
hint – for example, for "unusual clothes":
*What's the story about the girl who wore red? She
met a wolf.* (Answer: Little Red Riding Hood)

4. Check by calling out the categories and
having students give their ideas.

NOTE

• For the sample answers on the opposite
page, we have primarily chosen stories that
became famous movies, because students
from various cultures are likely to know of
them.

Strategy exercise: Summarizing

Summarizing is a useful skill in storytelling
and after listening to stories. As homework,

have students watch a video or TV program
or listen to an English song or radio
broadcast. Ask them to write a summary of
what they heard. Then, in class, they share
their summaries with their classmates. Each
student should prepare a list of words in the
summary that classmates might not know.

Optional activity

(For use anytime during or after the unit.)

EXPANSION ***Story cards.*** Before class, make
  copies of the Unit 11 Activity
Sheet on page T61. You will need one copy
for every four students. In class, divide
students into groups of four and give one
sheet to each group. The students cut the
cards apart.

Activity 1. Story race: Students put the
cards facedown on a table. Each person
takes three cards. T: *Here is the first sentence
in a story: Once upon a time, there was a little
girl.* Learners work to finish the story.
Anyone can add one or more sentences,
but they must include one word from one
of their cards. As students add to the story,
they lay that card faceup on the table. The
winner is the first person to use all of his or
her cards.
Variation: As above, but learners must
paraphrase what the previous person said
before making their addition to the story.

Activity 2. Guess the story: First, players
work in groups of four to think of a story. It
must include items from at least nine of the
cards. They lay out the story cards in the
correct order. Then each group joins
another. They look at their new partners'
card arrangement and try to guess the
story by asking yes/no questions.
Variation: To increase language practice,
have learners do the second part in pairs
instead of groups of eight. One member of
each group pairs up with a member from
the joining group.

Listening Task 1
Are you still carrying her?

> **Listening skills:** Understanding a story, understanding details

Note: The tapescript for Unit 11 begins on page T20.

1. T: *Look at page 37.*

2. Play the introduction and instructions: *This is a very old story from Japan. It's about two monks (holy men). Years ago, monks weren't allowed any contact with women. Listen. Where should the woman be in each picture? Write this symbol in the correct place.*

3. (Optional) If your students will find this task very difficult, do the Additional Support procedure.

4. Play Listening Task 1 on the tape. Gesture for students to draw the symbol. **Note:** We don't recommend stopping after each picture to check as that will cause students to lose the "flow," or continuity, of the story. However, you might want to pause the tape after each segment to give the learners time to think/visualize.

5. If necessary, play Listening Task 1 a second time. You probably want to do so before students answer the "What does this story mean?" question. Check by having volunteers show where they drew the symbol in each picture.

6. Have students answer the question in Step Two. Check by asking the students what they think the story means. (The answer appears in blue on the opposite page.) Ask students to give reasons.

7. Read the last set of instructions: *Now work with a partner. Do you agree with the moral of the story? Why or why not? Compare answers.* Allow students time to work.

8. You may want to have several pairs give their opinions.

ADDITIONAL SUPPORT Have students work in pairs. Tell them to describe exactly what is happening in each picture – for example: There are two men. They look like religious people. They are walking., etc. Then tell students that there is a woman in each picture. They can't see her. Have the learners draw a circle in the place they think the woman might be. Then, as they listen, they see if their guesses were correct.

NOTES

• This is a Buddhist story from Japan. Rules for monks and priests vary among religious sects. In Japan, for example, monks in some sects are allowed to marry. In Thailand, it is considered a sin for a woman to touch a monk, even by accident.

• The dark blue robes are typical of priests and monks in Japan. In other countries, the dress varies. Robes may be saffron, brown, or other colors.

• Most stories are told in past tenses. The simple past is used to describe those events seen as complete, single actions (The older priest walked up to the woman. Silently he looked at her. He picked up the woman . . .). The past progressive (*was wearing, was standing*) is used to view an event as one that is background for another action, which was in progress when that action occurred.

Culture corner

1. Have learners read the Culture Corner and answer the follow-up questions in pairs or groups.

2. (Optional) Before class, make a copy of the Culture Corner and cut all the sentences apart. Spread them out on the photocopier and make copies. You will need one copy for every two students. In class, give out the copies. Have students try to put the sentences in order. Then they look in their books to check. This activity helps students notice organization.

Are you still carrying her?

This is a very old story from Japan. It's about two monks (holy men).
Years ago, monks weren't allowed any contact with women.

❑ Listen. Where should the woman be in each picture?
Write this symbol ♀ in the correct place.

1.   2.   3.   4.

❑ What does this story mean? What is the moral? Check (✔) your answer.

☐ Remember the past. It tells us how to live.

☑ Forget the past. It's over. Think about the present.

☐ The past, the present, and the future are all the same.

❑ Now work with a partner.
Do you agree with the moral of the story? Why or why not?
Compare answers.

CULTURE CORNER

Every culture has stories. Stories serve different purposes. Some entertain.
Others teach history or help people understand their own culture. In many
cultures, stories are used to teach the difference between right and wrong.

This story is from the Buddhist religion. It has a moral. So do stories from other
religions such as the parables of the Bible (Judaism and Christianity) and the
Hadiths (Islam).

What kinds of stories are traditional in your culture? Do you know any stories
that teach a lesson?

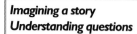
The story in your mind

❏ You will hear part of a story. It's about traveling through time.
In your mind, you'll imagine the rest of the story.
Close your eyes. Listen. Don't write anything. Just imagine.

❏ Now listen to these questions. Write your answers.

1. *It was …* _____

2. _____

3. _____

4. _____

5. _____

6. ☐ yes   ☐ no _____

YOUR TURN TO TALK

Work in a group of four people. Tell about your story. Listen to what happened to your partners. What was the same? What was different?

Example
A: I think I was in Europe.
B: I was too. In a small village.
C: I wasn't. I was here, but it was very different from now.

Listening Task 2
The story in your mind

Listening skills: Imagining a story,
understanding questions

1. T: *Look at page 38.* **(Optional)** Read the title: *"The story in your mind."* Ask: *What do you think this will be about?* Elicit answers. (Answer: thinking of a story)

2. Play the instructions: *You will hear part of a story. It's about traveling through time. In your mind, you'll imagine the rest of the story. Close your eyes. Listen. Don't write anything. Just imagine.*

3. (Optional) If your students will find the task very difficult, do the Additional Support procedure.

4. Gesture for students to close their eyes and relax. Play the story on the tape.

5. (Optional) If you want students to listen a second time, don't have them open their eyes and write their answers the first time they hear the questions. Either play the story again before they hear the questions or, for more support, play the questions once so that students know what the key elements are. Then play the tape again.

6. T: *Now listen to these questions. Write your answers.* Pause the tape after each question to allow time for students to write.

7. It probably won't be necessary to check answers at this point since students will talk about their stories during the Your Turn to Talk activity.

ADDITIONAL SUPPORT Write the following words and phrases on the board in a list:

Back in time. You are there. People? Clothes? Buildings? Where? Messenger. Follow. Small building. Person. Hands. Present. Coming back.

Play the story on the tape. Instead of having students close their eyes, have them look at the words. (For extra support, you may want to point at each item as it is mentioned.) After students have heard the story while looking at the key words, have them listen again with their eyes closed.

NOTE

- The main part of this activity is a "guided fantasy." It is essentially an imagination exercise, with the tape providing structure for the students' imaginations. The students close their eyes so they can focus on "the story in their mind." Note that even though the "content" of the story comes from the students' imaginations, they are following and responding to directions and questions from the tape. Also, by ending with a question about whether or not the student would like to return to the place of the story, the task asks learners to process the story at a level of evaluation and appreciation, a very sophisticated level of comprehension.

Your turn to talk

1. Divide the class into groups of four. T: *Tell about your story. Listen to what happened to your partners. What was the same? What was different?*

2. (Optional) Demonstrate by reading the example in the book. Then tell the first part of your own story. Gesture for two or three students to compare it to theirs: *I think I was in Africa . . . .*

3. (Optional) For additional support, on the board write either the key words from the story (see Additional Support above) or the questions:

1. How far back in time did you go?
2. Where did you go?
3. What was the building like?
4. Who did you meet?
5. What was the present?
6. Would you like to go back? Why (not)?

4. (after about 10 minutes) Ask: *Would you like to go back to that place? Why or why not?* Encourage several students to answer.

UNIT 12
Decisions, decisions

Content area: Deciding on schools and
living situations
Listening skills: Understanding details,
identifying key information (Listening
Task 1); understanding reasons
(Listening Task 2)
Grammar/vocabulary: *Wh*-questions

Warming Up

1. T: *Look at page 39.*

2. Divide the class into pairs. Read the
instructions. Pause when you see the
symbol ♦ to give students time to answer
the questions.

> *Work with a partner. Imagine that you want
> to study English in another country. Which
> country would you choose? Check your
> answer. ♦ When you're choosing a school,
> what information do you need? Write the
> questions you should ask. ♦ What else
> should you know? Write at least three more
> questions.*

3. As students work, circulate and help
pairs having difficulty. If pairs can't think
of other questions, gesture or give hints of
other items (cost, weather, safety, etc.).

4. T: *Now join another pair. Read your questions.
Listen to theirs. Which questions were different?*
Circulate as students compare. You may
want to have students write some of their
questions on the board. (Sample answers
appear in blue on the opposite page.)

5. You may want to compare answers as a
full class, having each student offer a
suggestion.

NOTE

• You may want to review *Wh*-questions
with "how":

> to ask about length: *How long does the
> course last?*

to ask about size: *How big are the
classes?/How large is the campus?*
to ask about numbers (count nouns):
*How many students from ____ are there?
How many students are in each class?*
to ask about quantity (noncount nouns):
How much is the tuition?

To ask about a general description, use
What is ____ like? – NOT *How is ____?*
(*Examples:* What is the campus like? What
are the dorms like? What is the city like?)

Strategy exercise: Listening with a purpose

Each time they listen, students need to
know why they are listening. You can use
hypothetical situations to help students
learn this skill. Students can work in pairs
to answer the question, "In your own
language, what do you listen to each day?"
Some answers might be, "I listen to the
weather report on the radio in the
morning." "I listen to the teacher tell us
about the homework." "I listen to my friend
tell me what she did last night." After
students list the ways they listen, have them
write down the information they listen for
(for example: in the weather report, the
temperature or whether it's going to rain).

Optional activity

(For use anytime during or after the unit.)

EXPANSION **Find someone who . . .** Before
class, make copies of the top
half of the Unit 12 Activity Sheet on page
T63. You will need one copy for each
student. In class, the whole class works
together. Learners walk around the room
and ask questions. If a classmate says "Yes,"
they write that person's name on the line.
If the classmate says "No," they ask another
question. Students write names only when
someone says "Yes."
Variation: Require students who say "Yes" to
add at least one extra piece of information.
Partners write it (in short note form) next
to the name.

Decisions, decisions

❑ Work with a partner.
Imagine that you want to study English in another
country. Which country would you choose?
Check (✔) your answer.

☐ the United States ☐ Great Britain
☐ Australia ☐ New Zealand
☐ Canada ☐ (other: _____)

❑ When you're choosing a school, what information
do you need? Write the questions you should ask.

SAMPLE
ANSWERS

• length of the course: *How long does the course last?*

• class size: *How big is the class?*

• location: *Is the school in the city or the country?*

• housing: *Where do most students live?*

• students' nationalities: *Where are most of the students from?*

❑ What else should you know? Write at least three
more questions.

• *How much does the course cost?*

• *How experienced are the teachers?*

• *Will I be able to meet local people?*

• *What kinds of classes are there?*

❑ Now join another pair.
Read your questions. Listen to theirs.
Which questions were different?

LISTENING TASK 1

Choosing a school

Hyung Jin is thinking about studying English in a foreign country.
He's talking to his teacher.

❑ Listen. What things are important to Hyung Jin? Write the information.

- class size: _small_
- location: _city_
- housing: _dorm or apartment_
- other: _He wants to use ... English a lot._
- Hyung Jin's English level: _high-intermediate_

Hyung Jin is at the "Study Abroad Fair."
Representatives are talking about their schools.

❑ Listen. Take notes. Write two important points about each school.

University of Pittsburgh
English Language Institute
Department Of Linguistics

1. _10 minutes from downtown,_
   good mix of nationalities

Australian
Centre for
Languages
Sydney
:acl

2. _flexible schedule_
   small classes

SEMESTER AT SEA

3. _travel around the world_
   English and academic classes

❑ Now listen to some questions. Follow the instructions.

1. _____   **2.** _____

CULTURE CORNER

Studying in English-speaking countries is popular with many students. Here are some good questions to ask when looking for a language school:

1. How much does it cost? (A 15-week course for $3,500 costs less per week than a 10-week program for $3,000.)
2. How experienced are the teachers? (Look for teachers with a lot of experience.)
3. Are there opportunities for meeting people and speaking English outside of class? It's also better if there are chances to meet local people.
4. What nationalities study at the school? (Look for a mix. You probably don't want to study at a school with too many people who speak your language.)

What different types of schools teach English in your country? What did you think about when choosing your school?

Listening Task 1
Choosing a school

Listening skills: Understanding details, identifying key information

Note: The tapescript for Unit 12 begins on page T21.

1. T: *Look at page 40.* (**Optional**) Read the title: *"Choosing a school."* Ask: *What do you think this will be about?* Elicit answers. (Answer: information about language schools)

2. Play the introduction, instructions, and the first part of the tape: *Hyung Jin is thinking about studying English in a foreign country. He's talking to his teacher. Listen. What things are important to Hyung Jin? Write the information.* Gesture for students to write their answers.

3. (**Optional**) If your students will find this task very difficult, do the Additional Support procedure.

4. Stop after the first part. Check by reading the question items and having students say their answers.

5. Play the rest of Listening Task 1: *Hyung Jin is at the "Study Abroad Fair." Representatives are talking about their schools. Listen. Take notes. Write two important points about each school.* (**Optional**) You may want to stop after the description of each school to check. Have students say what they wrote. This will help weaker students decide what is and what isn't really important. (Answers appear in blue on the opposite page.)

6. Check answers to the final questions in Step Three. Encourage students to give reasons.

ADDITIONAL SUPPORT Before students listen, they read the page. Alone or in pairs, they answer the items at the top (class size, location, etc.) with their own preferences. They look at the brochures and think of one question they would ask about each school.

NOTES
- Hyung Jin is Korean.
- Note that in this task (and the one on page 41), students are making evaluations and decisions about the best options. There are no absolute right or wrong answers. Obviously, much of life is like that. Just as importantly, it gives the students experience in processing and understanding information at the level of evaluation and judgment – a level much higher than simply "catching the main data" as they often do.
- In this unit, students may be surprised to hear non-native speakers who are not at an advanced level. Remind them that the voices are students who are working on their English. Also, in real life, English is used more by non-native speakers than by natives. Point out that hearing people with various accents speaking at different levels is always good practice.

Culture corner

1. Have the students read the Culture Corner and answer the follow-up questions. When talking about the types of schools in their country, it is probably best to have students work in pairs so they can share information.

2. (**Optional**) Before students read the Culture Corner, have them work in pairs. They imagine they are going to a language school in another country. What questions would they ask? They write as many questions as possible in five minutes. Then they join another pair and combine lists. Finally, they read the Culture Corner. They underline any questions they wrote that are included in the book. This activity encourages prediction.

Listening Task 2
A place to live

1. T: *Look at page 41.* **(Optional)** Read the title: *"A place to live."* Ask: *What do you think this will be about?* Elicit answers. (Answer: advantages and disadvantages of different living situations)

2. Play the introduction and instructions: *Maria is studying in the United States. She has lived for four weeks with a homestay family. Now she wants to live closer to school. Work with a partner. Look at Maria's housing choices. Write one good point and one bad point about each choice.* As students work, circulate and help. You may want to have various groups write their answers on the board.

3. T: *Now listen. Maria is talking to a friend about places to live. Write the good and bad points about each place. If they say an idea you already wrote, put a check next to it.* Play the tape. Gesture for students to write their answers.

4. **(Optional)** If your students will find this task very difficult, do the Additional Support procedure.

5. **(Optional)** Stop after each segment and have students answer. This will help weaker students focus on the main advantages and disadvantages.

6. Check by having students volunteer their answers. (Answers appear in blue on the opposite page.) Students don't need to decide which option is best since they will do so in the Your Turn to Talk activity.

ADDITIONAL SUPPORT Write all the students' ideas on the board as suggested in Step 2 above. Then have the students listen in pairs. Stop after each housing choice is discussed. Allow students time to share what they understood before asking them to say their answers.

NOTES

• Maria has been on a homestay; that is, she has been the "paying guest" of a family. Students often prefer homestays when studying abroad, especially if their time in the foreign country is limited.

• Many Americans live away from home for the first time during college, where they live in dormitories or share apartments with other students.

Your turn to talk

1. T: *Look at Maria's housing choices. Which one is best for her?*

2. Divide the class into pairs. T: *Rank Maria's choices from 1 to 4 (1 is the best).*

3. (after about 5 minutes) T: *Now join another pair. Tell your choices. Give reasons. Listen to their choices. Then try to agree on the best choice for Maria. Which would be the best for you? Why?*

4. **(Optional)** You may want to divide the class into four groups, one for each of the housing choices. Students join the group with the choice they prefer. They list as many reasons as possible why it is the best choice. Then each group presents their ideas to the full class.

Optional activity

(For use anytime during or after the unit.)

EXPANSION *Roleplay.* Before class, make copies of Activity Sheet 12B on page T63. You will need one copy for every four students. In class, learners work in groups of four. They cut apart the cards and each partner takes one. They read the card and pretend to be the person on the card. They look at their information from Listening Task 1. Everyone decides on the best school for them. They tell others their decisions and reasons. Then they compare their real preferences to the ones on the cards.

LISTENING TASK 2 *A place to live*

Maria is studying in the United States. She has lived for four weeks with a homestay family. Now she wants to live closer to school.

❑ Work with a partner.
Look at Maria's housing choices.
Write one good point (**+**) and one bad point (**−**) about each choice.

❑ Now listen. Maria is talking to a friend about places to live.
Write the good and bad points about each place.
If they say an idea you already wrote, put a check (✔) next to it.

1. + *don't have to cook   or clean*

    − *can be noisy*

2. + *good for English*

    − *might not understand problems/values*

3. + *understand problems*

    − *need to speak English inside and outside school*

4. + *could help each other*

    − *different customs/values*

YOUR TURN TO TALK

Look at Maria's housing choices. Which one is best for her?

Work with a partner. Rank Maria's choices from 1 to 4 (1 is the best).

Now join another pair. Tell your choices. Give reasons. Listen to their choices. Then try to agree on the best choice for Maria.

Which would be the best for you? Why?

Your type of personality

In parts of Asia, some people believe your personality is controlled by your blood type.

❏ Work with a partner.
Read these descriptions.
<u>Underline</u> one key idea for each blood type.

A
- always on time
- works hard/likes things perfect
- wants someone else to be the leader

B
- emotional, with a strong personality
- a natural leader – hates being told what to do
- has many new ideas

O
- likes doing new things, even if they're difficult
- competitive – loves to win in business, at school, in life
- thinks helping friends is important

AB
- a mixed personality
- doesn't like showing emotions
- thinks friends are very important
- likes science and art

❏ Answer these questions for yourself and your partner.

	You		**Your partner**	
1. What is your blood type?	☐ A	☐ B	☐ A	☐ B
	☐ O	☐ AB	☐ O	☐ AB
	☐ don't know		☐ don't know	
2. If you know your blood type: Do you match the description? Why or why not?	☐ yes	☐ no	☐ yes	☐ no
3. If you don't know your blood type: Which description matches your personality the best? Why?	☐ A	☐ B	☐ A	☐ B
	☐ O	☐ AB	☐ O	☐ AB

Your type of personality

Content area: Talking about personality types

Listening skills: Inferring personality characteristics (Listening Task 1); understanding and appreciating a cartoon, following instructions (Listening Task 2)

Grammar/vocabulary: Habitual present, imperatives, descriptive adjectives

Warming Up

1. T: *Look at page 42.*

2. Divide the class into pairs. Read the introduction and instructions: *In parts of Asia, some people believe your personality is controlled by your blood type. Work with a partner. Read these descriptions. Underline one key idea for each blood type.* As students work, circulate and help pairs having difficulty.

3. Check by having a few pairs say the words they underlined.

4. T: *Answer these questions for yourself and your partner.* Demonstrate by directing one pair through the questions as the others watch. Allow time for students to do the task.

5. (Optional) You may want to poll the entire class to see how many believe the descriptions match their own personalities.

NOTES

• It really doesn't matter which key ideas the students choose in Step 2 of the lesson plan. The point is to get them to really think about the information presented.

• While the blood-type/personality connection is popular in several Asian countries, we don't mean to suggest that everyone believes in it. Most people are very skeptical. Perhaps it should be considered in the way horoscopes are thought of in the West: interesting and a possible topic of conversation, but only a few people really think they are true.

• In many countries in Asia, elementary school children wear name badges when they go to school. In addition to listing the child's name, the badges usually list blood type. As a result, children know their own blood types from a very early age. This is different from many Western countries where, unless people need to know their blood type for medical reasons, it isn't uncommon not to find out until college age or later.

Strategy exercise: *Personality and language learning*

Personality has an effect on how people learn. After doing either Listening Task 1 or 2, students should look at the Warming Up again. In pairs or small groups, they look at the characteristics of the four blood types and try to find as many consequences as they can for language learning for each trait. For example, Type A people who like things perfect might get very upset when they miss a test question.

Optional activity

(For use anytime during or after the unit.)

EXPANSION **My partner's personality.** Before class, make a copy of the Unit 13 Activity Sheet on page T65. You will need one copy for each student. Learners work in pairs to ask each other the questions. They should get one extra piece of information about each answer. When they finish, they try to make three statements about their partner's personality.

Listening Task 1
It's in my blood.

Note: The tapescript for Unit 13 begins on page T25.

1. T: *Look at page 43.*

2. Play the instructions: *Listen. If the information on page 42 is true, what do you think these people's blood types are? What helped you guess? Write two or three things about each person.* Play the first part of the tape. Gesture for students to write their answers.

3. (Optional) If your students will find this task very difficult, do the Additional Support procedure.

4. (Optional) You may want to stop after Jenny speaks to check that item. The "hint words" that students said gave them the clues are just as important as getting the correct answer. Then play the rest of Listening Task 1.

5. If necessary, play Listening Task 1 a second time.

6. Check by having students call out their answers and the words that give them the clues. (Answers appear in blue on the opposite page.)

7. (Optional) Have each student write a short "mini-speech" like the ones they heard on the tape. It should contain the clues as to their blood type. Then students stand and circulate. Everyone finds a partner. They read what they wrote. Partners guess their blood types.

ADDITIONAL SUPPORT Write these sentences on the board:

"Getting angry doesn't help."
"I'm well organized."
"I don't like my boss."
"I work hard and I play hard."

Have students, alone or in pairs, decide which blood type each speaker would have. Then they do the listening task.

NOTE

• Be sure students understand that this is an inference activity. The speakers don't talk about blood types. They only describe their own personalities. Those descriptions provide the clues for the learners to match the personalities to the blood types.

Culture corner

1. Have students read the Culture Corner. Then, in pairs or small groups, have them answer the follow-up questions.

2. (Optional) After students read the Culture Corner, tell them that you are going to read it aloud and that you'll make some mistakes. Learners should try to find the mistakes. Read the first sentence, with these mistakes: *Blood types were invented nearly 1,000 years ago, in Vienna, Australia.*

Have students identify the mistakes. Then they work in pairs. One student reads, making three to five mistakes. The partner listens and finds the mistakes. Then they change roles. **Note:** If the listener's book is open, this is mainly a reading/listening activity. If the listener's book is closed, it is a listening/memory activity.

Optional activity

(For use anytime during or after the unit.)

• *Class poll.* Divide the class into four groups, one group for each blood type. Each group looks at the Warming Up page and thinks of three questions connected with their own blood type and personality. For example, those in Group A might ask ten people, "Do you like things perfect?" Then have the whole class stand up. Each student asks ten other people the questions. After groups finish, they report their results to the class.

It's in my blood.

❏ Listen. If the information on page 42 is true, what do you think
these people's blood types are?
What helped you guess? Write two or three things about each person.

1. Charles
Blood type: ☐ O

competitive

likes a

challenge

_____

_____

2. Jenny
Blood type: ☐ B

leader

likes to

organize

likes freedom

_____

3. Valeria
Blood type: ☐ AB

doesn't like

anger

a few close

friends

_____

4. Daniel
Blood type: ☐ A

organized

likes to know

what to do

_____

_____

CULTURE CORNER

Blood types were discovered nearly 100 years ago, in Vienna, Austria. About 10
years later, scientists in Europe began suggesting that there might be a
connection between a person's blood type and his or her personality. Recently,
this belief has become popular, especially in parts of Asia. Because many people
believe the blood-type/personality connection, different products and services
make use of it. For example, computer-dating services will often use blood type
information to put people together. Key holders, soft drinks, and lighters have
been designed to match people's types. Some companies even ask job applicants
their blood type during interviews.

Do people in your country believe blood type affects personality? Do you? What
other ways do people find out about personality?

Personality types

This cartoon shows four basic types of people.

❏ Look at the cartoon. Listen.

THE FAR SIDE   By GARY LARSON

The glass is half full!

optimist

The glass is half empty.

pessimist

Half full... No! Wait! Half empty!.. No, half... what was the question?

indecisive

Hey! I ordered a cheeseburger!

complainer

The four basic personality types

❏ Now listen to someone talking about the people in the cartoon. Who are they describing? Follow the instructions.

❏ Now listen to some questions. Follow the instructions.

❏ Work with a partner. Compare answers.

YOUR TURN TO TALK

Work with a partner. Do you know people who fit these descriptions? Who? Why do you think so? Give examples. Think of one person for each personality type.

- an optimist
- a pessimist
- a leader

- an emotional person
- an unemotional person
- an indecisive person

- someone who likes challenges
- a complainer
- a perfectionist (someone who likes things perfect)

Example: My neighbor is a complainer. When he can hear other people's music – even in the daytime – he gets angry.

Listening Task 2
Personality types

Listening skills: Understanding and appreciating a cartoon, following instructions

1. T: *Look at page 44.*

2. Play the introduction and instructions: *This cartoon shows four basic types of people. Look at the cartoon. Listen.* Play the cartoon narration.

3. T: *Now listen to someone talking about the people in the cartoon. Who are they describing? Follow the instructions.*

4. (Optional) If your students find this task very difficult, do the Additional Support procedure.

5. Check by having students call out their answers. You may want to draw a grid representing the cartoon on the board and write the words to make it easier for students to check spelling.

6. T: *Now listen to some questions. Follow the instructions.* Play the rest of Listening Task 2 on the tape. Gesture for students to write their answers. You may want to pause the tape between items to give students time to think and write.

7. If necessary, play the last part of Listening Task 2 a second time.

8. T: *Work with a partner. Compare answers.* It may help students' discussions if you write these instruction summaries on the board:

- Which type are you?
- Do most people fit these types?
- Do you understand the joke?
- Is it funny?

ADDITIONAL SUPPORT Explain the "half-empty/half-full" idea with a real glass of water. Make sure students understand that someone who says it is half full is positive. That person is saying, "Great. I have water to drink." The person who is says it is half empty is being negative. It's like saying, "I don't have much – maybe not enough." Then write the words on the board to help with spelling as students do the task: *indecisive, pessimist, optimist, complainer.*

NOTES

- This activity is another example of "learning by doing." The students don't simply overhear information. They hear instructions and do something based on their own opinions. Basing the answers on the students' own opinions and reactions requires them to do high-level processing.

- Humor in a foreign language can be extremely hard to understand, even for learners whose language ability is quite high. The humor in this cartoon comes from taking a standard expression (The glass is half full/half empty.) and first having it become a problem because of the person's inability to decide. The second part of the joke (I ordered a cheeseburger.) is funny because it is so unexpected. The other speakers are talking about views of life, and he is acting as if they are in a restaurant.

- This cartoon is by an American named Gary Larson. His comic strip was called *The Far Side* and often represented scientific or philosophical themes in the shape of ordinary people or animals.

Your turn to talk

1. Divide the class into pairs. T: *Do you know people who fit these descriptions? Who? Why do you think so? Give examples. Think of one person for each personality type.*

2. (Optional) To help students get started, give an example of someone you know. Talk about a friend, family member, or neighbor. Don't say the person's name. Demonstrate that you can describe someone without being too specific, especially about the negative items.

UNIT 14

You've got to have art.

Content area: Discussing examples of fine art

Listening skills: Following instructions (Listening Task 1); identifying supporting details (Listening Task 2)

Grammar/vocabulary: Imperatives, present tenses: simple present and present progressive

Warming Up

1. T: *Look at page 45.*

2. Divide the class into pairs. Read the instructions: *Look at the paintings and the sculptures. Work with a partner. What's your feeling about each piece of art? Which do you like the most? Why? Which don't you like? Why not?*

3. As students work, circulate and help pairs having difficulty. If pairs are having a hard time getting started, have them look at each picture and write one adjective that describes it.

4. (Optional) Poll the class to see which items are the most and least popular. Have students raise their hands to show their favorites. Encourage a few students to give their reasons.

NOTES

• The works pictured are top left: *The Water Lilies,* Claude Monet; center left: *Painted wood sculpture of a dog,* Guatemalan art; bottom left: *Eighth Avenue,* Jane Wooster Scott; top center: *Abstrakter Kopf,* Alexej Von Jawlensky; bottom center: *Woman with a Water Jug,* Jan Vermeer; right: *The Kiss,* Constantin Brancusi.

• The unit title, *You've got to have art,* is a pun (play on words). It sounds similar to *You've got to have heart,* which means "You should be kind" or "You should have courage."

• Art is part of everyday life, and students often respond to visual information more quickly than to what they hear or read. In this unit, we are trying to build on this basic human interest. Also, we believe that since art is basic, it can and should be part of everyone's education. However, we realize that some students have already "learned" that art is for other people, not for them. For that reason, this unit concentrates on the unusual art of surrealism. If learning about art itself is not of interest to some individuals, the strangeness and the humor will, we hope, get them involved.

Strategy exercise: *Linking learning to the world*

This unit gives students an opportunity to think about how much they know about the world outside the classroom and how they use that knowledge in the classroom. If you have a museum nearby, you might consider a class trip. You may also ask students to visit a museum, find a work of art they like, buy a postcard of it (or draw a simple reproduction), and bring it to class to share with their classmates.

Optional activity

(For use anytime during or after the unit.)

EXPANSION *How many in one minute?*

Before class, make copies of the Unit 14 Activity Sheet on page T67. You will need one copy for every five students. In class, students work in groups of five. Each group selects a leader. Only the leader can see the Activity Sheet. The leader reads each topic. If the players are unsure, leaders can read the examples next to the topics. The players try to give as many examples as possible in one minute. They get one point for each example. The leader listens and marks the points on the Activity Sheet. After one minute, the leader says "Stop" and goes on to the next topic.

You've got to have art.

❑ Look at the paintings and the sculptures.

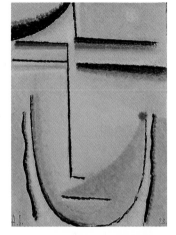

❑ Work with a partner.
What's your feeling about each piece of art?
Which do you like the most? Why?
Which don't you like? Why not?

❑ Now join another pair.
Are their opinions the same as or different from yours?

LISTENING TASK 1

It's ~~sure real~~ surreal.

Surreal art is very unusual. This picture is surreal.

❏ Listen. Look at the picture. Answer the questions.

1. V M S

2. E M L N L

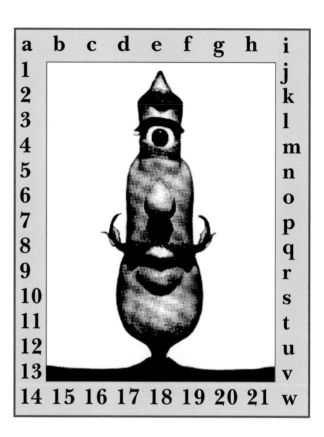

	a	b	c	d	e	f	g	h	i
1									j
2									k
3									l
4									m
5									n
6									o
7									p
8									q
9									r
10									s
11									t
12									u
13									v
14 15 16 17 18 19 20 21									w

❏ Now you're going to do an unusual activity. You'll need a piece of paper. Listen and follow the instructions.

CULTURE CORNER

Surrealistic art began in Paris in 1924. It soon spread throughout Europe and then to North America, Asia, and Australia. Surrealism is known for its strange images. They are sometimes humorous and bizarre. This artistic movement was influenced by psychology, and often challenged existing thinking about art … and about life. Among the most famous surrealists were Salvador Dalí, Joan Miró, and René Magritte. Other artists like Pablo Picasso and Man Ray were influenced by the surrealism movement.

Many of the strange and surprising images that we see in current music videos show a strong influence of surrealism.

Is unusual art popular in your country? What kind?

Listening Task 1
That's ~~sure real~~ surreal.

Note: The tapescript for Unit 14 begins on page T26.

1. T: *Look at page 46.*

2. Play the introduction and instructions: *Surreal art is very unusual. This picture is surreal. Listen. Look at the picture. Answer the questions.*

3. **(Optional)** If your students will find this task very difficult, do the Additional Support procedure.

4. Play the questions on the tape. Gesture for students to circle their answers. Since these are opinion questions, there are no real "right" and "wrong" answers but you may want to have students show their answers by raising their hands.

5. Make sure students have a piece of paper ready before going on to the next part of the activity. Ideally, the paper should be blank and be at least the size of the picture. Play the rest of the task: *Now you're going to do an unusual activity. You'll need a piece of paper. Listen and follow the instructions.* **Note:** It will take some people a little time to see the image of the artist. If necessary, play the segment a second time.

ADDITIONAL SUPPORT This task basically involves students' understanding the instructions and interacting with the page. Play the tape. Pause after each sentence or group of sentences. Allow time for students to think and respond. You may want to repeat the questions and instruction sentences. If it is very difficult, have students work in pairs.

NOTES

• This photo was made by Philippe Halsman. He photographed the famous artist Salvador Dalí. He printed the picture showing a partial view of Dalí's face, then reversed the negative so the same image was printed in reverse.

• Go over the meanings of these direction adverbs: *horizontally* = parallel to the ground; *vertically* = from top to bottom; *diagonally* = from corner to corner.

Culture corner

1. Have students read the Culture Corner and answer the questions in pairs or small groups: *Is unusual art popular in your country? What kind?* Encourage students to take a wide view of art, including film, performance, etc., in addition to traditional types such as painting.

2. **(Optional)** After students read the Culture Corner, have them look through it again, underlining all the words of three or more syllables. Then students call out the words as you write them on the board. Read each word twice. The second time, learners repeat it. They stand up on the accented syllable. This activity is especially useful for students whose native language has a stress system different from that of English. It also increases physical activity. If students feel silly standing up and sitting down, you can also do it by having them raise their hands. However, if you're willing to stand/sit, they probably will be too. (Answers: Surrealistic, America, Australia, Surrealism, images, humorous, artistic, influenced, psychology, existing, surrealists, Salvador, Picasso, surprising, videos, unusual, popular)

Optional activity

(For use anytime during or after the unit.)

• *Art for the city.* Students imagine this city (or area) will soon celebrate a major birthday. They work in groups of three to decide on a new sculpture that would best symbolize the city. What would the sculpture look like? Where is the best place to put it?

Listening Task 2
The Lovers

1. T: *Look at page 47.*

2. Play the introduction and instructions:
This painting is called The Lovers. *It was
painted by René Magritte. Listen. Two friends
are in an art museum. They're talking about*
The Lovers. *What do they think the painting
means? Write two details for each interpretation.*
Play the task on the tape.

3. (Optional) If your students will find this
task very difficult, do the Additional
Support procedure.

4. If necessary, play Listening Task 2 a
second time. If you do, you will probably
want to stop the tape before the final
questions.

5. Check the details by having some
students say what they wrote. (Answers
appear in blue on the opposite page.)

6. T: *Now listen to some questions. Write your
answers.* Have students share their answers,
either in pairs or with the whole class.

ADDITIONAL SUPPORT Before students
listen, have them work in pairs or small
groups. Have them look at the
interpretations (*Blind love* and *Cold,
untouching people*). Students talk about what
they think each interpretation means. In
particular, they note things in the picture
that might lead to each idea. They may
need to do this in the native language(s)
first and then choose a few words of
English to describe each idea.

NOTE

• Students may need to answer the last
question in their native language(s).

Remember that listening is a receptive skill.
As such, learners can understand things
that they can't say themselves. Since this
painting will touch a deep emotional level
with many learners, they may want to
describe emotions that they haven't yet
learned to describe in English.

Your turn to talk

1. Divide the class into pairs. T: *Look at the
picture on the cover of this book. Of course, all of
the people are listening to things. Imagine that
there is a deeper, stranger meaning to the picture.
Write the meaning.*

2. As students work, circulate and help. If
pairs are having difficulty, ask leading
questions such as: *Who are these people? What
are they listening to? Do you think they're happy?
What's the connection between them?*

3. (after about 5 minutes) T: *Now join two
other pairs. Tell about your meaning for the
picture. Listen to theirs. Which was the most
unusual?*

4. You may want to have a few pairs tell
their ideas to the whole class.

Optional activity

(For use anytime during or after the unit.)

• *That's wrong.* Find pictures of famous
works of art. You will need one for each
student. There can be duplicates, but it is
best if there are at least eight different
pictures. Students work in pairs. They study
their partner's picture for one minute,
trying to remember exactly what is in the
picture. After a minute, they give the
picture back to the first student. That
student describes the picture, making at
least three "mistakes" in the description.
The other partner listens and tries to find
the mistakes. Then they change roles.
When they finish, they change partners
and continue.

LISTENING TASK 2

The Lovers

This painting is called *The Lovers*. It was painted by René Magritte.

❑ Listen. Two friends are in an art museum. They're talking about *The Lovers*. What do they think the painting means? Write two details for each interpretation.

Interpretation 1
Blind love
- can't see ... *anything bad*
- not thinking about ... *anything else*

Interpretation 2
Cold, untouching people
- *aren't touching*
- *almost like masks*

❑ Now listen to some questions. Write your answers.

1. _____   2. _____

YOUR TURN TO TALK

Work with a partner. Look at the picture on the cover of this book. Of course, all of the people are listening to things. Imagine that there is a deeper, stranger meaning to the picture. Write the meaning.

Now join two other pairs. Tell about your meaning for the picture. Listen to theirs. Which was the most unusual?

47

I wonder how that works.

❑ Work with a partner.
   Think of machines you both know how to use.
   Write as many as you can in three minutes.

computer	telephone
fax machine	lawn mower
vacuum cleaner	CD player
dishwasher	car
hair dryer	TV

❑ Choose one machine. Imagine that you're
   meeting someone who has never used it before.
   Write the instructions for how the machine works.

First, *press the OPEN button.*

Then *put in the disk. Don't touch the bottom of it.*

Next, *close the door.*

After that, *put the headphones on your ears.*

Finally, *press the PLAY button.*

❑ Now change partners. Read your instructions. Don't say
   the name of the machine. Your partner will guess.
   Then change partners again and continue.

UNIT 15

I wonder how that works.

Content area: Talking about how machines work
Listening skills: Identifying steps in a process (Listening Task 1); identifying steps in a technical process (Listening Task 2)
Grammar/vocabulary: Simple present, sequence markers

Warming Up

1. T: *Look at page 48.*

2. Divide the class into pairs. Read the instructions: *Work with a partner. Think of machines you both know how to use. Write as many as you can in three minutes.* As students work, circulate and help pairs having difficulty. If some pairs can't think of machines, give hints as to what some machines do – for example: *We use this to turn the TV off and on.* (See the first Note below for possibilities.)

3. (Optional) Have each pair call out one or more machines and list them on the board. OR Divide the class in half. Have the teams compete to see who can list the most on the board.

4. (after 3 minutes) T: *Choose one machine. Imagine that you're meeting someone who has never used it before. Write the instructions for how the machine works.* As students work, circulate and help.

5. T: *Now change partners. Read your instructions. Don't say the name of the machine. Your partner will guess. Then change partners again and continue.* **Note:** This step goes more smoothly if students stand and circulate.

NOTES

• Here are some common machines that many students will know how to operate:

(those illustrated on this page) abacus, coffee maker, fax machine, remote control device, exercise machine, rice cooker

(at home) mixer, blender, food processor, can opener, electric frying pan, washing machine, vacuum cleaner, hair dryer, clothes dryer, computer, cassette or CD player, VCR, TV, radio

(other) vending machine, ATM (Automatic Teller Machine/bank cash machine)

• You may want to review sequence markers used for describing a process – for example: *first, second, third, then, next, after that, before, while, finally, last.*

Strategy exercise: *Focusing on specific words*

This might be a good time to focus again on the idea of anticipating the knowledge students need to listen effectively. After doing Listening Task 2, they can listen again and follow the process. They should keep track of the number of times they hear each of the following illustrated words: *analog, digital, pits, videotape, laser, disk, computer, audiotape.*

Optional activity

(For use anytime during or after the unit.)

EXPANSION *Process strip stories.* Before class, make copies of the Unit 15 Activity Sheet on page T69. You will need one copy for every two students. In class, have students work in pairs. Give each pair one sheet and have them cut the sentences into strips. Tell the students that there are two separate processes (recipes) described. Have them go through the strips, first identifying each recipe and the sentences that go with it. Then they try to put the steps in each recipe in order.
Variation: Each partner is responsible for one of the recipes. They work out the order and then explain the process to their partner.
Note: To make the task easier, tell students the names of the recipes and the order of the first two sentences in each. (Answers: French toast: g, p, a, j, d, m, t, i, e, s
Stir-fried vegetables: o, f, k, c, b, r, q, n, h, l)

Listening Task 1 How does a vending machine work?

Note: The tapescript for Unit 15 begins on page T27.

1. T: *Look at page 49.*

2. Play the instructions: *Listen. How does a vending machine know that you have put in the correct coin? Complete the chart.* Play Listening Task 1 on the tape. Gesture for students to write their answers. **(Optional)** To make sure students understand what to do, stop after the first part. Have volunteers say what they wrote.

3. (Optional) If your students will find this task very difficult, do the Additional Support procedure.

4. If necessary, play Listening Task 1 a second time. Before you do, you may want to have students compare answers in pairs.

5. Check by having students call out their answers. (Answers appear in blue on the opposite page.)

ADDITIONAL SUPPORT Have students work in pairs. They look at the illustration and guess (in English or their native language) how the process works. Then they listen to confirm.

NOTES

• There are various types of vending machines, so technologies differ. The process described here is typical of newer machines.

• The term "vending machine" is used to refer to any machine that sells products. The machines are also called by their specific product names: soda machine, etc.

Culture corner

1. (Optional) Before students read, write these words on the board: *candy, eggs, frozen food, glasses, rice, soft drinks, tools, vegetables, videos.* Students copy the list. They circle all the items they think might be sold in vending machines. As they read, they correct their answers, if necessary. (All items listed are in the reading.)

2. Students read the Culture Corner and answer the follow-up questions alone or in small groups. When students are thinking of things they wish were sold in vending machines, encourage them to use their imaginations.

3. (Optional) After students read the Culture Corner, have them work with English phrasing. Read the text. Have students mark the places you pause (♦): *In many countries, ♦ vending machines are used ♦ to sell soft drinks, ♦ candy, ♦ and many other items. ♦ In some places, ♦ what is sold in vending machines might surprise you. ♦ For example, ♦ in the United States, ♦ there are machines that sell videos, ♦ tools, ♦ and frozen food. ♦ In Japan, ♦ you can buy rice, ♦ fresh vegetables, ♦ and even eggs ♦ (fresh that day!) ♦ from machines. If you are about to get on an airplane in Great Britain ♦ and realize you've forgotten your reading glasses, ♦ don't worry. ♦ Some British airports ♦ have vending machines ♦ that sell glasses. ♦ There are three strengths. ♦ Customers read a card ♦ through different types of glass ♦ to decide which pair of glasses ♦ they need to buy.*

Have students work in pairs to take turns reading the sentences in the text and comparing answers. This activity helps create an awareness of English phrasing as well as reinforcing the idea of chunking (reading in related units of meaning rather than word-by-word).

Optional activity

(For use anytime during or after the unit.)

• ***Process pantomime.*** Students work in an even number of groups. In their groups, they should think of a process to act out. They prepare their pantomime and then perform it for another group, who tries to guess what the process is.

How does a vending machine work?

❑ Listen. How does a vending machine know that you have put in the correct coin? Complete the chart.

Step 1

The machine checks *what the coin is made of* .

How? It uses *electricity* .

Step 2

The machine finds out *how much it weighs* .

How? The coin goes between *two magnets* . This *slows down the coin and checks speed* .

Step 3

The machine makes sure *the coin is the correct size* .

How? The coin goes between *two lights* .

They *measure the size* .

❑ Now complete the sentences.

The machine checks the coin's *content* , *weight* , and *size* .

If those are right, *the machine will accept it and you'll get what you paid for* .

CULTURE CORNER

In many countries, vending machines are used to sell soft drinks, candy, and many other items. In some places, what is sold in vending machines might surprise you. For example, in the United States, there are machines that sell videos, tools, and frozen food. In Japan, you can buy rice, fresh vegetables, and even eggs (fresh that day!) from machines. If you are about to get on an airplane in Great Britain and realize you've forgotten your reading glasses, don't worry. Some British airports have vending machines that sell glasses. There are three strengths. Customers read a card through different types of glass to decide which pair of glasses they need to buy.

Are vending machines popular in your country? What do they sell? What do you wish they sold?

LISTENING TASK 2

How do they make CDs?

Step 1

❏ Look at the pictures. One shows "digital" sound recording, and the other shows "analog" sound recording.

❏ Now listen. Friends are talking about different ways of recording sound. Write "digital" or "analog" under each picture.

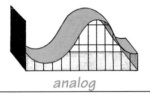

analog

digital

Step 2

❏ Listen. Kathy and Mike are talking about making CDs. Number the steps (1–5). There is one extra step.

4   pits (holes)

1   videotape

3   glass disk and laser

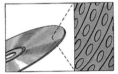
2   computer

  audiotape

5   laser's light bounces off pits

YOUR TURN TO TALK

Work in groups of three. How many different machines can you list? You have one minute for each item.

- machines in your home
- machines you put money into
- machines that make your life easier
- machines that make your life more difficult

Now each person chooses one of these topics. Try to talk about it for two minutes without stopping. Your partners will listen. Then they will ask at least two questions each.

- A problem you had with a machine
- If you could invent a machine to do anything, what would it do?

Listening Task 2
How do they make CDs?

Listening skill: Identifying steps in a technical process

1. T: *Look at page 50.*

2. Play the instructions: *Step One. Look at the pictures. One shows "digital" sound recording, and the other shows "analog" sound recording. Now listen. Friends are talking about different ways of recording sound. Write "digital" or "analog" under each picture.* Play Listening Task 2 on the tape. Gesture for students to write their answers.

3. (Optional) If your students will find this task very difficult, do the Additional Support procedure.

4. Stop after Step One. Check by having students tell you which picture is which. **(Optional)** You may want to have learners check their understanding by working with a partner. One partner explains the difference between analog and digital sound (probably in their native language). The other partners listen to see if the speakers' understanding is the same as their own.

5. T: *Step Two. Listen. Kathy and Mike are talking about making CDs. Number the steps (1–5). There is one extra step.* Play Step Two on the tape. Gesture for students to write their answers.

6. If necessary, play Listening Task 2 a second time. Before replaying the tape, you may want to have students compare answers in pairs.

7. Check by having students say their answers. (Answers appear in blue on the opposite page.)

ADDITIONAL SUPPORT Because the topic of technology scares some people, have students do the task in pairs. Remind them that they don't need to catch every word or every bit of information. If they can label the "analog" and "digital" pictures and number the pictures in Step Two, they have understood what they needed and have successfully completed the task.

Your turn to talk

1. Divide the class into groups of three. T: *How many different machines can you list? You have one minute for each item.*

2. Read off the list, one item at a time.

3. (after students have listed machines for all four items) T: *Now each person chooses one of these topics. Try to talk about it for two minutes without stopping. Your partners will listen. Then they will ask at least two questions each. Topics: A problem you had with a machine; If you could invent a machine to do anything, what would it do?*

4. Allow students a minute or two to think about their topic. Then have them do the task.

NOTE

• To do the first part of this activity as a game, give one point for each machine. Players can compete within their teams, or teams can compete against each other. OR Do the activity as a chalkboard race. Students have their books closed. You need as many teams as you have board space. Players line up about three meters (ten feet) from the board. Give the first person on each team a piece of chalk. Call out the first topic. The first player on each team goes to the board, writes an answer, runs back to the team, and gives the chalk to the next player. That person runs to the board, writes an answer, and returns. Students continue. Allow about one minute for each topic. You may want to add a few more topics such as the following:

  • machines you don't have but would like
  • machines you have already used today
  • machines that are dangerous

A matter of values

> **Content area:** Debating and explaining difficult decisions
> **Listening skills:** Understanding and evaluating opinions (Listening Task 1); identifying problems and reasons (Listening Task 2)
> **Grammar/vocabulary:** Future with *will* and *going to*, transition words for contrast

Warming Up

1. T: *Look at page 51.*

2. Read the instructions: *What do you think is most important to society? Look at this list of items. Then add two more things.* Read the list aloud. Make sure students understand the meaning of everything on the list.

3. Ask: *What were the extra things you wrote?* Encourage several people to give answers. (Sample answers appear in blue on the opposite page.)

4. Divide the class into pairs. T: *Work with a partner. Look at your list again. Decide on the five most important things. Number them (1–5).* As students work, circulate and help pairs having difficulty. Difficulty usually comes in ranking items that are of nearly equal importance. If so, ask "forced-choice" questions – for example: *Which would you rather have, a society with freedom and some crime or one with no crime but less freedom?*

5. T: *Now join another pair. Compare answers. When your answers are different, give reasons.*

6. You may want to poll the class to see how many students rated each item as most important.

NOTES

• Nearly everyone would agree that all the items listed are important – and, one would hope, achievable. In reality, however, societies can rarely try to do everything at once. They have to make hard choices and

set priorities. The goal of this unit is to help students look at making choices and talk in English about their own priorities.

• You may want to review transition words for showing contrast: *but, or, although, on one hand/on the other hand.* Their meanings are similar, but the differences in their grammar are significant:

But and *or* join two nouns, phrases, or sentences: *She can't decide whether to X or Y. She wants to X, but he wants to Y.*

Although must be used with two clauses. The phrase that follows it becomes a dependent clause that must be joined with a complete sentence: *Although she loves him.* is not a correct sentence in English. It could be: *Although she loves him, she won't marry him.*

Strategy exercise: *Reviewing*

Students can profit from learning how others review. A useful review technique is "spiraling." Spiraling means reviewing material on the day you learn it, then the next day, then two days later, then at ever-increasing intervals. The key is putting the information into contexts (new sentences, associations, etc.). Different systems of review work for different kinds of learners. Encourage students to learn new ways from their peers and to try at least one new way this week.

Optional activity

(For use anytime during or after the unit.)

EXPANSION **What's important to you?** Before class, make copies of the Unit 16 Activity Sheet on page T71. You will need one copy for every two students. Cut each copy into two parts: **A** and **B**. In class, divide students into pairs. They take turns reading the questions below the box. Both partners write their own answers to each question. Then they tell their partner what they wrote. The other student should try to get extra information about each item by asking at least two follow-up questions. If any question is too personal, the students can say, "I'd rather not say."

A matter of values

❏ What do you think is most important to society?
Look at this list of items. Then add two more things.

   ____ a clean environment

   ____ education

   ____ a relaxed lifestyle

   ____ keeping old traditions and customs

   ____ no crime

   ____ freedom

   ____ a job for everyone

   ____ helping other people

SAMPLE   ____ *family*

ANSWERS   ____ *religion*

❏ Work with a partner.
Look at your list again. Decide on the five most
important things. Number them (1–5).

❏ Now join another pair. Compare answers.
When your answers are different, give reasons.

LISTENING TASK 1

Who's right?

Radio talk shows usually present two sides of an argument.

❏ Listen. What is the topic of the debate? Complete the sentence.

"_Tourism_ is/isn't good for the island."

Which things does Ms. Selles say? Write "S" in the boxes.
Which things does Mr. Williams say? Write "W." There are three extra sentences.

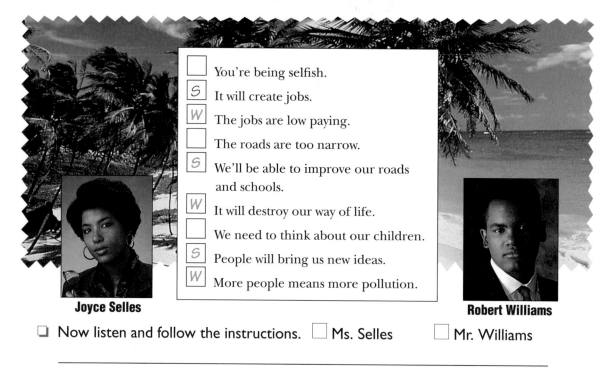

☐	You're being selfish.
S	It will create jobs.
W	The jobs are low paying.
☐	The roads are too narrow.
S	We'll be able to improve our roads and schools.
W	It will destroy our way of life.
☐	We need to think about our children.
S	People will bring us new ideas.
W	More people means more pollution.

Joyce Selles

Robert Williams

❏ Now listen and follow the instructions. ☐ Ms. Selles ☐ Mr. Williams

---

CULTURE CORNER

Travel is big business around the world, and most countries encourage tourism. Of course, there are advantages and disadvantages. Tourism creates jobs, but many are low paying. Tourism can also drive up prices. In Hawaii, for example, 25 percent of all jobs are related to tourism, but the average income is only $21,641. The cost of an average house is $270,000, more than twice the average for the rest of the United States. Tourism can also be hard on the environment. The Mediterranean coast is the most-visited tourist area in the world. By 2025, it will receive 760 million visitors per year. But that will require more food and water than the area can support.

What places are popular with tourists in your country? What are the advantages and disadvantages?

52

Listening Task 1
Who's right?

Note: The tapescript for Unit 16 begins on page T28.

1. T: *Look at page 52.*

2. Play the introduction and instructions: *Radio talk shows usually present two sides of an argument. Listen. What is the topic of the debate? Complete the sentence: BLANK is or isn't good for the island. Which things does Ms. Selles say? Write "S" in the boxes. Which things does Mr. Williams say? Write "W." There are three extra sentences.*

3. (Optional) If your students will find this task very difficult, do the Additional Support procedure.

4. Play Listening Task 1 on the tape. Gesture for students to write their answers. **(Optional)** To make sure students understand what to do, stop after one or two interactions. Ask: *What did Ms. Selles say? What did Mr. Williams say?* Encourage students to answer. Then play the rest of Listening Task 1.

5. If necessary, play Listening Task 1 a second time. If you do so, you'll probably want to stop the tape before the final questions so that students listen again before deciding on their own choice.

6. Check by reading the statements and having students say who the speaker was. (Answers appear in blue on the opposite page.)

7. Have students raise their hands to show which speaker they agree with. You may want to have a few students give their reasons.

ADDITIONAL SUPPORT Have students work in pairs. They look at the list in the middle of the page. They decide on and underline the one or two most important words in each sentence. Then they listen. This task makes them more aware of what they will be hearing.

NOTES

• Development vs. preservation of the environment is an issue in nearly every country. You may want to encourage students to see if the arguments presented here are similar to issues in their own country.

• "On the other hand" connects two sentences, but it can go at the beginning, at the end, or in the middle of the second sentence. In writing, there must be a period or semicolon between the two sentences and commas around the transition word: *On the other hand, I could make a lot of money.* OR *I could, on the other hand, make a lot of money.*

Culture corner

1. Have students read the Culture Corner and answer the follow-up questions. You may want students to answer the questions in pairs or small groups. Have them write their lists and then compare with another pair or group.

2. (Optional) Before class, make a copy of the Culture Corner. On the copy, block out all the prepositions. Then make copies, one copy for every two students. In class, give the copies to the pairs. Have them read the paragraph and try to guess the missing words. Then they read in their books to check. This activity helps students make use of context to understand the passage.

Listening Task 2
Tough choices

Listening skill: Identifying problems and reasons

1. T: *Look at page 53.*

2. (Optional) Read the title: *"Tough choices."* Ask: *What do you think this will be about?* Elicit answers. (Answer: making difficult decisions)

3. Play the instructions: *Listen. People are talking about problems. Write the problem. Then write the important factors in each choice.*

4. Play Listening Task 2 on the tape. Gesture for students to write their answers.

5. (Optional) If your students will find this task very difficult, do the Additional Support procedure.

6. If necessary, play Listening Task 2 a second time. Before replaying the tape, you may want to have students compare answers: *Work with a partner. Look at your partner's answers. How many were the same as yours?*

7. Check by having students say what they wrote for each item. (Answers appear in blue on the opposite page.) You don't need to have students decide what they think the people should do yet. They'll do that in the Your Turn to Talk activity.

ADDITIONAL SUPPORT Have students listen to each segment twice. The first time, they only try to understand the topic: What is the choice? The second time, they try to catch the details. Have students compare factors with a partner before you ask for their answers.

NOTE

• You may prefer to check after each item rather than waiting until students have heard all four conversations.

Your turn to talk

1. Divide the class into pairs. T: *Decide what you think the people should do about these problems. Write down your reasons. Which problem is the most difficult to decide? Circle it.* Allow time for students to work.

2. (after about 5 minutes) *Now take a survey of at least ten people. Which solutions do they suggest for each problem? Which problem did each person find the most difficult?*

3. (Optional) Divide the class into smaller groups. Each group is made up of members who found the same item to be the most difficult. As a group, they list as many possible solutions as they can. Then they rank each solution as "good," "so-so," or "not good." Finally, as a group, they decide on the best course of action.

NOTE

• You may want to remind students that the people may have more choices than "Do X" or "Do Y." For example, in number two, the man could refuse to give his friend the questions but offer to help him study economics.

Optional activities

(For use anytime during or after the unit.)

• *Hero/Villain of the Year.* Learners work in groups of three or four. Who is the person who had the best impact on the world this year? Who is the person who made the worst impact? Students make a list of the good and bad things each person did. You may want to have them post the results on the board and have the whole class try to agree.

• *The best teacher.* Learners work in groups of four. What makes a teacher excellent? Students make a list of the qualities that an excellent teacher needs to have. Then they rank those qualities (1=the most important). You may want to combine groups or list items on the board and have the whole class rate each.

Tough choices

❏ Listen. People are talking about problems. Write the problem.
Then write the important factors in each choice.

1. She can't decide whether to …

marry Allen *or* marry Stan.

What's important?

good to her	she loves him
has money	has no money
wedding already planned	

2. His friend wants him to …

copy the exam questions *but* that's cheating.

What's important?

economics	doesn't want to
difficult	lose teacher's
his best friend	respect

3. He has to decide to use the money for …

his daughter's college *or* his mother's house repairs.

What's important?

accepted at good university	house needs
	major repairs
good future	mother has always
	helped him

4. She has to choose between …

a job as a sales representative for a computer company *or* an office job working with computers.

What's important?

travel – exciting	no travel – maybe
salary would	dull
depend on sales	safe – salary
	pretty good

YOUR TURN TO TALK

Work with a partner. Decide what you think the people should do about these problems. Write down your reasons. Which problem is the most difficult to decide? Circle it.

Now take a survey of at least 10 people. Which solutions do they suggest for each problem? Which problem did each person find the most difficult?

Food for thought

❑ Work in groups of three.
Think about food. One person chooses an item below.
How many answers can your group say in one minute?
Then the next person chooses another item.
Continue for six items.

Foods people ate 100 years ago that you rarely eat now
Unusual foods you've tried
Foods you've never eaten but would like to
Healthy foods you like
Foods that are becoming more popular
Unhealthy foods you love
Healthy foods you don't like
Foods you often eat that people didn't have 100 years ago
Foods from your country that people all over the world would like

❑ Now think about your answers.
How is your country's diet changing? Why do you think it is?
Which things are getting better? Which are getting worse?
Give as many reasons and examples as you can.

Food for thought

> **Content area:** Explaining food trends and customs
> **Listening skills:** Understanding topics, interpreting charts and graphs (Listening Task 1); identifying places, recognizing details (Listening Task 2)
> **Grammar/vocabulary:** Simple present, food and health words

Warming Up

1. T: *Look at page 54.*

2. (Optional) Demonstrate the activity. Do one item as an entire class. Say a category: *Foods you have already eaten today* and encourage as many students as possible to answer within one minute. Make a mark on the board for each answer.

3. Divide the class into groups of three. T: *Work in groups of three. Think about food. One person chooses an item below. How many answers can your group say in one minute? Then the next person chooses another item. Continue for six items.*

4. As students work, circulate and help groups having difficulty. Help by giving hints about examples.

5. (after most groups are finished) T: *Now think about your answers. How is your country's diet changing? Why do you think it is? Which things are getting better? Which are getting worse? Give as many reasons and examples as you can.* Have a few students share their ideas with the whole class.

NOTES

• Nearly every country's diet is changing. The growth of international fast-food restaurant chains is one example. A more positive example is that often the volume and quality of food available increase with economic development.

• Relative clauses follow a noun to describe it. They usually begin with a relative pronoun: "who" (to refer to people), "which" (to refer to things), or "that" (to refer to people or things). The relative pronoun comes at the beginning of the clause and replaces either the subject or object of the sentence.

Strategy exercise: *Associations*

Students bring a wealth of knowledge to the classroom. Indeed, prior knowledge can help or sometimes interfere with listening. One way to remind students of this is to have them brainstorm feelings and memories associated with certain kinds of food. Students work in an even number of groups. Each group brainstorms names of foods. They exchange lists with another group. Each group now must brainstorm associations they have with the food. They then combine groups and listen to one another's associations.

Optional activity

(For use anytime during or after the unit.)

• *Tell me more.* Ask students to think of something that happened to them that is connected to food. It could be a strange or an unusual food they have eaten, a very nice (or terrible) dinner, or something that happened while at a restaurant. Students work in groups of about four. One person begins telling his or her own story. The other students ask a lot of questions about the speaker's story (Where was the restaurant? Who were you with?). The speaker must answer all the questions – even if only with "I don't know." The people asking questions try to ask so many that the speaker can't finish the story within three minutes. This is based on an activity we learned from Charles Browne.

Listening Task 1
Food trends

> **Listening skills:** Understanding topics, interpreting charts and graphs

Note: The tapescript for Unit 17 begins on page T31.

1. T: *Look at page 55.* **(Optional)** Read the title: *"Food trends."* Ask: *What do you think this will be about?* Elicit answers. (Answer: foods that are becoming more and less popular)

2. Play the introduction and instructions: *Charts and graphs help explain information. Listen. You will hear information about food. Number the graphs and charts (1–4). Then write the names of the foods on the lines. There is one extra graph or chart.*

3. Play Listening Task 1 on the tape. Gesture for students to write their answers.

4. **(Optional)** If your students will find this task very difficult, do the Additional Support procedure.

5. **(Optional)** To make sure students understand what to do, stop after the first item and ask: *Which graph is it? What's the food?* (Answer: d. beef) Then play the rest of Listening Task 1.

6. If necessary, play Listening Task 1 a second time.

7. Check by having students say the answers and identify the foods. (Answers appear in blue on the opposite page.)

ADDITIONAL SUPPORT Have students listen twice. The first time, they listen only for numbers. Each time they hear a number, they raise their hands. Then they listen again and identify the correct graph or chart. By raising their hands, students are both showing that they heard a number and providing a cue for others who may have missed it.

NOTE

• A "graph" shows the relationship or comparison of two or more pieces of information. A "chart" is any presentation of information in visual form. Items b, c, and d are graphs; items a and e are charts. While this distinction exists, it is not uncommon to refer to them all as charts.

Culture corner

1. Have students read the Culture Corner. Alone or in small groups, they answer the follow-up questions: *Is rice popular in your country? How is it prepared?*

2. **(Optional)** Before students read the Culture Corner, they work in groups of three. Two players open their books to the map on pages 68–69. The third student reads the Culture Corner aloud. The partners listen. When they hear a country mentioned, they write one or two words on the country to describe the rice that is eaten there. When they finish, they take turns calling out the "hint" words. The other partners, without looking at their books, try to remember the countries. This activity helps students focus on key words.

NOTES

• *"Arroz"* is the Spanish word for "rice." Foreign words are frequently used in English when describing food.

• The Culture Corner refers to wild rice, traditionally a Native American food. It is now enjoyed by many people but is very expensive and so is considered a delicacy.

Food trends

Charts and graphs help explain information.

❏ Listen. You will hear information about food.
Number the graphs and charts (1–4). Then write the names of the foods on the lines. There is one extra graph or chart.

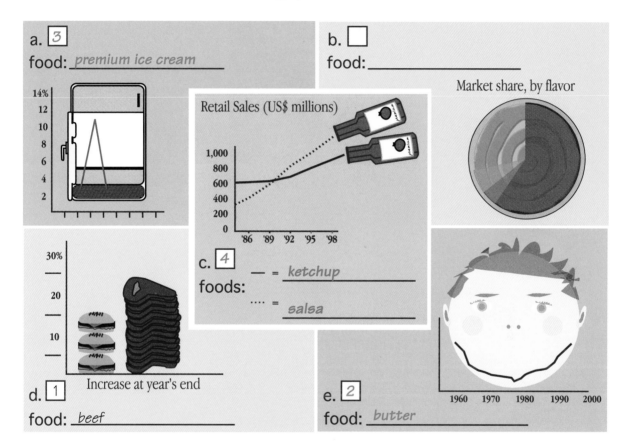

a. 3
food: _premium ice cream_

b. ☐
food: _____

14%
12
10
8
6
4
2

Retail Sales (US$ millions)

1,000
800
600
400
200
0
'86 '89 '92 '95 '98

Market share, by flavor

c. 4
foods: — = _ketchup_
        .... = _salsa_

30%
—
20
—
10
—

Increase at year's end

d. 1
food: _beef_

e. 2
food: _butter_

1960   1970   1980   1990   2000

CULTURE CORNER

One of the most popular foods in the world is rice. It is common in many places. However, the type of rice people like varies greatly. In North America, many people prefer brown rice because it is healthier than white rice. In Southeast Asian countries like Thailand, people eat light, flaky rice. In Japan, sticky rice is used for making sushi. Indians often eat bright yellow rice that is colored with the spice turmeric. In Mexico, *arroz* is served with vegetables and small pieces of fried meat. In the northern U.S. and parts of Canada, people sometimes eat wild rice, a delicious type that is black, brown, and white.

Is rice popular in your country? How is it prepared?

What's on the menu?

Some foods are popular in some places and avoided in other places.

❏ Listen. Do people in the places listed eat or avoid these foods?
If people eat the food, check (✔) the place. If people don't (or didn't)
eat it, put an ✗. Then write one extra fact about each food.

1. milk and milk products
- ✔ North America
- ✔ Europe
- ✗ parts of Africa
- ✗ China

In U.S., children drink milk every day.

2. beef
- ✗ Egypt
- ✗ Greece
- ✗ India

*Ancient people thought
bulls were gods.*

3. horse
- ✔ Sweden
- ✔ Finland
- ✔ France
- ✔ Italy

*In France, special stores
sell horse meat.*

4. fish
- ✗ parts of Africa
- ✗ parts of Southwest U.S.
- ✗ parts of Southeast Asia
- ✔ Switzerland/Iraq

*Fish must be sold alive in
Switzerland.*

5. chicken
- ✔ U.S./Canada
- ✗ Philippines
- ✗ Vietnam
- ✗ Middle East

*In the Philippines and
Vietnam, women don't eat it.*

YOUR TURN TO TALK

Work with a partner. Imagine that someone from another country is visiting you.
What kind of food would you serve? Plan two meals – one that is very fancy and one
that is typical. In your country, which of these would you include?

• an appetizer • a main dish • salad • vegetables • something to drink • dessert

Now join another pair. Explain your menus and the reasons you chose those foods.

Listening Task 2
What's on the menu?

Listening skills: Identifying places, recognizing details

1. T: *Look at page 56.* **(Optional)** Read the title: *"What's on the menu?"* Ask: *What do you think this will be about?* Elicit answers. (Answer: foods that are and aren't eaten in certain places)

2. Play the introduction and instructions: *Some foods are popular in some places and avoided in other places. Listen. Do people in the places listed eat or avoid these foods? If people eat the food, check the place. If people don't (or didn't) eat it, put an X. Then write one extra fact about each food.*

3. **(Optional)** If your students will find this task very difficult, do the Additional Support procedure.

4. Play Listening Task 2 on the tape. Gesture for students to write their answers. **(Optional)** You may want to stop after the second item to check. Have students call out their answers.

5. If necessary, play Listening Task 2 a second time. You may want students to concentrate on catching the place names the first time they listen and writing an extra fact for each the second time.

6. Check by reading the place names and having students say "yes" or "no." Encourage several students to say what they wrote as extra information. (Answers appear in blue on the opposite page.)

ADDITIONAL SUPPORT Have students look at the places listed. They find the places on the map on pages 68–69. They circle each place on the map. Then they listen once, looking only at the map. They check the place names as they hear them. After that, they go back to page 56 and listen for items eaten and not eaten.

NOTE

- You may prefer to check after each segment rather than waiting until students have heard all five items.

Your turn to talk

1. Divide the class into pairs. T: *Imagine that someone from another country is visiting you. What kind of food would you serve? Plan two meals – one that is very fancy and one that is typical. In your country, which of these would you include? An appetizer? A main dish? Salad? Vegetables? Something to drink? Dessert?*

2. (after about 10 minutes) T: *Now join another pair. Explain your menus and the reasons you chose those foods.*

3. **(Optional)** Have the groups combine their menus to come up with a single menu for each type of dinner.

Optional activity

(For use anytime during or after the unit.)

- *How long can you go?* Each student chooses one of the questions from the Warming Up on page 54. It doesn't matter whether or not it was one the student worked with during the warming-up activity. Students work in pairs. They decide who will speak first. The speakers see how long they can talk without stopping or saying something that is not English. The partners listen and keep time. The speaker is out when he or she (a) pauses for more than five seconds or (b) says a word that is not English. When the speaker's turn is over, students change roles and the other partner speaks. If time permits, you may want learners to change partners when they finish and do the same task with a new partner. **Note:** This is a monologue, not a conversation. However, you might want to require partners to ask at least one follow-up question to make sure they are really thinking about the speaker's meaning.

U N I T   1 8

We mean business.

Content area: Talking about successful
people and companies
Listening skills: Listening for specific
information (Listening Task 1);
understanding main ideas (Listening
Task 2)
Grammar/vocabulary: Simple present,
simple past, possible and unreal
conditionals

Warming Up

1. T: *Look at page 57.*

2. Divide the class into pairs. T: *Work with a
partner. Choose one set of questions. Answer the
questions. Give examples and extra information.*

3. Point out the choices on the page: *The
questions on the left are about the job you have.
It can be any job, including a part-time job. The
questions on the right are about businesses you
know.*

4. As students work, circulate and help
pairs having difficulty. If there is a question
they really can't answer, have them skip it.
They may want to come back to it at the
end.

5. (Optional) Have pairs merge into
groups of four to compare answers.

NOTE

• Encourage students to give very specific
examples. For example, "I like my boss.
She's nice." or "I like *X* store. It's nice."
really doesn't give much information.
Reasons and examples should be more
interesting and informative. The more
interesting, the better they are for getting
conversations started. For example, "I like
my boss. She gives me a lot of
responsibility. Last month, she gave me a
raise." or "I like *X* store. The clothes are
very fashionable, and the prices are
reasonable."

Strategy exercise: *Rules for language learning*

Listening Task 2 presents some rules for a
successful business. Have students work in
groups to make a list of rules for successful
language learning. Keep the atmosphere
light. Remind them that the idea of "rules"
for language learning is a little silly because
everyone learns in a different way.
However, rules are useful reminders of
those different ways. Students may want to
work with large pieces of poster paper and
post their rules around the classroom.

Optional activity

(For use anytime after learners have done
Listening Task 1.)

EXPANSION **The Big-Mac™ Index.** Before
class, make copies of the Unit
18 Activity Sheet on page T73. You will
need one copy for every two students. Cut
each copy into two parts: **A** and **B**. In class,
divide students into pairs. First, they do a
peer dictation: Each Student **A** reads the
first sentence, and **B** writes the missing
words. Then **B** reads and **A** writes. Students
continue until both partners of every pair
have a complete story. Finally, each partner
draws arrows from the countries and prices
on his/her sheet to the correct position in
the sandwich. Students **A** and **B** then take
turns reading the countries/prices from
their sheets so that their partners can write
them in the correct places. If possible, they
should also figure out the price of a Big
Mac™ in U.S. dollars for their own
country. (For answers, combine the
information on the two parts of the activity
sheet.)
Note: This is based on the following
source: "U.S. Dollar to take bite out of NT
dollar." Report in *China News,* 4 May 1996: 3.
(All prices are given in U.S. dollars so
students can compare values.)

We *mean business.*

❑ Work with a partner.
Choose one set of questions.
Answer the questions.
Give examples and extra information.

Your job	Businesses you know
1. What do you really like about your job? Why?	**1.** What's a store or other business that you like? Why?
2. What don't you like about your job? Why not?	**2.** What store or business don't you like? Why not?
3. When do you feel you're doing a good job?	**3.** Is there a store or business that makes you feel like a special customer? How?
4. What does your boss do very well?	**4.** If you could own a business, what kind would it be? How would you make it different from other companies?
5. If you were the boss, what would you do differently? Why?	

Billions sold!

Business Today is a radio program. Today they're talking about McDonald's restaurants.

❏ Listen. What happened in each of these years? Write the missing information.

1960
200 restaurants

1959
100 restaurants

1954
Ray Kroc: *12* restaurants

1950
Over *1 million* sold

1948
Fast food: limited *menu*

1940
McDonald brothers
first hamburger stand

1973
New product: *Egg McMuffin™*
Importance: *created fast-food breakfast*

1963
New product: *Filet-O-Fish™*
Importance: *local restaurant meets customers' needs*

McDonald's now

18,000 restaurants worldwide

90 countries

25 million customers daily

20 % of U.S. restaurant meals

96 % of people in U.S. eat there

®

CULTURE CORNER

Part of McDonald's success is their limited menus. They sell large numbers of a few types of food. However, in some places, they change the menu to match local tastes. Here are some McDonald's food items that are sold in different markets:

- Norway: *MacLak™*, a salmon sandwich
- Thailand: Samurai pork sandwich
- the Philippines: *MacSpaghetti™*
- Japan: bacon and potato pie teriyaki burgers

What items in fast-food restaurants are designed for your country's tastes? If you were going to add a food, what would it be?

Listing Task 1
Billions sold!

Listening skill: Listening for specific information

Note: The tapescript for Unit 18 begins on page T32.

1. T: *Look at page 58.* **(Optional)** Read the title: *"Billions sold!"* Ask: *What do you think this will be about?* Elicit answers. (Answer: a history of McDonald's restaurants)

2. Play the introduction and instructions: Business Today *is a radio program. Today they're talking about McDonald's restaurants. Listen. What happened in each of these years? Write the missing information.*

3. Play Listening Task 1 on the tape. Gesture for students to write their answers.

4. **(Optional)** If your students will find this task very difficult, do the Additional Support procedure.

5. **(Optional)** To make sure students understand what to do, stop after Jane's first long speech. Ask: *What happened in 1948?* Encourage students to answer. Then play the rest of Listening Task 1.

6. If necessary, play Listening Task 1 a second time. If so, you may want to stop the tape just after they talk about the Egg McMuffin™. Students listen first to the time line, then to the information about the company today.

7. Check by calling out the years and other items and having students say their answers. (Answers appear in blue on the opposite page.)

ADDITIONAL SUPPORT Write the dates on the board, in the same design as they appear on the page. As you play the tape, point to the year just before it is mentioned. This will help students follow the flow of the conversation.

Culture corner

1. Have students read the Culture Corner and answer the questions, alone or in small groups.

2. **(Optional)** Before class, make enlarged copies of the Culture Corner. Post the copies on the front and back walls. Before students read from the book, they work in pairs. Their books are closed. One partner quickly goes to a copy on the wall and begins reading. That student remembers as much as possible, then goes back and dictates it to the partner, who writes. Then that partner goes to the copy, remembers the next part, and returns to dictate it. They continue until they've written the entire passage. Then they read it in their books to check. This activity builds speed and memory.

Optional activity

(For use anytime during or after the unit.)

• **Fast food.** Students work in groups of three. They imagine they are opening a new fast-food restaurant. The restaurant must serve food that is typical of their country. They must decide on these things:
  - a name for the restaurant
  - the menu (They can serve only eight items. The items should appeal to as wide a range of customers as possible.)
  - a way their restaurant will be different from most fast-food restaurants.

After they have decided, have each person change partners so there are new groups of three. They explain their restaurant plan. The new group listens to all three plans and combines ideas to make the best possible restaurant.

Note: If students are from different countries, they can either create a restaurant serving food of the country they are in, any type of food they are all familiar with, or a restaurant that serves specialties from all their countries.

Listening Task 2
The richest man in America

Listening skill: Understanding main ideas

1. T: *Look at page 59.* (**Optional**) Read the title: *"The richest man in America."* Ask: *What do you think this will be about?* Elicit answers. (Answer: the business beliefs of a very successful businessperson)

2. Play the introduction and instructions: *Sam Walton was the richest person in America. His chain of WAL-MART stores has sold more products than any other group of stores in the world. Listen. These are Sam Walton's ten rules for business. What does each rule mean? Check your answers. Then write the extra rule on the line at the bottom.*

3. (**Optional**) If your students will find this task very difficult, do the Additional Support procedure.

4. Play Listening Task 2 on the tape. Gesture for students to write their answers. (**Optional**) To make sure students understand what to do, stop after one or two items and check. Then play the rest of Listening Task 2.

5. If necessary, play Listening Task 2 a second time. Before replaying the tape, you may want to have students compare answers: *Work with a partner. Look at your partner's answers. How many were the same as yours?*

6. Check by reading the rules and having students say what they mean. (Answers appear in blue on the opposite page.)

ADDITIONAL SUPPORT Have students read through all the rules. First, they underline one or two key words in each meaning. Then they circle the box they think will be the answer in each item. Finally, students listen to see if they guessed correctly. Note that there is no reason or way they "should"

be able to figure out the answers before they listen. But reading and underlining first will make sure students think about the meaning. Making guesses often makes students more focused since they will want to see if they were correct. You may want to pause the tape between items to give students more time to think.

Your turn to talk

1. Divide the class into groups of three. T: *Imagine that you are managers of a business. It can be a place you work at or a store or business you know. It could even be your school. Look at Sam Walton's list again. How could you apply his business rules? Think of specific actions that you could take. Try to find at least one action for each rule.*

2. As students work, circulate and help. If students can't think of or don't know a business, have them use their school. (Even if a school is not really a business, most of the rules still apply.) To help learners get started, ask questions based on the rules: *How could you show that you really believe in what you do?* (Get to work before anyone else. Always talk positively., etc.)

3. (after about 10 minutes) T: *Now join another group. Tell them your ideas. Listen to theirs. Then decide on the five best ideas.*

NOTE

• Another type of conditional sentence (see Unit 7) is the unreal conditional; these are about situations that are not true or possible – they are often hypothetical. They are about present or future time but use the past tense in the *if*-clause to show they are not real: *If I were a manager* (I'm not really one). The result clause in the sentence usually uses the modal "would" or "could" to show it is a hypothetical case: *If I were a manager, I would share profits with the employees.*

The richest man in America

Sam Walton was the richest person in America. His chain of WAL-MART stores has sold more products than any other group of stores in the world.

❏ Listen. These are Sam Walton's ten rules for business. What does each rule mean? Check (✔) your answers. Then write the extra rule on the line at the bottom.

1. COMMIT to your business.
[✔] Believe in what you do.
[ ] Never change careers.

2. SHARE your profits.
[ ] Give money to good causes.
[✔] People who work for you should get extra money if business is good.

3. MOTIVATE your workers.
[✔] Find ways to challenge people.
[ ] Give workers more vacation.

4. COMMUNICATE everything you can.
[ ] Give interviews to magazines and newspapers.
[✔] The more people know, the more they care.

5. APPRECIATE everything people do.
[ ] Give hard workers extra money.
[✔] Praise people often.

6. CELEBRATE your success.
[✔] Do something original.
[ ] Go out to dinner.

7. LISTEN to everyone in the company.
[✔] Listen to store clerks. They know what customers really think.
[ ] Lots of talking leads to good ideas.

8. EXCEED your customers' expectations.
[ ] Serve your customers on time.
[✔] Make sure customers are always happy.

9. CONTROL your expenses.
[ ] Lower costs mean bigger profits.
[✔] Lower costs mean lower prices.

10. SWIM upstream.
[✔] Don't do things the way other people do them.
[ ] Relax and exercise.

One more rule: _Break all the rules._

Work in groups of three. Imagine that you are managers of a business. It can be a place you work at or a store or business you know. It could even be your school.

Look at Sam Walton's list again. How could you apply his business rules? Think of specific actions that you could take. Try to find at least one action for each rule.

Now join another group. Tell them your ideas. Listen to theirs. Then decide on the five best ideas.

Everything we know is wrong.

When you were a child,
what did you believe?

❑ Work with a partner.
Make lists of things you used to believe
that you don't believe now.

I thought ... ,
but my partner didn't.

We both thought ... .

- _____
- _____
- _____
- _____

- _____
- _____
- _____
- _____

❑ Look at the lists again. Answer these questions.
  1. When did you learn the truth?
  2. How did you feel when you found out?
  3. What else do you remember?

Everything we know is wrong.

> **Content area:** Explaining and challenging "common knowledge"
> **Listening skills:** Understanding and evaluating information (Listening Task 1); following instructions, giving opinions (Listening Task 2)
> **Grammar/vocabulary:** Comparative and superlative of adjectives

Warming Up

1. T: *Look at page 60.*

2. Divide the class into pairs. T: *When you were a child, what did you believe? Work with a partner. Make lists of things you used to believe that you don't believe now.*

3. **(Optional)** Demonstrate with a pair as the rest of the class watches. Ask each partner a question – for example: *Did you believe in Santa Claus (fairies, monsters, etc.)?* If one person believed it, he or she writes it on the left. If they both believed it, they write it on the right.

4. As students work, circulate and help pairs having difficulty by asking about the beliefs illustrated or beliefs common among children in the learners' culture(s).

5. (after about 5 minutes) T: *Look at the lists again. Answer these questions. 1. When did you learn the truth? 2. How did you feel when you found out? 3. What else do you remember?* Have students try to answer. Some will have clear memories. Others will have forgotten. Students can skip any that they don't remember.

6. You may want to see which beliefs were most common. Have students say the beliefs they wrote. Other students raise their hands if they also believed it.

NOTES

• When the manuscript for this book was being reviewed before publication, one of the reviewers wrote about this unit: *This is a kick.* Yes, the unit is surprising and strange. We wrote it for several reasons. First, we wanted students to have fun. The unit comes off as humorous. Humor is very hard for students to process in a foreign language. However, the humor here is based on being surprised. Various times in this *Teacher's Edition,* we have mentioned the importance of getting students to think about information at the level of "appreciation." Surprising and humorous tasks can help get at this high level of processing. Also, Listening Task 1, at least, is non-fiction. The information may be strange, but the students are almost certain to learn things they didn't know before.

• Dragons have different traditions in Asia and in the West. In the West, they are usually thought of as evil and dangerous creatures. In Asia, they are often symbols of good luck.

• Although Santa Claus comes out of the European tradition, awareness of him has spread throughout the world. Many children who do not come from a Christian tradition still believe in him.

Strategy exercise: *Seeing progress*

Sometimes it is difficult for students at this level to see their own progress. When they were beginners, everything they learned was clearly new. Now, although they are moving ahead, they may not see it because the steps they take are smaller in relation to all the English they already know. To help students see their progress over the term, choose a listening task that they found challenging earlier in the course. Before they listen, have them work in pairs, listing whatever they remember about doing the activity (the speed, difficult vocabulary, etc.). Then play the tape. Most students will be surprised to see how much easier it is.

Listening Task 1
Of course that's true . . . isn't it?

Listening skill: Understanding and
evaluating information

Note: The tapescript for Unit 19 begins on
page T34.

1. T: *Look at page 61.*

2. Play the instructions: *Read the statements.
What do you think? Are they true or false? Check
your answers.* Circulate and help with
vocabulary. Students may have no idea at
all about some of the items. In that case,
they should just guess.

3. Play the instructions and Listening Task
1 on the tape. Gesture for students to write
their answers.

4. (Optional) If your students will find this
task very difficult, do the Additional
Support procedure.

5. If necessary, play Listening Task 1 a
second time.

6. Check by reading the items. Have
students call out their answers and extra
information. (Answers appear in blue on
the opposite page).

ADDITIONAL SUPPORT Have students listen
twice. The first time, they are only trying to
catch if the item is true or false. The second
time, they try to catch extra information.

NOTE

• Comparatives (*-er/more*) are used to
compare one thing relative to something
else; superlatives (*-est/most*) describe
something as at the top or bottom of its
category, most often in comparison with
two or more items.

We use *-er/-est* with adverbs and adjectives
of one syllable (*hotter, coldest*) and with most
two-syllable words that end with a vowel
sound (*shallower, loveliest*). We use *more/the
most* with all other words, including those
of three syllables or more.

Culture corner

Have students read the Culture Corner
and answer the follow-up question alone or
in pairs.

EXPANSION **(Optional)** Before class, make
copies of the Unit 19 Activity
Sheet on page T75. You will need one copy
for every three students. In class, learners
work in groups of three. They open their
books to page 61 but place the books facedown on their desks. Give one activity sheet
to someone in each group. That person
reads the first question twice. When the
questioner says, "Go!" the partners look at
the Culture Corner and try to be first to
answer. That person must point out where
he or she found the answer so the other
students can check. Then the books are
again put facedown, and groups continue
with the next question.

Optional activity

(For use anytime during or after the unit.)

• *To tell the truth.* Learners begin in
groups of three. Each partner thinks of an
interesting experience he or she has had.
Then partners take turns briefly describing
their experiences. The group chooses one
of the stories. The "owner" then gives the
partners as much information as possible.
Finally, the group decides on a one-
sentence summary of the story. (*Example:
Last winter vacation, I rode an elephant.*)
Each group joins another group. One team
begins with each person saying the
summary sentence – with each student
pretending that the experience is his or
her own. The new partners ask questions to
get more information. They use the
questions and answers to try to decide
which person is telling the truth. After
about five minutes, they vote. Then the
person who really had the experience
identifies him or herself. Finally, the other
team tells their story.

Of course that's true ... isn't it?

❏ Read the statements. What do you think? Are they true or false?
Check (✔) your answers.

❏ Now listen. What's really true? Correct your answers.
Then write one more piece of information about each item.

1. Thomas Edison invented the light bulb. ☐ true ✔ false
   It was invented by ... *Sir Joseph Swan.*

2. Bulls hate the color red. ☐ true ✔ false
   They hate motion.

3. Big Ben is a clock. ☐ true ✔ false
   It's a bell.

4. Brown eggs are healthier than white eggs. ☐ true ✔ false
   There isn't any difference.

5. The fastest animal in the world is the cheetah. ☐ true ✔ false
   It's the falcon.

6. Hot water freezes faster than cold water. ✔ true ☐ false
   Steam carries away the heat.

7. Mosquitoes are more dangerous than tigers. ✔ true ☐ false
   They carry diseases.

8. Frankenstein, the monster, was invented by
   a crazy doctor. ☐ true ✔ false
   Frankenstein was a student.

CULTURE CORNER

Two countries have names that seem to be mistakes. Iceland and Greenland
seem to have their names reversed. Iceland is not really very icy. Only about 13%
of the country is covered with snow and ice. Greenland, on the other hand, isn't
very green. Most of the country is covered by ice up to 4,300 meters (14,000 feet)
thick. People can live on only about 5% of the land.

The names seem like mistakes, but they aren't. Vikings were the first Europeans
to visit the areas. They didn't want other people to come to Iceland, so they gave
it an unfriendly-sounding name. They gave Greenland its name to further
confuse people.

Are there any surprising place names in your country?

LISTENING TASK 2

The flat earth

Most people know the earth is round. However, some say it's flat.

❏ Listen. A "flat earther" is trying to prove the earth is flat.
Try the experiments he suggests. Circle your answers.

1. The earth moves.		
Did you get the same result?	yes	no
Do you believe him?	yes	no
2. Earthquakes come from the center of the earth.		
Did you get the same result?	yes	no
Do you believe him?	yes	no
3. We can't see across large lakes.		
Did you get the same result?	yes	no
Do you believe him?	yes	no
4. Photos from space show the earth is round.		
Did you get the same result?	yes	no
Do you believe him?	yes	no

❏ Now work with a partner.
Do you think the flat earther *really* believes the earth is flat? ☐ yes ☐ no
Why? _____

YOUR TURN TO TALK

Work in pairs. Think of as many true but unusual or surprising facts as you can. On small pieces of paper, write at least three. Write them in question form. Write the answers on the back.

Example: True or false? The printing press was invented in Germany.
(False. It was invented in Korea.)

Now join two other pairs. Take turns asking your questions. Your pair gets one point for each correct answer.

Stay in your group of six. Exchange questions with another group. Continue to play.

Listening Task 2
The flat earth

Listening skills: Following instructions, giving opinions

1. T: *Look at page 62.*

2. Play the introduction and instructions: *Most people know the earth is round. However, some say it's flat. Listen. A "flat earther" is trying to prove the earth is flat. Try the experiments he suggests. Circle your answers.*

3. Play Listening Task 2 on the tape. Gesture for students to write their answers.

4. (Optional) If your students will find this task very difficult, do the Additional Support procedure.

5. (Optional) You may want to stop after each section and have students explain each experiment. Then have them try the experiments.

6. If necessary, play Listening Task 2 a second time. Before replaying the tape, you may want to have students compare their answers in pairs.

7. T: *Now work with a partner. Do you think the flat earther* really *believes the earth is flat? Why?*

8. Check by reading the items. Have students raise their hands to show if they agree or not.

ADDITIONAL SUPPORT Write the following series of words on the board:

    earth – turtle – moves
    heavy – elephants – earthquakes
    reflection – flat areas – distorted
    photos – focus – circle

Have students listen once. Point to each series of words as the related topic is discussed. Then have the students listen again. Stop after each section. Have students explain the experiment. They then work in pairs. They direct their partner through each experiment.

NOTE

• Some students might feel strange doing the experiments (putting their ears on the desk, holding out a book, etc.). In most cases, if you are willing to do the experiment, they will be too.

Your turn to talk

1. Divide the class into pairs. T: *Think of as many true but unusual or surprising facts as you can. On small pieces of paper, write at least three. Write them in question form. Write the answers on the back.* Circulate and help.

2. (after about 10 minutes) T: *Now join two other pairs. Take turns asking your questions. Your pair gets one point for each correct answer.*

3. (as groups run out of questions) *Stay in your group of six. Exchange questions with another group. Continue to play.*

NOTE

• This is a trivia game, similar to the one heard in Listening Task 1. Most students know a lot of small facts. However, it takes a little while to remember them. You can help to remind students by writing categories such as the following on the board: *history, important dates, music, geography, famous people, books, politics, your country, other cultures.*

Optional activity

(For use anytime during or after the unit.)

• *Why?* Students think of a fact they know is true. They work in pairs. One partner says the fact. The other asks, "Why?" The speaker gives a reason. Again, the partner asks, "Why?" They continue until the first speaker can't think of a reason. Then they change roles. (*Example:* **A:** *The sky is blue.* **B:** *Why?* **A:** *It reflects light from the ocean.* **B:** *Why?* **A:** *Because . . .*) We learned this game from Yoko Narahashi.

Poetry

> **Content area:** Appreciating and creating poetry
> **Listening skills:** Identifying poetry types (Listening Task 1); creating a poem/song (Listening Task 2)
> **Grammar/vocabulary:** Verb + present participle, literary terms

Warming Up

1. T: *Look at page 63.*

2. Read the poem aloud (or play the tape). Talk about the vocabulary that is defined under the poem and then read the poem again.

3. T: *Work with a partner. What do you think the poem means? Does the writer really mean* fire *and* ice*? Or are those words symbols of something else? How does the poem make you feel?*

4. Allow time for students to work. Circulate and help. If students have difficulty, help them think figuratively by asking leading questions: *How might the world end?* (war, earthquakes) *What could* fire *be a symbol of?* (anger, hate, fighting)

5. T: *With your partner, write four sentences about the poem.*

6. (after about 5 minutes) You may want to have a few students read their sentences. However, we don't recommend that you spend too much time "analyzing" the poem. If students understand the general meaning, that's enough.

NOTES

• The most common interpretation of the poem is that the lack of caring and love among people (ice) is just as dangerous as active hatred (fire).

• Robert Frost (1874–1963) is thought of as one of the U.S.A.'s greatest and most loved poets. He won three Pulitzer Prizes.

Strategy exercise: *Looking for opportunities to listen*

As the course ends, students should be encouraged to seek opportunities for practice outside class. This can be made into a class project. Students can work in teams to find out the names of places where they can listen to or practice English. This might include a list of radio stations and any special programs they have, lists of upcoming movies or TV shows, or any supplemental books students could recommend. Students studying in English-speaking countries may investigate volunteer programs that would put them in touch with the local community.

Optional activity

EXPANSION *Newspaper poem.* Before class, make copies of the Unit 20 Activity Sheet on page T77. You will need one copy for every two students. Bring to class some old English-language newspapers. Students work in groups of four. Give each group at least one newspaper. If possible, also give them large pieces of paper, glue or tape, and markers. Cut the activity sheet in half and give two copies of the top half to each group. Tell students the poem came from newspaper headlines and someone's reaction to them. Read the poem aloud. Students look through their newspapers and find four to eight headlines or parts of headlines that they could respond to with "Me too" or "Not me." They can change the punctuation any way they want. They work together to create a newspaper poem. After they finish, they practice reading it aloud with feeling. Then each group displays their poem on the wall or a desk. Two students stay with the poem, reading it aloud as other learners look at it. The other two members of the group circulate and look at other poems. After a few minutes, they change roles.

Poetry

❏ Read this poem.

Fire and Ice

Some say the world will end in fire,
Some say in ice.
From what I've tasted of desire
I hold with those who favor fire.

But if it had to perish* twice,
I think I know enough of hate
To say that for destruction** ice
Is also great
And would suffice.***

— Robert Frost

Vocabulary:
*perish = to end, be destroyed
**destruction = when things are destroyed
***suffice = be enough

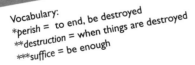

❏ Work with a partner.
What do you think the poem means? Does the
writer really mean *fire* and *ice?* Or are those
words symbols of something else? How does
the poem make you feel?

❏ With your partner, write four sentences about the poem.

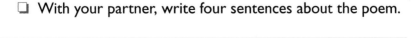

Four poems

❏ Listen to these poems.

Rivers [1]

Rivers,
beautiful, clear
gurgling,* rushing, chasing
swift or slow they're fun to play in
creeks, streams.

* gurgling =
the sound a
river makes

5 parts, about nature

The Boy from Baghdad [2]

There once was a boy from Baghdad,
A curious sort of a lad.
He said, "I will see
if the sting has a bee."
And soon he found out that it had.

humorous, rhymes, tells story

*Across the calm path
Branches snake, telling people,
"Do not come in here."* ☐

White [3]

White is
  a soft breeze
  or a snowflake on my nose.
White is
  a wedding
  a shower of love.
White is
  soft, not too rough,
  white is a beautiful color.

uses the same word over and over

❏ Now listen to someone describing three of the poems.
  Write the numbers (**1.** quintet, **2.** limerick, **3.** fugue) in the
  boxes above. Then write one more thing about each poem.

❏ Now listen and answer the question. _____

CULTURE CORNER

Some people think of poetry as a "high culture" art form. They see poetry as "high class" and something that only a few people enjoy – like fine arts, classical music, and traditional literature.

Actually, there are many types of poetry that everyone meets almost every day. A lot of poems are part of popular culture. Rap music is one example. It is poetry based on rhyme and rhythm that often creates an image instead of telling a complete story. The lyrics (words) to many popular songs are similar. Jingles – the short rhymes you hear in radio and TV commercials – are quick poems meant to remind you of a company or product.

What kinds of poetry do you often hear? Which do you like? Which don't you like? Are there any that are especially easy to remember?

Listening Task 1
Four poems

Note: The tapescript for Unit 20 begins on page T36.

1. T: *Look at page 64.*

2. Play the instructions: *Listen to these poems.* Play the tape of the poems being read.

3. T: *Now listen to someone describing three of the poems. Write the numbers (1. quintet, 2. limerick, 3. fugue) in the boxes above. Then write one more thing about each poem.* Play the next part of the tape. Gesture for students to number the boxes and write one more thing.

4. (Optional) If your students will find this task very difficult, do the Additional Support procedure.

5. (Optional) You may want to stop after each description to check. Have students say which poem number and extra information they wrote. Then continue.

6. If necessary, play the segment again.

7. Play the final question. You may want to play the tape of the poems again as students listen and decide on their favorite.

8. Check if you haven't already done so. (Answers appear in blue on the opposite page.) You may want to have students raise their hands to show which poem they liked best. Also, have a few students give reasons.

ADDITIONAL SUPPORT Stop after each item. Read (or dictate) the key elements of each type of poem (see the Unit 20 Activity Sheet on page T77). Then have students notice the elements in the poems.

NOTES

• The poem not identified is a haiku. Haiku are three-line poems. The first and last lines have five syllables each. The middle line has seven. They are in present tenses and often mention nature or the seasons.

• Quintets are sometimes referred to by the French name *"cinquain."*

• "Gurgling" is an example of *onomatopoeia,* that is, a word that is an imitation of the natural sound. This device is often used in poetry. Similar words include "buzz," "crack," and "hiss."

Culture corner

1. Have students read the Culture Corner and answer the follow-up questions alone or in pairs.

2. (Optional) After students read the Culture Corner, have them work in groups of four. First, they think of a radio or TV jingle in their first language. Then they divide into pairs. Each pair translates the jingle into English. They should think about the rhythm and overall feeling, in addition to the meaning of the words. When the pairs finish, they join other pairs to compare their results.

Optional activity

(For use anytime after Listening Task 1.)

EXPANSION *A poem of your own.* Make sure you have the copies you made earlier of the Unit 20 Activity Sheet – the bottom half. This sheet lists the key features of the types of poetry in Listening Task 1. Students work alone or in pairs. They choose one of the poetry types. They write one (or more) poems that fit the descriptions. As they work, circulate and help with vocabulary. If some learners are having difficulty getting started, encourage them to choose haiku, quintet, or fugue. These poems are often based on feelings and senses, and it is easier to think about what one sees, hears, or feels. After students have written their poems, have them work together in groups of five to eight. They each read their poem while the other partners listen.

Listening Task 2
Talking blues

Listening skill: Creating a poem/song

1. T: *Look at page 65.*

2. Play the introduction and instructions: *The words in blues songs are one form of African-American poetry. There are many styles of blues. One style is called "talking blues." Read the words.* Allow time for students to read the words.

3. T: *Now listen. Follow the instructions.* Play Listening Task 2 on the tape. Gesture for students to write their ideas.

4. (Optional) If your students will find this task very difficult, do the Additional Support procedure.

5. (Optional) You may want to play the tape twice. The first time, don't have the students write. They just listen and think about their song. The second time, they write their parts of the song.

6. T: *Work with a partner. Read your "talking blues." Then listen to your partner's poem.*

7. (Optional) You may want to have students change partners a few times and continue. OR A few students might want to perform their song for the class.

ADDITIONAL SUPPORT If students have difficulty, it is probably not a listening problem. They just may not be feeling very creative today. (Do they have the blues?) Pause the tape for each blank. As a whole class, have students suggest as many words as they can that could fit the blank. Then individual students choose the one(s) they want to use.

NOTES

• In this unit, the focus is not on poetry as great literature. Rather, it's a chance for students to think of poetry as a form of communication. Also, we hope it will help students notice the poetry around them in their daily lives.

• Students sometimes have a stereotype of blues as a very slow, sad type of music. Actually, like most types of music, there is a great variety. "Talking blues" is one type where the words are spoken, rather than sung.

• It might at first appear that students can fill in all the blanks without listening. However, only by listening to the tape do they know exactly what kind of information to put in the blanks. Also, the tape gives them the rhythm necessary for the final step.

Your turn to talk

1. T: *One kind of poem is called an acrostic. It's a spelling poem. Write your name down the page. Then write words that begin with those letters. The words should be about the same thing. The poem can be about anything – food, places, things you like, and so on. When you finish writing the words, write a final line.*

2. Read the example (the poem by Bob).

3. Allow time for students to write. Some students (especially those with short names) will finish very quickly. Have them continue by writing acrostic poems based on their family names, the place they live, etc.

4. (when students are finished) T: *Now work in groups of six. Take turns reading your poems.*

LISTENING TASK 2

Talking blues

The words in blues songs are one form of African-American poetry. There are many styles of blues. One style is called "talking blues."

❏ Read the words.

❏ Now listen. Follow the instructions.

SAMPLE ANSWERS

My talking blues

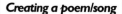

Woke up this morning
Feeling so *sad*   .

Yes, I woke up this morning
I was feeling so *sad*   .

Went *to the shopping center*   ,
Started feeling so *happy*   .

I saw somebody walking.
I had to say *hello*   .

Well, I saw somebody walking.
I just had to say *hello*   .

And you know that somebody
Acted *like a friend*   .

❏ Work with a partner.
Read your "talking blues."
Then listen to your partner's poem.

YOUR TURN TO TALK

One kind of poem is called an acrostic. It's a spelling poem.

Write your name down the page. Then write words that begin with those letters. The words should be about the same thing. The poem can be about anything – food, places, things you like, and so on. When you finish writing the words, write a final line.

Example: This person's name is Bob. He wrote:

> **B**ig trains
> **O**ld trains
> **B**lack and silver trains.
> I love them all.

Now work in groups of six. Take turns reading your poems.

Activation:
a speaking and listening game

The teaching procedure for this activity begins on page T39.

- Work in groups of 3 or 4.
- Each player puts a place marker on *Start here.*
- Close your eyes. Touch the *How many spaces?* box. Move that many spaces.
- Read the sentences. How much can you say about the topic?
- Each partner asks one question about what you said.
- Take turns.

When you have to make a difficult decision, who do you talk to?

Tell about a time you saw something surprising.

Start here

Think of a time you met someone from another country. What did you say? What did the other person say?

Did you believe in ghosts when you were younger? Do you now? Have you ever seen one?

Think of a poem in your language. Can you say it – or explain it – in English?

What is something you believed as a child but don't believe now?

If you could have a date with a famous person, who would it be? Why?

What story did you love when you were a child?

What topics do you usually talk about when you meet someone? What don't you talk about?

What was a very difficult decision to make?

Who's your hero? Why?

Tell about an advertisement or a commercial you hate. Why don't you like it?

If you could change something about your personality, what would it be?

Have you ever been afraid of an animal? When? What happened?

What do you do to stay healthy? What else should you do?

If you could invent a robot, what would it do?

What song has a special meaning for you? Why?

What's a superstition that many people believe? Do you?

Tell about an unusual health technique you've tried. If you haven't tried one, what would you like to try?

Have you ever seen a piece of art that you thought was ugly or stupid?

| What don't you like to do to learn English? | What's the most unusual food you've ever eaten? | *You can ask any player one question.* | What's a custom in your country that is hard for foreigners to understand? How could you explain it? | What do you do for the environment? What else could you do? |

How many spaces?

2	1	3	1	3	2
1	3	4	2	3	1
3	1	2	1	2	3
1	2	1	3	5	2
3	5	2	1	2	3
2	1	3	4	3	1

Tell about an advertisement or a commercial you think is really good. Why do you think so?

What do people do that you think is very rude? What would you like to say to them? Do you?

What are five words or phrases that describe your personality?

Do you know of a custom from another country that you like? What is it?

What food is becoming more popular in your area?

Anyone can ask you one question.

What do you listen to in English? How many different things can you list?

What would make your area a better place to live?

Have you ever made a mistake that was funny or embarrassing?

What is your idea for "the perfect date"?

Have you ever had a pet? Tell about it. If you haven't, would you like one? What kind?

If you could have seen an important event in history, what would it be?

Does new technology make your life easier or more difficult?

Would you rather be a boss or work for someone else? Why?

What helps you learn English?

Tell about a sound you'll never forget.

Have you ever seen a piece of art that you thought was wonderful?

Do you do anything to bring good luck?

World map

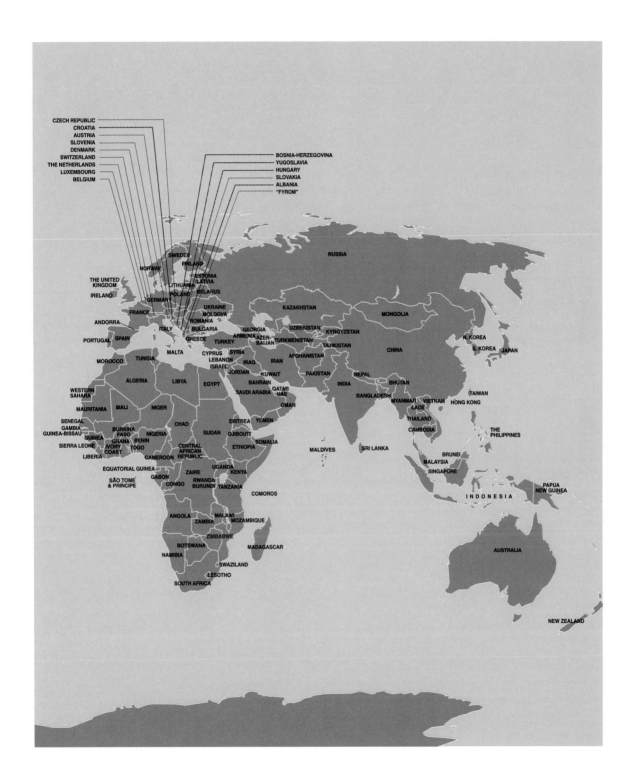

CZECH REPUBLIC
CROATIA
AUSTRIA
SLOVENIA
DENMARK
SWITZERLAND
THE NETHERLANDS
LUXEMBOURG
BELGIUM

BOSNIA-HERZEGOVINA
YUGOSLAVIA
HUNGARY
SLOVAKIA
ALBANIA
"FYROM"

RUSSIA

SWEDEN
FINLAND
NORWAY
ESTONIA
LATVIA
THE UNITED
KINGDOM
LITHUANIA
POLAND
BELARUS
IRELAND
GERMANY
UKRAINE
MOLDOVA
FRANCE
ROMANIA
ANDORRA
ITALY
BULGARIA
KAZAKHSTAN
MONGOLIA
PORTUGAL
SPAIN
GREECE
TURKEY
GEORGIA
UZBEKISTAN
KYRGYZSTAN
ARMENIA
AZER-
BAIJAN
TURKMENISTAN
N. KOREA
MALTA
CYPRUS
SYRIA
TAJIKISTAN
CHINA
S. KOREA
JAPAN
MOROCCO
TUNISIA
LEBANON
IRAN
AFGHANISTAN
ISRAEL
IRAQ
JORDAN
KUWAIT
PAKISTAN
NEPAL
BHUTAN
ALGERIA
LIBYA
EGYPT
BAHRAIN
QATAR
INDIA
TAIWAN
WESTERN
SAHARA
SAUDI ARABIA
UAE
BANGLADESH
MYANMAR
VIETNAM
HONG KONG
OMAN
LAOS
MAURITANIA
MALI
NIGER
THAILAND
SENEGAL
ERITREA
YEMEN
CAMBODIA
GAMBIA
BURKINA
CHAD
GUINEA-BISSAU
FASO
NIGERIA
SUDAN
DJIBOUTI
THE
PHILIPPINES
GUINEA
GHANA
BENIN
SIERRA LEONE
IVORY
TOGO
CAMEROON
ETHIOPIA
SOMALIA
MALDIVES
SRI LANKA
BRUNEI
COAST
CENTRAL
AFRICAN
MALAYSIA
LIBERIA
REPUBLIC
SINGAPORE
EQUATORIAL GUINEA
UGANDA
GABON
ZAIRE
KENYA
PAPUA
SÃO TOMÉ
NEW GUINEA
& PRÍNCIPE
CONGO
RWANDA
BURUNDI
TANZANIA
INDONESIA
COMOROS
ANGOLA
MALAWI
ZAMBIA
MOZAMBIQUE
ZIMBABWE
BOTSWANA
MADAGASCAR
AUSTRALIA
NAMIBIA
SWAZILAND
LESOTHO
SOUTH AFRICA

NEW ZEALAND

Art and text credits

Illustrations

Lloyd P. Birmingham 4 (*bottom left*), 12, 13, 14, 26, 38, 49, 50
Edgar Blakeney T45 (*all except baby*), T53 (*all except car, broccoli, flamingo*), T61
Susan Ferris Jones 19, 24 (*bottom*), 36, 48, 54
Blaine J. Graboyes 55
Randy Jones 7, 20, 25, 28 (*top*), 31, 62

Patricia Ossowski 65
Janet Pietrobono 8, 16, 23, 29, 32, 33, 37, 39, 41
Anna Veltfort 3 (*top*), 4 (*top and bottom right*), 9, 10, 13 (*bottom*), 21, 24 (*top*), 30 (*top*), 33 (*top and bottom*), 34 (*bottom*), 42, 46 (*left*), 65, 66, 67
Sam Viviano 34 (*top*), 60

Photographic credits

The authors and publisher are grateful for permission to reprint the following photographs.

3 (*clockwise from top*) © David Hanover/Tony Stone Images; © Jon Feingersh/The Stock Market; © Bob Torrez/Tony Stone Images; © Ken Fisher/Tony Stone Images; © Jon Riley/Tony Stone Images
5 (*from top to bottom*) © Jon Feingersh/The Stock Market; © Randy M. Ury/The Stock Market
6 (*clockwise from top*) © John Waterman/Tony Stone Images; © Henley & Savage/The Stock Market; © Chuck Savage/The Stock Market
8 © Rob Gage/FPG International Corp.
11 © John Gajda/FPG International Corp.
12 (*from left to right*) © Western History Collections, University of Oklahoma Library; silhouetted photo of Belle Starr © Roeder, Fort Smith, AR. Courtesy of the Oklahoma Historical Society, Barde Coll. 19383.172
17 (*from top to bottom*) © H. Lambert/SuperStock; © Ron Chapple/FPG International Corp.
18 © Jim Cummins/FPG International Corp.
20 © Anna Veltfort
21 (*clockwise from top*) © Lori Adamski Peek/Tony Stone Images; © Tony Garcia/Tony Stone Images; © William Westheimer/The Stock Market; © Marc Dolphin/Tony Stone Images
30 (*from middle to bottom*) © Rob Goldman/FPG International Corp.; Michael Goldman/FPG International Corp.
35 © Kay Chernush
39 © Anna Veltfort
40 (*from top to bottom*) © English Language Institute, University of Pittsburgh; © The Australian Centre for Languages; © Institute for Shipboard Education: Semester at Sea
43 (*clockwise from top*) © Michael Keller/The Stock Market; © Chuck Savage/The Stock Market; © Michael Keller/The Stock Market; © Ed Bock/The Stock Market
45 (*clockwise from top*) Photo of Claude Monet's "Water Lilies" © Neue Pinakothek, Munich/SuperStock, © 1996 Artists Rights Society (ARS)/ADAGP, Paris; Photo of Alexej Jawlensky's "Abstrakter Kopf" © Christie's, London/SuperStock,

© 1996 Artists Rights Society (ARS), New York/VG Bild-Kunst, Bonn; Brancusi, Constantin, The Kiss, c. 1912, Philadelphia Museum of Art: The Louise and Walter Arensberg Collection, © 1996 Artists Rights Society (ARS), New York/ADAGP, Paris; Photo of Jan Vermeer's "Woman with a Water Jug" © Metropolitan Museum of Art, New York/Lerner Fine Art Collection/SuperStock; Photo of Jane Wooster Scott's "Eighth Avenue" © Collection of Ron Sunderland/SuperStock; Photo of painted wood sculpture of dog © Private Collection/SuperStock
46 Copyright © 1954 Salvador Dali et Philippe HALSMAN, Copyright © renewed 1982 Salvador Dali. Yvonne Halsman. Jane Halsman Bello et Irene Halsman
47 Photo of René Magritte's "The Lovers" © Richard S. Zeisler Collection, New York, © 1996 C. Herscovici, Brussels/Artists Rights Society (ARS), New York
50 © R. Heinzen/SuperStock
51 (*clockwise from top*) © Tom and DeeAnn McCarthy/The Stock Market; © Jon Feingersh/The Stock Market; © Paul Barton/The Stock Market; © Craig Tuttle/The Stock Market
52 (*clockwise from top*) © David Brooks/The Stock Market; © Reggie Parker/FPG International Corp.; © Ron Chapple/FPG International Corp.
56 (*from left to right*) © Paul Redman/Tony Stone Images; © Wayne Eastep/Tony Stone Images; © Peter M. Fisher/The Stock Market; © Jose Fuste Raga/The Stock Market
57 (*clockwise from top*) © Don Smetzer/Tony Stone Images; © Mark Ferri/The Stock Market; © Bruce Forster/Tony Stone Images; © Terry Vine/Tony Stone Images; © Mug Shots/The Stock Market
58 © McDonald's Corporation
59 © 1992 by Estate of Samuel Moore Walton. Used by permission of Doubleday, a division of Bantam Doubleday Dell Publishing Group, Inc.
61 (*from top to bottom*) © SuperStock; © Christian Michaels/FPG International Corp.; © SuperStock
63 © Anna Veltfort

Text credits

The authors and publisher are grateful for permission to reprint the following items.

35 List of the Ten Worst Faux Pas © MISS MANNERS®.
40 English Language Institute, University of Pittsburgh; Information reproduced by the kind permission of The Australian Centre for Languages, Sydney, Australia; Institute for Shipboard Education: Semester at Sea
59 From SAM WALTON: MADE IN AMERICA by Sam Walton. Copyright © 1992 by Estate of Samuel Moore

Walton. Used by permission of Doubleday, a division of Bantam Doubleday Dell Publishing Group, Inc.
63 From: THE POETRY OF ROBERT FROST edited by Edward Connery Latham. Copyright © 1951 by Robert Frost. Copyright 1923, © 1969 by Henry Holt and Company, Inc. Reprinted by permission of Henry Holt and Company, Inc.
64 "Rivers" and "White" reprinted courtesy Edna Kovacs.

Tapescript

The following tapescript, which includes all of the listening tasks in the text, reflects *Active Listening*'s emphasis on natural, spoken English. There are, of course, differences between spoken and written English. This is a transcription of the spoken language.

You may occasionally want students to see the tapescript. For that reason, permission is granted to photocopy the script. However, the authors strongly suggest that this be done only occasionally and for specific reasons. Many students are too "word-level dependent." That is, they try to catch each individual word and piece together the meaning from the individual parts, rather than relying on their overall understanding of what they hear. If they insist on reading along with the script for every lesson, it can actually hurt their ability to listen and understand.

Here are two examples of situations where you might want to give out copies of the script:

- After students have completed the tasks in their text, you may want them to go back and note the uses of a particular grammatical form. In that case, you might give out the script and play the tape again, having students underline the times the form is used.
- If a class found a particular listening segment extremely difficult, you may want to give them a copy of the script. Have students read along silently as you play the tape. This increases their reading speed as well as letting them combine reading with listening to understand the segment. Then have them put away the script. Play the tape again and let them see how much they understood.

Before you begin: Getting ready to listen and learn

Page 2, A letter from the people who wrote this book.

Listen to the letter.

READER: Dear students:

You've learned a lot of English so far. We hope this book will help you learn even more. We also hope that you enjoy learning it.

Before you begin, we would like to give you some hints about learning how to listen. First of all, it is important to think about your task. *Why* are you listening? What do you need to know?

Work with a partner. You want to take an English class. What do you need to know? Write the questions you need to ask. [*pause*]

What is the most important question for you? Check it. [*pause*]

You also need to think about your knowledge. What do you already know? To help you answer this question, each of the units in this book begins with a Warming Up activity. This helps you think about the words and ideas you will hear. It makes listening and understanding easier.

We hope you will be *active* when you listen. Sometimes you will work in pairs or small groups. Help your partners. Listen to their ideas. When you don't understand something, ask your teacher or another student.

Good luck with learning English. You can do it!

Sincerely,
Marc Helgesen
Steven Brown
Dorolyn Smith

Page 3, Listening Task 1: What do you need to know?

We listen for different reasons. Work with a partner. Look at the ad.

APARTMENT FOR RENT. CALL 555-2938.

What questions might people ask about this apartment? Why? Write your answers. [*pause*]

Listen. People are calling about the apartment. What's the most important question for each person? Why do you think it's important? Write your answers.

NUMBER 1
[*Telephone rings*]
MANAGER: Grange Real Estate.

WOMAN: Hello. I'm calling about the apartment you have for rent.

MANAGER: Yes, the apartment's $650 a month for two bedrooms. It's close to the university, and . . . uh . . .

WOMAN: Um, what I need to ask first is whether you allow pets.

MANAGER: No dogs, but if you have a cat, that's fine.

WOMAN: Great. OK, that's $650 a month. And when is it available?

NUMBER 2

[*Telephone rings*]

MANAGER: Grange Real Estate.

MAN: I'm calling about the apartment.

MANAGER: Yes. What would you like to know about it?

MAN: Well, first of all, the most important thing, really, is where it's located.

MANAGER: OK. It's near the university. Do you know Oak Street?

MAN: Is that the street the library's on?

MANAGER: No, that's Pine. Oak is one block up.

MAN: OK. Oak Street. So that's about ten minutes from the university, right?

MANAGER: About a ten-minute walk, yeah.

MAN: Sounds good. How much is it?

NUMBER 3

[*Telephone rings*]

MANAGER: You have reached Grange Real Estate. We are unable to come to the phone right now. Please leave your name and number, and we will return your call as soon as possible.

WOMAN: My name is Sara Fox. I'm calling about the apartment you've advertised. I'd like a little more information. What I'm most concerned about is the size. I need two bedrooms. If it's a two-bedroom apartment, please call me back. That's Sara Fox, and my number is 555-8921. Thanks very much.

NUMBER 4

MAN: Uh-huh . . . OK. Just one more question. How much is the rent?

MANAGER: The apartment is $650 a month. The rent's due on the first of the month. The late fee is $25.

MAN: Oh, just one more thing. I can't believe I almost forgot the most important thing. You don't mind if I share with a roommate, do you?

MANAGER: No, that's fine. There are two bedrooms. They're kind of small, so I wouldn't want more than two people.

MAN: I understand. It's just my brother and me. So, if we wanted to take it . . .

NUMBER 5

WOMAN: Well, those are all my questions. The apartment sounds really good. When can I move in?

MANAGER: The current tenant is going to move out this Monday the 30th. Any time after that is fine.

WOMAN: I'd like to move in as soon as possible. How about Tuesday?

MANAGER: Tuesday the first. That's fine with me, but you'd better call first to see if the apartment is ready. Give me a call Monday night after seven. I'll know more then.

WOMAN: Great. I'll talk to you then. And I should give you a check . . .

Page 4, Listening Task 2: What do you already know?

Before you listen, you need to think about what you already know. Read the message below. [*pause*]

Look at these things. What do you think Ken will tell Erika? [*pause*]

Page 5, Listening Task 2: What do you already know? (Continued)

Ken is talking to Erika. Look at Erika's questions. If you know Ken's answers, check them. [*pause*]

Now listen. Check the answers you didn't know.

[*Telephone rings*]

ERIKA: Hello?

KEN: Hi, Erika. I got your message. I thought I'd give you a call.

ERIKA: Oh, hi, Ken. I'm glad you called. What are you doing today?

KEN: I'm going to work soon. I just wanted to call and let you know about the park. [*pause*]

ERIKA: Thanks for getting back to me so quickly. I won't keep you long – I know you have to get to work. Now, you've been to the National Park, right?

KEN: Yes. I went last summer.

ERIKA: That's what I thought. [*pause*] What's the best way to get to the National Park?

KEN: Well, Route 12 is really pretty. It goes through the forest, and there are lots of trees and animals. But, really, the best way . . . the fastest way . . . is to take Route 5.

ERIKA: Route 5 all the way?

KEN: Right. [*pause*]

ERIKA: So, would you like to go with us on the 17th?

KEN: Sorry. I'd really like to, but I can't. I have plans for the 17th. [*pause*]

ERIKA: Oh, you're busy. Too bad. What are you going to do that day?

KEN: I'm going to a concert. My favorite band is coming to town, and I bought tickets for the first show. [*pause*]

ERIKA: How about the weekend after that? Any plans?

KEN: Saturday the 24th? That sounds good. Let's get together then.

ERIKA: Great. I'll call you next week, and we'll make plans.

KEN: Great. Listen, I've got to go. Talk to you later.

ERIKA: OK. Bye.

Unit 1 What do you say first?

Page 7, Listening Task 1: A good first impression

"First impressions" are what you think when you meet someone for the first time. Your opinion is based on what the person says and does.

Listen. People are meeting for the first time. What do they say? Write the missing words.
What do the people do to make a good first impression? Write their strategies.

NUMBER 1

[*Sounds of office*]

ANN: You're new here, aren't you?

SUE: Yes, I just started this week.

ANN: I'm Ann Rogers.

SUE: I'm Sue Kelly.

ANN: It's nice to meet you, Sue.

SUE: Nice to meet you, too.

ANN: I was just going for my coffee break. Would you like to join me, Sue? [*pause*]

COMMENTATOR: Ann's strategy? Remembering names. She tries to remember the names of people she meets. Notice that she said, "It's nice to meet you, *Sue*" and "Would you like to join me, *Sue*?" The strategy: Try to remember people's names by using them.

NUMBER 2

[*Sound of jazz*]

WOMAN: Nice music, isn't it?

MAN: Yes. I really like jazz.

WOMAN: So do I. Especially Wynton Marsalis and Miles Davis.

MAN: I like them too. [*pause*]

COMMENTATOR: This strategy is to add extra information. The woman didn't just say, "I like jazz, too." She said the names of two musicians she likes. It's really difficult to have a conversation with someone who just says "yes" or "no" or gives very short answers. Try to give extra information, especially when you're asked a question. Don't just say "yes" or "no."

NUMBER 3

[*Sound of classroom*]

TONY: Have you ever taken a class with this teacher before?

JAN: No, I haven't. But I've heard she's good.

TONY: I had her for a course last year. She's really good.

JAN: I'm glad to hear that. Oh, by the way, I'm Jan.

TONY: Nice to meet you. I'm Tony. [*pause*]

COMMENTATOR: The key here is to start a conversation by finding something you and the other person have in common – something that's the same, or that affects both of you. Here, the speakers are at school. They start by talking about the class and the teacher. At a party, you might mention the food or the music. What about other times? Anything that you and the speaker have in common – even the weather. You both already know it's cold or hot or rainy. But people talk about the weather because it's something they have in common. The strategy is to find something that is the same for you and the person you're talking to.

NUMBER 4

MAN: Well, I'm a little shy. Of course I like meeting people, but it's kind of difficult. So before I meet someone, I sometimes think about what I want to say. I'll think of something about school or work. It depends where I am. Anyway, I usually do that before I say my name. So I guess planning what I want to say is important for me. I don't practice or memorize it or anything . . . I just think about it. [*pause*]

COMMENTATOR: His strategy is to think about what he wants to say. By thinking about the topics, he knows what he wants to say – or at least what he wants to talk about. That makes it easier.

What do you say when you meet people? When English-speaking people meet, they often follow a pattern.

Listen. What do the people talk about? Number the items (1 through 3).

[*Elevator door closes*]

TERRY: Sure is hot out today.

JEAN: It really is. It might rain tonight, though.

TERRY: I hope so. Uh . . . I've seen you around the office, but I don't think we've met. I'm Terry Moss. I work in the financial section.

JEAN: Nice to meet you, Terry. I'm Jean Grant. I'm in the advertising department, up on seven.

TERRY: The advertising section. Really? What do you do in advertising?

JEAN: I'm a copywriter. [*pause*]

COMMENTATOR: A good way to start a conversation is to find something that you and the other person have in common. Here, they talked about the weather. It affects them both. Second, they said their names. They introduced themselves. People often say their names *after* they've already started talking. Third, the man asked the woman about her job. Asking a question is a good way to move into a real conversation.

Listen. You're going to get ready to have a conversation. Follow the instructions.

Situation 1: In class

Step 1:

WOMAN: Since you're studying English, you're probably in a class right now. If you wanted to meet someone in your class, naturally school is what you have in common. If you're both studying English, you might say, "I really like English" or even, "I don't really like English much. I'm taking this class because I have to."

Now it's your turn. What would you say about school, or about your class, or about English? Write one sentence. [*pause*]
When you say something about school, the person you're talking to will usually respond with his or her opinion or something about what you said. [*pause*]

Step 2:

WOMAN: Next, you need to introduce yourself. You might say something like, "I don't think we've met. I'm . . ." then your name. Or you

might just say, "By the way, my name's ____."
How will you introduce yourself? Write an answer. [*pause*]

Step 3:

WOMAN: Then you might want to ask a question. For example, you might ask if your classmate knows anything about the teacher. Or what other classes he or she is taking. What will you ask? Write a question. [*pause*]

Now try it again.

Situation 2: At a party

Step 1:

WOMAN: Now think of a different situation. Imagine you're at a party. You want to introduce yourself to someone. What do you and the other person have in common? The party, of course. What could you say about the party, the food, the music, the person giving the party, or anything else about the party? Write one sentence. Or write a sentence about a general topic, like the weather. Write your sentence. [*pause*]

Step 2:

WOMAN: Sometimes you can ask the person's name at the same time you say your own: "I didn't catch your name. I'm . . ." and then say your name. You might want to add some extra information about yourself. For example, you could say the job you do or where you go to school. What could you say? Write it. [*pause*]

Step 3:

WOMAN: Next, think about how you're going to keep the conversation going. What's a question you could ask? It could be about the other person's job or something else about the party. Write your question.

Unit 2 Sights and sounds

Page 10, Listening Task 1: The five senses

Listen. People are talking about the senses. What are they talking about? Write "hearing," "sight," "taste," "smell," or "touch."
How did you guess? Write at least one thing for each sense.

NUMBER 1

MAN: This sense changes while we use it. When we first use this sense, we're very aware of it, but after some time, we don't think about it anymore – like when we wear a wool sweater.

This sense can replace other senses – for example, blind people can learn to read using this sense. They use books that are written in Braille. Animals may use their tongues or their noses or their feet when they use this sense. Humans use their hands.

NUMBER 2

WOMAN: We remember things we experience through this sense for a long time, but we usually don't remember what we just experienced. That's because it's difficult to describe this sense in words. Scientists have studied this sense a lot. They're interested in how strong it is. Through tests, they have found that it's quite strong. A mother, for example, can pick out her baby's shirt from many shirts that look the same. If a mother is given five shirts, she'll know which one belongs to her baby.

This sense becomes very strong before a rain storm. It's also very strong high in the mountains.

NUMBER 3

MAN: This is one of the strongest senses. Most people use it a lot. Recently, people have begun to wonder if some famous painters had trouble with this sense. This is surprising since the sense is connected to their art.

Vincent van Gogh painted in ways that people thought were strange. He painted rings around lights and made the sky very unusual. People wonder if van Gogh might have had a problem with this sense. Some of the paints he used might have made him sick.

Another artist, El Greco, was famous for painting people as if they were taller and thinner than they really were. Some art historians think he may have had a problem called astigmatism. Astigmatism can change the shape of things. This might have been what happened to El Greco.

NUMBER 4

WOMAN: This sense can help us deal with stress. Our bodies can make chemicals that help us deal with stress in our daily lives. The chemicals are made from the food we eat. Some scientists think that when we need these chemicals, our bodies tell us to eat food that contains them or that helps our body make them. For example, when we eat sweet food like chocolate, our bodies feel calm; the stress goes away. So when we're feeling stress, we might feel like eating a box of cookies. Sometimes in winter, when we feel tired because it's cold and dark, we want to eat pasta or noodles. We love the taste. What the food does explains why: the carbohydrates – a chemical in pasta and noodles – make us feel better. Salty foods like potato chips might also be good for us in this way – but *only* in this way.

Page 11, Listening Task 2: Colors and sight

A scientist is talking on television. He's talking about color vision, the way we see colors.

Listen. Try the experiment.

[*Music*]

MAN: Welcome to "Science Corner." Today we're going to try an experiment with color. First, we're going to look at the green square. Stare at it for thirty seconds or so. Don't blink. Look right at it. [*Music*]

Now look away from the green square. Look at the white part of the page. You should see a red or pink square. Not a green one – a red or pink one. It may move a little, but close your eyes quickly and when you open them, the red or pink square will be back. What you've seen happens all the time. It's an "afterimage." Bright images or pictures make dark afterimages; dark ones make light ones. Green makes red, and red makes green. The eye – or the mind – tries to make the opposites come together. Now try it again. Look at the green square for thirty seconds. Then look at the white part of the page. [*Music*]

Work with a partner. Describe what you saw. Did you and your partner have the same experience? Check your answer. [*pause*]
At night, we really see black and white like this picture. Why?

Listen. Check the answer.

[*Music*]

MAN: Here's something else to try. Do you see colors at night? Think for a minute. Of course the sky isn't blue. But are the leaves green? Think about the grass. What color is it? That's right: Our eyes lose their ability to see color at night. What we see is black and white and gray – just like an old black-and-white movie.

Try this experiment. If possible, turn off the lights in this room. Close the curtains. Make the room as dark as possible. Wait a little while for your eyes to get used to seeing in the dark. Then look at the cover of this book. You know the cover is green, yellow, red, and blue; but if the room is dark enough, you just see black and white.

Why is that? Well, the eyes have two structures inside them. One set is cone-shaped, like ice cream cones. The other is rod-shaped, like pencils. We use the cones to see color. The problem is that they aren't useful in weak light. The rods, on the other hand, can "see" in a very little bit of light; they just can't see color. So when it becomes dark, the parts of our eyes that *can* see color aren't useful anymore.

Most people don't notice this loss of color because our brain puts the color where it thinks it is. But next time you're outside at night, pay close attention to colors. You'll be surprised by how little color you see.

Unit 3 Pirates and such

Page 13, Listening Task 1: Pirates of the Caribbean

Read this passage. [*pause*]

Now listen. Some information is wrong. The tape is correct. Find the mistakes. Write the correct information.

WOMAN: The word "pirates" makes us think of sailors who attacked ships in the Caribbean Sea during the sixteenth and seventeenth centuries. Most pirates were English, French, or Dutch. They mainly attacked Spanish ships that were carrying gold to Spain from colonies in South America and Mexico. Sometimes pirates attacked towns where the gold and silver were stored before it was taken to Spain. When pirates attacked a town, they stole the riches that were hidden there, robbed rich families' houses, and then burned the town down.

There were other adventurers living on the Caribbean islands. These men were hunters. They learned to make smoked meat, called "boucan," from the Tupi Indians in the Caribbean. "Boucan" was the Indian word for smoked meat; the hunters became known as buccaneers. At the beginning of the 1600s, buccaneers were only hunters and adventurers who sold boucan and other food to pirates. However, by 1650, they had become pirates too and began attacking ships for the gold. The gold that pirates and buccaneers stole was usually in the form of a coin called a piece of eight. The symbol for a piece of eight was the number 8 written on top of the letter *P*. This symbol eventually became abbreviated to the letter *S*

with a vertical line through it, and this became the symbol for the American dollar.

Page 14, Listening Task 2: Sunken treasure

Since the 1500s, many ships carrying valuable cargo have sunk in the ocean. These ships were carrying gold and silver when they sank.

Listen. Where did these ships sink? Write the numbers in the circles.

NUMBER 1: the Egypt

MAN: The *Egypt* was a British cargo ship that carried goods between England and India in the early part of the 20th century. In 1922, the *Egypt* left London for Bombay with 44 passengers and 294 workers; 450 more passengers were expected to join the ship in southern France. As the ship sailed around the coast of Brittany in northwestern France, the fog was very thick. The ship's officers couldn't see the sun – they could only guess the location of their ship. Around 7 o'clock in the evening, they heard the horn of another ship. They thought the ship was going in the opposite direction, but suddenly it appeared in front of them. It hit the *Egypt*, which quickly sank in the water off the coast of France. The other ship wasn't damaged, and its crew was able to save many of the people on the *Egypt*. Unfortunately, though, 88 people from the *Egypt* died.

NUMBER 2: the ships at Vigo

WOMAN: In 1702, a group of Spanish ships left Cuba to carry gold to Spain. Just before the ships arrived in Spain, war broke out between Spain on one side and England and Holland on the other. The gold ships usually went to the port of Cádiz, in southern Spain. But the English and Dutch ships were waiting near Cádiz, so the Spanish decided to go to the port of Vigo, in the north of Spain. The ships arrived safely, but the Spanish authorities wouldn't allow them to remove the gold for several days. During this time, the English heard of the ships' location and sailed to Vigo. In October 1702, there was a battle and several of the Spanish ships with gold sank off the coast of northwestern Spain. The Spaniards threw some of the gold and silver into the sea to prevent the English from getting it.

NUMBER 3: the Nuestra Señora de la Concepción

MAN: The *Nuestra Señora de la Concepción* left Cuba for Spain in 1641. It was carrying double the amount of gold and silver it usually carried because no ships had taken gold to Spain in 1640. But soon after it left Havana, a hurricane developed. The *Nuestra Señora de la Concepción* became damaged by the waves. Then it got lost in a dangerous area of the Caribbean Sea near the island that is now Haiti and the Dominican Republic. In November 1641, the *Nuestra Señora de la Concepción* hit some rocks.

NUMBER 4: the Lutine

WOMAN: England and France were at war from 1793 to 1815, a period called the Napoleonic Wars. During this time, the British navy captured a French warship called the *Lutine*. In 1799, the *Lutine* sailed from England toward Germany with gold to pay soldiers fighting against France. It was also carrying gold and silver from English bankers to use in business in Germany. The *Lutine* was probably carrying gold and silver that was worth four million six hundred thousand dollars. During the first evening at sea, the *Lutine* was sailing near the coast of Holland. A storm arose, and the ship hit a sandbank. The waves from the storm destroyed the *Lutine* during the night, and by the next day – October 9, 1799 – the ship had disappeared.

Now listen to some more information. What was the total value of the cargo? How much is still at the bottom of the ocean? Write the numbers.

NUMBER I

MAN: The *Egypt* was carrying an unusual cargo: the Bank of England was sending gold bars, silver bars, and gold coins to banks in India. The value of the gold and silver was about six million two hundred thousand dollars. Over the next ten years, treasure hunters from several countries – England, Sweden, France, Germany, and Italy – searched for the *Egypt*. It was difficult to find the ship because the exact location wasn't known, and sometimes bad weather caused problems. One time, a group found the ship and marked its location, but the bad weather moved the marker. Finally, in 1930, an Italian crew found the *Egypt* and successfully marked its location. At first, they didn't find any gold or silver – only guns, silk, and Indian money – but three years later they found the gold and silver, and the crew was able to bring up around five million dollars' worth of valuable cargo. That means there's one million two

hundred thousand dollars waiting under the sea – waiting for someone to find it!

NUMBER 2

WOMAN: When the ships at Vigo sank during the battle between the English and the Spanish, there was a total of approximately one hundred forty million dollars' worth of gold on the ships. About twenty million dollars' worth has been found. So if there had been a total of a hundred and forty million dollars – and only twenty million dollars have been found – then there must be around a hundred twenty million dollars' worth of gold left at the bottom of Vigo Bay.

NUMBER 3

MAN: When the *Nuestra Señora de la Concepción* sank, how much gold and silver was the ship carrying? Over 21 million dollars! In 1687, a man found the ship underwater. He brought up around one million five hundred thousand dollars' worth of gold, silver, and jewels. That's right: in 1687! That was the first time gold had been recovered from a shipwreck. But there's still nineteen million, five hundred thousand left at the bottom of the sea.

NUMBER 4

WOMAN: A week after the *Lutine* disappeared, a Dutch fisherman found a bar of gold on the sandbank. Soon many fishermen were looking for gold! Over the last 200 years, approximately eight hundred fifty thousand dollars has been found. If the total was worth four million six hundred fifty thousand dollars – and eight hundred fifty thousand dollars has been found – then there must be around three million eight hundred thousand dollars' worth of gold near the coast of Holland. Imagine, three million eight hundred thousand dollars! And guess what? I don't think the water is very deep near the coast of Holland!

Now you will hear a question. Write your answer.

MAN: Look at the amounts that are left at the bottom of the ocean. How much money is waiting to be found? [*Musical scale*] The answer? One hundred forty-four million five hundred thousand dollars. One hundred forty-four million, five hundred thousand dollars! Would you like to have a look? [*Sound of splash*]

Unit 4 Dating

Page 16, Listening Task 1: Which way is best?

Listen. Some students are talking about ways people meet and begin dating or get married. What is an advantage and a disadvantage of each way? Complete the chart.

MAN: Hey, look. I just got a letter from Chen.

FIRST WOMAN: From Chen? Back in Taiwan?

MAN: Yeah. Guess what? He's getting married.

FIRST WOMAN: Getting married? That's great! But when – and who? I didn't even know he had a girlfriend.

MAN: He says he just met her two months ago. Someone introduced them – a matchmaker.

FIRST WOMAN: A matchmaker?

SECOND WOMAN: That's not so unusual in Asia . . . in parts of Asia, anyway. Many people – when they want to get married – have a matchmaker introduce them . . . you know, to someone else who wants to get married. Lots of people act as matchmakers: uh . . . relatives, friends of the family . . . there are even some professional matchmakers.

FIRST WOMAN: Really?

SECOND WOMAN: Yes. Lots of people go to a matchmaker. It's very common.

MAN: So the matchmaker just . . . arranges the marriage?

SECOND WOMAN: Not exactly. Eh . . . the matchmaker just introduces the people. I know this seems unusual to you, but actually there are a lot of advantages. Both people find out about each other's background . . . and schools, jobs, money. It's a pretty open and honest system. You can't lie. Well, most people don't.

FIRST WOMAN: But if Chen's only known this woman for two months, . . . does he really love her? How could you know in such a short time?

SECOND WOMAN: Remember, they're ready to get married. They *want* to fall in love.

MAN: Um . . . but what if they don't?

SECOND WOMAN: They usually do, but – yes – that's the disadvantage. Sometimes people get married but never really fall in love. That can lead to a bad marriage. [*pause*]

FIRST WOMAN: You know, I guess going to a matchmaker isn't really all that different from being introduced by a friend – or someone in your family – like when they know someone they want you to meet. It's just a little more formal.

MAN: So when friends or someone in the family introduces you, they're acting like matchmakers? Yeah, I think you're right.

FIRST WOMAN: Uh-huh. And everybody knows who everyone is. Plus your friends know what your interests are, so they introduce you to people with similar interests. People who are your friends like you, and they like the other person, too. It's the best of both worlds.

MAN: I don't know. The problem with friends – or even worse, your mother! – is . . . well, there's pressure. "So what do you think?" "She's great, isn't she?" I guess that I think who I fall in love with is a pretty personal decision. I don't really want the pressure. Sort of like "Thank you very much, but it's none of your business." [*pause*]

SECOND WOMAN: I think the best way is by chance. You know, a love match. You just meet someone. Maybe someone at school. Maybe someone who likes the same things you do. You learn more about the person and do things together. You date – go to restaurants, movies. You know, just fall in love. I like the idea of meeting the right person . . . just by chance.

FIRST WOMAN: Yeah. But what if you don't? What if you never meet "Mr. Right"? You could go your whole life and never fall in love. That would be awful.

SECOND WOMAN: Well, at least you're not in a bad marriage.

Page 17, Listening Task 2: How did they meet?

Listen. First, you will hear people talking about how their parents met. Write the correct letter in the boxes:

    a. through a matchmaker, b. by chance,
    c. a "blind date" arranged by a friend,
    d. through the young woman's mother,
    e. in high school

Next, write the parents' first impressions of each other. Do they still think the same thing? Circle "yes" or "no."

NUMBER 1

ANNE: Craig, how did your folks meet?

CRAIG: It's kind of funny, Anne. They met on a blind date. They didn't even know each other before their first date.

ANNE: And what happened?

CRAIG: Well, my dad worked on cars. He's a mechanic. And this guy he worked with knew this woman, Mary. So Dad's friend says, "I've got this friend. Her name is Mary. She's really nice, and she's got a really great sense of humor. She loves jokes, and she tells really funny stories. Why don't you take her to the movies?" Dad says, "OK." And they met. And Mary – my mom – was really funny. And they fell in love. [*Music*]

INTERVIEWER: You're Craig's father, right?

CRAIG'S FATHER: Uh-huh.

INTERVIEWER: You met your wife on a blind date, didn't you? What was your first impression? What did you think when you met her?

CRAIG'S FATHER: My first impression? That she was really funny. We went to a movie and then to a restaurant. And she started telling stories. She made me laugh. She had a great sense of humor.

INTERVIEWER: Your first impression was that she was funny. What do you think now?

CRAIG'S FATHER: Well, we've been married almost thirty years now. And, yeah, I still laugh. Mary's the funniest person I've ever met. She's wonderful.

NUMBER 2

ANNE: Do you know how your parents met, Dave?

DAVE: They were high school sweethearts. They started dating in high school. My dad had just moved to town. He didn't know anyone, and he didn't talk very much. Anyway, they were in the same French class. But Dad was really quiet. He never said anything in class. Now, Mom was very outgoing – she still is. So the teacher asked her – my mom – to help my dad when they were doing speaking activities. The teacher was worried about Dad's French. So Mom and Dad started to study together outside of class, too. Then they started dating. After high school, they went to the same college . . . dated the whole time . . . and, the week after they graduated, they got married. [*Music*]

INTERVIEWER: And you're Dave's mother. What was your first impression of your husband?

DAVE'S MOTHER: He was really quiet in class. I thought he was shy. In fact, I thought he was the shiest person I'd ever met.

INTERVIEWER: Was he?

DAVE'S MOTHER: That's the funny part: When we were studying together, his French was wonderful. He never told anyone he had lived in France for a year. His language was perfect. He didn't say much in class because what we were learning was much too easy for him. He wasn't

shy – he was clever. He wanted to ask me out. Really, he got the teacher to put us together. Clever, very clever. His French was great – he didn't need help at all!

NUMBER 3

SARA: Maybe everyone has a relative who likes getting involved in things that . . . well, maybe it's the relative's business – but maybe not. For my parents, it was my grandmother – my mom's mom. You see, Grandma liked to make things happen. My mother didn't date much – and Grandma wanted grandchildren – so she set it up. Grandma had this dentist who loved boats . . . and sailing. That's all he talked about. And naturally, dentists do most of the talking, since your mouth is always full of stuff. Right? Well, anyway, Grandma decided that this dentist was the perfect match for her daughter. See, Mom loved sailing too. So my grandmother made an appointment for my mom to get her teeth cleaned. And Mom and Dad talked. They talked about boats. And on their first date, they went sailing. [*Music*]

INTERVIEWER: What did you think on your first date with Sara's mother – your wife?

SARA'S FATHER: I thought she knew a lot more about boats than I did. I was amazed – she was a wonderful sailor.

INTERVIEWER: What do you think now?

SARA'S FATHER: I was right. We've been sailing for what – twenty years?

NUMBER 4

LISA: My parents met through a matchmaker. My father was 30 years old and wanted to get married. But he didn't know anyone. He had his own business and was working all the time, so he really didn't have a way to meet anyone. So my grandfather called this man he knew, and they just arranged an introduction between my mother and father. [*Music*]

LISA'S MOTHER: That's right. We met through a matchmaker. Lisa's father wanted to get married, and I wanted to get married. But our first meeting was a disaster! He was nervous. Oh, he was so nervous. He came to my house. I made him coffee. But he was so nervous, he spilled it on his pants and then all over the floor. Then he dropped a box of chocolates all over me. What a mess! He did not make a good impression. Anyway, we had dinner, and after dinner, I was about to wash dishes and he said, "Can I help?"

And I said, "No, you just sit down. You don't need to wash dishes." Actually, I was afraid he'd break them. He'd already broken my favorite cup. It was not a good introduction. But I could see he was so nice. He was so nice – but so nervous. But that was then. We started dating. We got married. The funny thing is that he's not a nervous person at all. He's very relaxed. It was just that time. And by the way, he usually does the dishes.

Unit 5 A broad view of health

Page 19, Listening Task 1: Reflexology

Reflexology is foot massage. It comes from ideas of traditional Chinese medicine. Reflexology believes that rubbing parts of the foot can help other parts of the body.

Listen. What body parts go with these areas of the foot? Write the body parts in the boxes. There are two extra boxes.

WOMAN: Did I tell you about the reflexology class I'm taking at the Asia Center?

MAN: The what class?

WOMAN: Reflexology. It's foot massage . . . you know, from Chinese medicine.

MAN: Foot massage?

WOMAN: Yeah. It's wonderful. Here, let me show you what I've learned. Take off your shoes and socks.

MAN: Are you serious?

WOMAN: Just try it.

MAN: OK.

WOMAN: The important thing to understand is that parts of your foot are connected to other parts of your body.

MAN: Yeah, my legs.

WOMAN: No, I mean certain places on your foot are connected to other places, other parts of your body. So when you massage a part of your foot, it's good for another part. For example, look at your big toe.

MAN: Uh-huh.

WOMAN: The area on the bottom of the big toe is connected to your brain. Do you have headaches?

MAN: Headaches? Sometimes.

WOMAN: So just rub the area on the bottom of your big toe. It will help your brain.

MAN: Huh? Huh. [pause] Actually, my eyes hurt more often than my head. My eyes get tired from using the computer at work.

WOMAN: Massaging your other toes can help your eyes. On the bottom of each toe, there's a small area. They're round, like circles. Well, rubbing these circles makes your eyes feel better. It relaxes tired eyes.

MAN: Here? This area under each toe?

WOMAN: Yeah. But that's not the only place for tired eyes. If your eyes really hurt, find the area under your two smallest toes . . . there by your two smallest toes.

MAN: Uh-huh.

WOMAN: It looks something like the letter "U." Massage that U. It will help when you feel really bad pain in your eyes. [pause]

MAN: What else?

WOMAN: Well, now move down your foot on the outside. Find the widest part of your foot. On the outside, there's an area related to your shoulders. Massage it firmly – not so hard that it hurts, but you should be firm. This will help the muscles in your shoulders.

MAN: Like stiff shoulders, that kind of thing?

WOMAN: Right. [pause] Now let's look at the other side of your foot. On the inside of your foot, put your fingers near the top – on the inside, just under the big toe. Slowly and firmly, rub from the top all the way to your heel . . . to the end of your foot. This area will heal your back. If you have backaches, rub this long, narrow area several times a day.

MAN: The whole inside edge helps the back?

WOMAN: That's right. [pause] How's your stomach? Do you get stomachaches?

MAN: Not very often . . . well, sometimes – if I eat too much.

WOMAN: Find the area in the center of your foot. It goes from the inside edge of your foot almost all the way to the other side. It's almost like a small egg. Massage it firmly. It can help your stomach.

MAN: Here, in the middle?

WOMAN: Right. [pause] You can work on your knees, too. If you have sore knees, move your hand to the bottom, outside edge of your foot – the sole of your foot, by the heel. Rub firmly. [pause]

MAN: You know, this is kind of interesting. But actually, you know what hurts the most? My feet. I get blisters a lot.

WOMAN: Blisters? Maybe you need bigger shoes.

Page 20, Listening Task 2: Relax!

There are many ways to relax. Some people play sports. Others read or watch TV.

Listen. This is an alternative relaxation technique. What are the steps? Complete the sentences.

[*Music*]

INSTRUCTOR: This is a good way to relax. It will help you get rid of stress. There are different ways to do it. Today, I'm going to teach you one.

First, sit in a comfortable chair in a quiet room. You don't need to sit any special way – as long as you're comfortable. [*pause*]

Next, close your eyes. Close your eyes and take a deep breath. Take a very long, deep breath. Relax. [*pause*]

After about thirty seconds, start thinking of a word. It should be a word with no special meaning. Let's use the word "La." Silently say the word "La" in your mind. [*pause*]

Now, in your mind, repeat the word slowly. Silently, over and over in your mind. La. La. La. La. La. La. Say it to yourself many times. La. La. La. La. [*pause*]

At times, you'll have other thoughts. You'll think about your life: about work . . . about school . . . about problems . . . about other things. You have those other thoughts because stress is being released. Don't worry about the other thoughts. They're natural. When you think other thoughts, just go back to the word. Just go back to "La." La. La.

Do this as often as you have other thoughts. La. La. La. [*pause*]

Do this for about twenty minutes. You notice that you aren't breathing very deeply. Your breathing is very shallow. That's because you're very relaxed. After the twenty minutes, slowly open your eyes. Take a deep breath and slowly open your eyes. [*Sound of deep breath*] [*pause*]

Now you're more relaxed. A lot of stress has left you. You feel much better.

Try doing this two times every day: twenty minutes in the morning, twenty minutes at night. You'll feel much better. You'll be more relaxed. [*pause*]

Would you like to try this technique? Check your answer.

Why or why not?

Unit 6 Advertising

Page 22, Listening Task 1: What's in a name?

Have you heard of these companies?
   A. Sara Lee B. Green Giant C. Wal-Mart
   D. Visa E. Exxon

The companies used to have different names. Can you match their names with the old names below? Write your guesses (A through E) on the lines. There is one extra name. [*pause*]

Now listen. Correct your answers. Why did the companies change their names? Check the reasons.

NUMBER 1
WOMAN: The original name for the Visa credit card was Bank-Americard. The company wanted to change its image and grow. They wanted to make the card international and to offer other services besides credit cards. They dropped the reference to America and the word "bank." They chose the name "Visa" because it's easy to pronounce in other languages and it gives the image of a passport to other, wonderful places.

NUMBER 2
MAN: Sara Lee is well known to Americans as a brand of baked goods – pies, cakes, and cookies. The company used to be named Consolidated Foods Corporation, and Sara Lee was only one of their line of products. When Consolidated Foods decided to change their name, they chose Sara Lee. It was their most famous brand, and many Americans recognize the name. Sara Lee, by the way, was the daughter of the man who started the original bakery company in 1951 – the Kitchens of Sara Lee.

NUMBER 3
WOMAN: An example of an invented company name is Exxon, the oil company. The Exxon company was originally called Standard Oil when it was started by John Rockefeller in 1870. It became Esso in 1926 – Esso is the pronunciation of the initials of Standard Oil, "S - O." By the 1960s, the company had many products and wanted one name for all its products. They spent three years finding a new name. They wanted a name that was different and had no negative meanings in other languages. In fact, they wanted a name that didn't exist in any other language. The "x-x" combination exists only in Maltese, the language

of Malta. It was easy to check that there were no Maltese words that were similar to "Exxon."

NUMBER 4

MAN: In 1903, in a small town in Minnesota, a company was formed called the Minnesota Valley Canning Company. This company canned fruits and vegetables for other companies to sell. In the 1920s, a new kind of green pea from England was found, called the Prince of Wales. This pea was larger than the typical green pea that Americans were used to eating, and the private companies refused to sell it. So the Minnesota Valley Canning Company decided to sell the pea itself. They called it "green giant" to emphasize its size. Then they developed the symbol of a green giant, a large green man dressed in green leaves. This symbol became so famous that in 1950 they changed the name of the company to Green Giant. Today the symbol is known as the "Jolly Green Giant."

Page 23, Listening Task 2: Lost in the translation

Some advertisements are effective in one language or country but not in another. This can be because of cultural differences or translation problems.

Listen. These companies had advertising problems. What was the problem? What should they have done? Complete the sentences.

NUMBER 1: China

MAN: This is funny.
WOMAN: What's that?
MAN: I'm reading this article about bad advertisements . . . you know, advertising mistakes.
WOMAN: Yeah?
MAN: Of course, you know Pepsi Cola, the soft drink company? Remember their old "Come alive!" commercials?
WOMAN: Sure. "Come alive!" . . . with all those young people drinking Pepsi and suddenly being full of energy and life.
MAN: Well, when Pepsi was sold in China, "Come alive!" was translated as "Pepsi brings your ancestors back from the dead!"
WOMAN: Well, I guess "Pepsi brings your ancestors back from the dead" is one way to come alive.
MAN: But I don't think that's what they had in mind.

NUMBER 2: the Middle East

MAN: Here's one I wouldn't have thought of. You know those "before and after" commercials for laundry soap?
WOMAN: The ones with a pile of dirty clothes on one side and then the same clothes after they've been washed? Sure.
MAN: There was an American company that had one of those ads. It was really successful in North America. In the ad there was a pile of dirty clothes on the left, a box of the laundry soap in the middle, and a pile of clean clothes on the right. So, the message was that a box of this detergent would make really dirty clothes clean.
WOMAN: Yeah?
MAN: So what do you think happened when they used the ad in the Middle East?
WOMAN: I don't know.
MAN: Think about it. In the Middle East, languages are written from right to left. People look at things from right to left.
WOMAN: So it looked like the soap made the clothes dirty?
MAN: "Our soap will make your clothes dirty!" Not a very smart ad campaign.
WOMAN: They should have changed the order of the pictures. They should have put the picture of the clean clothes on the left side and the dirty clothes on the right.
MAN: Really.

NUMBER 3: Mexico

MAN: Oh, here's another one. Some shirt maker put an ad in a Mexican magazine.
WOMAN: And?
MAN: Well, the ad was supposed to say, "When I wore this shirt, I felt good." But they made a translation mistake.
WOMAN: What did they say?
MAN: Instead of "When I wore this shirt," the ad said, "Until I wore this shirt, I felt good."
WOMAN: "Until I wore this shirt, I felt good"? Gee, changing one little word gave it the opposite meaning.

NUMBER 4: Japan

MAN: The article says sometimes it's not just the advertising slogan that gets companies into trouble. Sometimes the company name can scare off business.
WOMAN: What do you mean?
MAN: Well, there was a large oil company in the United States called Enco: E-N-C-O.
WOMAN: Yeah, I remember them.

MAN: They opened some gas stations in Japan, and they advertised using their American name. Unfortunately, they didn't know what the word means in Japanese.

WOMAN: What does it mean?

MAN: "Enco" is a short way of saying "Engine stop" in Japanese.

WOMAN: Great. Would you buy gasoline from a company that said your car engine would stop?

MAN: No, and neither did the Japanese.

Unit 7 Superstitions

Page 25, Listening Task 1: The real meaning

Listen. What do these superstitions mean? Check your answers.

NUMBER 1

WOMAN: Oh, I saw another scorpion this morning. That's the third scorpion I've seen this week!

MAN: Scorpions are coming down from the mountain. The god of the mountain is getting angry. Soon strong winds will begin to blow. Then it will rain. I can tell. Scorpions come, then winds blow, then it rains – whenever the mountain god is angry.

NUMBER 2

WOMAN: In the past, people never lent milk or butter to anyone. It was dangerous. The person might be a witch. He or she could put a magic spell on your cow. And then the cow would stop giving milk.

NUMBER 3

MAN: "Don't eat any of those mangoes. They look good, but you'll get sick if you eat them. You'll get very, very sick." That's what the land owners would tell their workers.

NUMBER 4

[*Sound of thunder*]

WOMAN: Ah. Ko-chan. Listen. It's thunder. We'd better cover you up or Kaminari-sama, the thunder god, will sneak up and steal your belly-button. Got to cover your belly-button.

[*Sound of baby*]

Now listen to the explanations. What do the superstitions really mean? Complete the sentences.

NUMBER 1

WOMAN: I don't understand. Why do you think the mountain god is angry?

MAN: I learned that story when I was very young. We still watch for scorpions. Scorpions can feel the wind long before people can. They can feel the wind early – and the wind usually starts to blow a couple of weeks before the rainy season starts.

NUMBER 2

MAN: Never lend milk? Why not?

WOMAN: Most cultures have proverbs about lending things – you know, warning against it. When proverbs were created – a long time ago, of course – most people were farmers. They were poor and really couldn't lend things. They didn't have very much. So the superstition is really a rule. It means, "Don't lend anything to anyone."

NUMBER 3

WOMAN: Mangoes would make the workers sick? How could fruit make them sick?

MAN: No, the mangoes wouldn't really make them sick. But the land owners used to tell that to their workers so they wouldn't eat the fruit that they were picking. If they ate the mangoes, the owners wouldn't have as many to sell. If they didn't have enough fruit to sell, they wouldn't make much money. Then they wouldn't be able to pay the workers.

NUMBER 4

MAN: The thunder god will steal his belly-button? Don't stories like that scare your baby?

WOMAN: No, they're just stories. Besides, there's a reason. During a thunderstorm, the temperature goes down. It can get cool very fast. So the real meaning is to cover your body so you don't catch a cold. You should keep warm during a storm.

Page 26, Listening Task 2: In my culture

Think about beliefs in your culture. [*pause*]

Now listen. Write the missing words in the circles. Then finish the sentences with beliefs you know. If you don't know a belief, cross out the sentence.

NUMBER 1

WOMAN: To have good luck, you should . . . [*Sound of bell*]. To have good luck, you should . . . [*Sound of bell*].

NUMBER 2

MAN: Don't . . . [*Sound of bell*], or you'll have bad luck. Don't . . . [*Sound of bell*], or you'll have bad luck.

NUMBER 3

WOMAN: In my culture, . . . [*Sound of bell*] is a lucky number. In my culture, . . . [*Sound of bell*] is a lucky number.

NUMBER 4

MAN: Some people say the number . . . [*Sound of bell*] is unlucky. Some people say the number . . . [*Sound of bell*] is unlucky.

NUMBER 5

WOMAN: If you get sick, you should . . . [*Sound of bell*]. If you get sick, you should . . . [*Sound of bell*].

NUMBER 6

MAN: Be careful if you see . . . [*Sound of bell*]. Be careful if you see . . . [*Sound of bell*].

Do you think the beliefs are true? Circle "yes" or "no."

Unit 8 Communication and culture

Page 28, Listening Task 1: It's our style.

Listen. People are describing conversation styles in three cultures. Which things are OK to do? Check the boxes. Which are not OK? Put an X in the boxes.

TEACHER: You know, a lot of people around the world often think their own way of speaking is the "natural" or "right" way. But how we speak is really determined by our culture. Different cultures have different ideas about what is "polite" or "good" behavior. So, what I have today is a set of questions. I thought I'd ask you to tell the rest of us about communication in your own culture. You don't have to answer for everyone in your culture – people have different ideas. Just answer for yourself. OK? Can you start, Luis?

LUIS: Sure.

TEACHER: You're from Latin America, aren't you?

LUIS: That's right. I was born in Colombia. I also worked for awhile in Brazil.

TEACHER: Do you ever touch the person you're speaking to?

LUIS: Oh, yes. In Latin America, personal connections with people are very important – and we're quite physical. So I often touch someone I'm talking to on the arm or shoulder. It means we're close. We feel close to each other.

TEACHER: How about interruptions? You know, stopping someone to add your idea.

LUIS: That's very common. Again, it's part of the closeness. It shows you are interested in what the other person is saying. It's usually not rude to interrupt. [*pause*]

TEACHER: How about in Korea, Soon Jin? Do you touch or interrupt people you're talking to?

SOON JIN: Do we touch? Well, of course, it depends on the situation. But if I'm talking to a friend – yes, we touch each other . . . usually on the hand or arm. But interrupting? We usually don't interrupt each other. That would be rude.

TEACHER: You don't interrupt.

SOON JIN: Well, usually we don't. Especially if the person is older or has a higher position – like your parents or your boss at work. I usually wouldn't interrupt them. That would be impolite. [*pause*]

TEACHER: How about in Saudi Arabia, Ali?

ALI: Oh, people touch each other a lot. You might hold the hand of the person you're talking to. Or the person might touch you to emphasize a point. But interrupting – we're different in that way from the Koreans. We don't see interruptions as rude . . . not at all. It's fine to do. It's just part of the conversation.

TEACHER: So it's OK to interrupt a speaker.

ALI: Oh, yes. I think it's part of being a leader. Becoming a leader is a very good thing, and one way to do that is by directing the conversation. So, yeah, interruptions are fine. [*pause*]

TEACHER: Any thoughts on saying "no," on disagreeing?

LUIS: I think as Latin Americans, we value the ability to speak well: to make good arguments and give good reasons. So we say "no" quite directly. We argue and disagree. We're not angry. It's just how we interact.

SOON JIN: It's very different in Korea. We don't usually say "no" – not directly. We tend to say "no" indirectly – again, especially if the person we're talking to is in a higher position, like an older person or someone above you in a company. In Korea age is very important, and you're supposed to show some respect to the old and to parents – people above you. And one way of doing that is by not saying "no" directly.

TEACHER: How about in the Arab world, Ali?

ALI: Disagreeing? It shows intelligence . . . leadership. It's fine to say what you think. Although – one thing you might know about our culture – showing respect to other people is very important. So if a friend asks you for help, you should never say "no." Because if you say "no" to that request, you are not showing respect. [*pause*]

TEACHER: You're all speaking directly with me here. How about when you're in your own country? How do you act in class?

LUIS: What do you mean?

TEACHER: For example, do you ask and answer questions a lot or wait for the teacher to answer . . . or what?

LUIS: Oh, I'm very active. I'm happy to answer the teacher's questions. Maybe it goes back to thinking that speaking ability – verbal ability – is important. I know that that's not true everywhere, but I still find it unusual that some people from other countries don't want to answer – even when they know their answers are right.

SOON JIN: I can understand it. A few years ago, I would have said, "No, we don't speak out." It wasn't the students' place. But I think that's changing now – especially in classes like English. So I think now it's OK to speak out, but a lot of people in Korea still aren't comfortable with that.

ALI: I try to answer the teacher . . . and answer quickly – even if I have to call out the answer. It's almost like a competition . . . like a sport. [*pause*]

TEACHER: I want to thank you all for sharing your views. I think the more we know about each other's culture, the easier it is to understand that it's not that one culture's way is good and another's is bad. Each way is right for that culture, . . . but there are differences.

Page 29, Listening Task 2: I didn't know that.

Many universities have an International Students' Association. This ISA is having a party. Students from several countries are getting to know one another. They're talking about mistakes they made when they were living abroad.

Listen. Write the information.

NUMBER 1: John, Ana, and Ken

[*Sound of party*]

ANA: Hi. My name's Ana.

JOHN: Nice to meet you, Ana. I'm John. Where are you from?

ANA: I am from Peru. Are you from the States?

JOHN: Yes, from Florida. Where in Peru are you from? I was an exchange student in Arequipa.

ANA: No kidding! I am from Lima, but my mother's from Arequipa. How did you like Peru?

JOHN: Oh, I loved it. It was a wonderful experience for me.

ANA: That's great to hear. Did you have any trouble with the language?

JOHN: Well, I didn't really have any problems with the language. I understand Spanish OK, . . . but sometimes I had trouble with the meaning.

ANA: What do you mean?

JOHN: There were some things I didn't know about . . . like time.

ANA: Yeah. That's often a problem for people from the U.S. and Canada.

JOHN: Actually, it was pretty funny! I was invited to a friend's house for a party. He said the party would begin at seven. You know, I didn't want to be too early, so I arrived about 15 minutes after 7. I knocked on the door, and no one answered. "That's strange," I thought. "I'm sure today's the right day." I knocked again, louder. Soon the door opened. It was my friend, but his hair was dripping wet. He was in the shower. I was going to say I was sorry to be late, but he asked me why I was so early! I later learned that you should add two hours to a party invitation. He was expecting me at nine!

ANA: Nine o'clock? That's when we often meet people for dinner in Peru. I made that kind of mistake when I first came to the U.S. A friend invited me for dinner. She didn't say an exact time. She just said, "Come over around dinnertime." So I got there about nine. She thought that I had forgotten about dinner. I was really late . . . and so embarrassed.

KEN: Hi, John. I couldn't help but hear your stories.

JOHN: Hi, Ken. Do you know Ana? She's from Peru. Ken's from Japan.

ANA: Hi, Ken. Nice to meet you.

KEN: Nice to meet you, too, Ana. You know, John, I had a similar problem here in the U.S.

JOHN: Really? But Americans are usually pretty much on time.

KEN: Compared to Latin Americans maybe, but not compared to Asians. When a Japanese says "seven o'clock," it means a little before seven. We usually have parties at restaurants, and they start at a set time. Anyway, I was invited to a professor's house for a party at eight o'clock. I arrived at a little before eight and rang the bell. After several minutes, the door opened, and the professor was wearing his bathrobe! He had been in the shower, too. He was really surprised to see me. And I was really embarrassed to see him!

JOHN: I guess you're right. Americans don't usually show up at parties until around fifteen or twenty minutes late.

ANA: So I'll be two hours late for a Japanese party – but only an hour and 45 minutes late for an American party!

NUMBER 2: Karen and Hakan

[*Sound of party*]

HAKAN: Here, Karen. I brought some tea.

KAREN: Thanks, Hakan. Too bad it's not apple tea, like in Turkey.

HAKAN: Yeah, too bad! You really liked living in Turkey, didn't you?

KAREN: Yeah, it was great. Turkish people are so warm and generous.

HAKAN: How did you like the food in Turkey, Karen?

KAREN: Oh, the food was fantastic! But you know what I couldn't get used to? How much people expected me to eat. I gained so much weight while I was living there!

HAKAN: Yes, it's so polite to be generous. We think people aren't polite if they don't offer a lot of food.

KAREN: I know. I also learned that it's not polite for the guest to accept the offer of food at first.

HAKAN: Yes, that's definitely true! If you're the guest, you must refuse the first two offers of food.

KAREN: The first time I had dinner at a Turkish home, I felt rude refusing food. So I ate everything. And I kept on eating . . . and eating. . . . Every time the host offered me something, I ate it.

HAKAN: Do you know how to stop the host from offering you food? You must leave some food on your plate. That way the host knows that you're full.

KAREN: Oh, is that the trick? In the United States, we usually eat everything. You don't want the host to think that you don't like the food.

HAKAN: That *is* a difference. You know what happened to me the first time I had dinner at an American home? When my host offered me a second helping of food, I said "no" the first time,

to be polite. But he didn't offer again! I really wanted some more, but I didn't know how to ask . . . and he didn't offer. I was still hungry when I left the house!

KAREN: Americans think it's not polite to insist. We don't want to force you to eat more if you don't want more. So if you say "no" the first time, we believe you and we don't offer again.

HAKAN: I learned that lesson the hard way. Now if someone asks me if I want something, I say "yes" the first time – even though I feel rude.

KAREN: Would you like something to eat?

HAKAN: Oh, yes, I would. Thank you!

Unit 9 People's best friends

Page 31, Listening Task 1: Your dog/cat IQ

How much do you know about dogs and cats? Read the statements. Do you think they're true or false? Check your answers. [*pause*]

Now listen. Correct your answers. Write a reason for each.

NUMBER 1

MAN: Your dog ate so fast. I think he's still hungry.

WOMAN: No, he always eats like that. If I give him more food, he'll just get sick.

MAN: How do you know?

WOMAN: Because dogs often do that – eat until they get sick. Thousands of years ago – when dogs were wild – they hunted in groups for food. They also ate in groups, so they had to compete with other dogs for food. If a dog didn't eat fast, another dog took his food away. As a result, dogs today will eat everything you give them really fast – and they'll eat until they get sick if you let them.

MAN: No kidding.

NUMBER 2

FIRST WOMAN: Oh, you have a dog *and* a cat! Don't they fight a lot?

SECOND WOMAN: No, they're good friends. When two animals grow up together, you know, they usually get along. See, they're playing now.

FIRST WOMAN: The dog is wagging his tail. That means he's happy, doesn't it?

SECOND WOMAN: Yes. Dogs wag their tails when they're happy or excited – but not cats. Cats move their tails when they get annoyed or angry.

FIRST WOMAN: Yes, I see that. He's moving the tip of his tail just a little, and the dog is trying to bite his head. Your cat must be annoyed! How do you know when he's happy?

SECOND WOMAN: He holds his tail straight up in the air. When cats were kittens, they held their tails up for their mothers. So they developed good feelings when they held their tails up. And that's how cats show that they're happy.

FIRST WOMAN: Huh. That's interesting.

NUMBER 3

FIRST MAN: What are you doing?

SECOND MAN: Working with my cat. I'm trying to train her.

FIRST MAN: Are you having any luck?

SECOND MAN: No, not really. It's hard to train cats. They're too independent.

FIRST MAN: That's true.

SECOND MAN: I've heard that thousands of years ago – when cats were wild – they used to hunt by themselves, alone. Because of that, they aren't used to working with other animals. You know, they don't know how to cooperate very well. They don't cooperate with humans easily either, and that's why they're difficult to train. The result is that people only use cats to catch mice and rats and for entertainment. They're beautiful to look at, so they make good pets.

FIRST MAN: So they're independent because they *can't* cooperate. I thought they just had bad attitudes.

SECOND MAN: Jeff!

NUMBER 4

MAN: Hey, you know what I did for the first time yesterday? I went to a dog show. It was interesting. I never realized there were so many different kinds of dogs.

WOMAN: Yes, it's amazing, isn't it? There really are a lot of different breeds. Have you ever been to a cat show? You'd be surprised at how similar cats look. There just aren't very many different breeds.

MAN: Do you know why that is?

WOMAN: They say it's because dogs are easy to train. Humans have bred them to do a lot of different kinds of jobs. In other words, dogs have been bred so their bodies match the job. So, for example, dogs that run a lot have long legs and long noses – long noses help them breathe more easily and stay cool. Other dogs have short,

strong legs to help them dig in the ground to find small animals.

MAN: And I guess since cats are so hard to train, people haven't bred them for as many jobs – and so they haven't developed as many different characteristics.

WOMAN: You learn pretty fast, don't you?

MAN: Grrr.

NUMBER 5

WOMAN: Oh, look! Isn't that your cat on the roof? I hope he doesn't fall.

MAN: Yes, that's my cat. But don't worry. He won't fall. And even if he falls, he won't get hurt.

WOMAN: Are you sure?

MAN: Yeah, I'm sure. It's because of the way cats' bodies are built. The bones in their back can turn very easily. When they fall, they can turn their bodies around so that their front legs and head are pointing toward the ground. Then they turn their back legs toward the ground. Finally, they put their legs out to protect themselves as they hit the ground.

WOMAN: But dogs are different, right?

MAN: Yeah, because dogs have strong backs and legs that don't turn or bend easily. Dogs need to be strong to run fast or dig. Cats need to be flexible so they can climb trees and jump easily. Besides, how's a dog going to get on the roof in the first place?

WOMAN: Oh, yeah. I didn't think of that.

NUMBER 6

[*Sound of doorbell; footsteps; door opening*]

FIRST WOMAN: Hi! Come on in. I'm glad you were able to come.

SECOND WOMAN: Thanks for inviting me. [*Sound of door closing*] Atchoo! Atchoo!

FIRST WOMAN: Bless you. Gee, I hope you're not catching a cold.

SECOND WOMAN: I don't think so. But I *am* allergic to cats. Atchoo! Do you have a cat?

FIRST WOMAN: Well, I'm taking care of my sister's cat for a few days. Are you sure it's not a dog allergy? I have a dog with long hair, and the cat has only been here an hour.

SECOND WOMAN: Oh, I'm sure. Atchoo! This only happens when I'm near cats. More people are allergic to cats than to dogs. It's not the hair, though. When cats clean themselves, they lick their fur. It gets wet, right? Well, when the fur dries, the saliva floats in the air like dust. It's the dried saliva that people are allergic to, not the hair itself. Atchoo!

Pets sometimes do amazing things.

Listen. You will hear two stories from the newspaper. Follow the instructions.

NUMBER 1

WOMAN: I got my dog, Lucky, about five years before I got married. Fortunately, John – my husband – also likes dogs. John and Lucky got along fine. Lucky was a nice dog but not a very good watchdog – she never barked, not even when someone came to the front door.

Anyway, a year and a half ago, we had a baby. When our son was born, I was worried that the dog would be jealous. But she wasn't at all interested in the baby. She paid no attention to the baby.

One evening I was in the kitchen fixing dinner when I heard a strange sound: Lucky barking. I thought, "That's funny. She never barks." So I called out, "Lucky! Be quiet! The baby's sleeping." But she continued to bark, louder and louder. Finally, I couldn't ignore her anymore. I went into the living room where the baby was sleeping. "Be quiet!" I said. Then I looked at the baby. He was . . .

What do you think the mother saw? Finish the story. Write or draw what you think she saw. [*pause*]

Now listen to the ending.

WOMAN: I went into the living room where the baby was sleeping. "Be quiet!" I said. Then I looked at the baby. He was walking toward the fire. He had climbed out of his crib and was almost in the fireplace. Lucky was standing between the baby and the fire – and barking. I ran over and picked up the baby. Lucky gave a soft bark. I looked at her and I thought, "Yes, Lucky. The next time you bark, I'll listen!"

NUMBER 2

MAN: I have a daughter named Lisa, and for her seventh birthday, we gave her a cat. Lisa was thrilled to have a cat. She named it Hero. He was a wonderful cat, and Lisa and Hero were like best friends. They often played in the woods behind our house. But one day the next winter, Hero didn't come home. The weather had turned cold, and it had started to snow. Lisa begged me to try to find the cat. I was afraid that Hero had run away. I thought it would be impossible to find him in such bad weather, but I knew we had to try. That afternoon we searched in the woods near the house. After an hour, Lisa said she was sure she had heard a soft meow coming from under an old tree. She pulled me by the hand to where the meow was coming from. I was amazed – we were amazed – to see the cat. But what was even more amazing to see was that Hero was lying on top of . . .

What was Hero lying on top of? Finish the story. Write – or draw – what Hero might have been lying on top of. [*pause*]

Now listen to the ending.

MAN: . . . we were amazed – to see the cat. But what was even more amazing to see was that Hero was lying on top of a little girl. Hero was keeping the little girl warm. The child had gotten lost in the woods and had lain down to sleep. I picked her up and took her to the hospital. The doctor later said that the cat had saved the little girl's life by keeping her warm. And Lisa said, "I knew it. My cat wouldn't run away. He was just being a 'Hero'!" [*pause*]

How are the two stories similar? Write your answer.

Unit 10 Mind your manners!

Page 34, Listening Task 1: It drives me crazy!

Listen. People are talking about rude behavior and how strongly they feel about it. Draw lines. How did you know their feelings? Write a few words.

NUMBER 1: *Chatting on a public telephone*

FIRST WOMAN: You know what bothers me? When you're waiting to use a pay phone – you know, waiting in line – and the person using the phone is having a long conversation. You can't hear what they're saying, but it sounds as if they're just chatting. Nothing important, but they keep talking and talking and talking.

FIRST MAN: I know what you mean.

FIRST WOMAN: And of course it only happens when you're in a hurry.

FIRST MAN: Absolutely.

NUMBER 2: *Using a mobile phone in a public place*

FIRST MAN: Oh, talking about phones. I was in a restaurant the other night, and the guy at the next table was having a conversation on one of those mobile . . . uh . . . cellular phones. You know, it wasn't terrible, but I think he should have gone outside or something. It just kind of took away from the atmosphere of the place.

NUMBER 3: Double-parking

SECOND MAN: You know what I just cannot stand? Double-parking! This happens to me a lot . . . when I'm driving home from work. There's a convenience store with a really small parking lot. So there are always two or three cars parked on the street, in front of the store. And it's a busy street, so two lanes of cars have to merge into one. It slows everyone down. It's so rude! Don't those people think about anyone else? It drives me nuts – makes you want to carry some eggs to throw at their cars.

SECOND WOMAN: Chill out, Marc.

NUMBER 4: Not giving up a seat on the train or bus

FIRST WOMAN: I'll tell you what else bothers me: When you're on the train or bus, and there's an older person – or maybe a mother or father holding a baby – and no one gives the person a place to sit. You'll see younger people . . . you know . . . regular healthy people just sit there. They act as if they don't notice. I have to admit I never thought about people holding babies until my son was born. Let me tell you: Babies are heavy! Anyway, I think it's really inconsiderate not to give up your seat when someone needs it more than you do.

NUMBER 5: Friends who are late

SECOND WOMAN: Oh, I've got one. I have this friend – a really nice guy, but always late. If he says we're going to meet at seven, he might get there by 7:30. I'm convinced he was born a half-hour late and hasn't caught up yet.

SECOND MAN: I was not!

SECOND WOMAN: No, not you. You're only late sometimes. This guy is always late. But it's not that big a deal . . . now that I know to expect it.

NUMBER 6: Students who are late for class

FIRST MAN: You know what I don't like is when other students are late for class. It disrupts things. The teacher has to go over stuff again. It's rude to the teacher, but it's also rude to the rest of us. It just wastes our time.

Page 35, Listening Task 2: Ask Miss Manners

Miss Manners is a newspaper columnist. She gives advice about manners and relationships.

Read her list of the five worst behavior "mistakes." The list is surprising. At first, the things on the list look good. [*pause*]

Now listen. Why does Miss Manners think the things can be bad?
Write examples and reasons.

NUMBER 1: Honesty

FIRST MAN: So, how do you like my new suit?

SECOND MAN: Uh . . . well . . . um . . . OK, I've got to tell you, John, that color really doesn't look so good on you. I mean, purple? Some people look good in purple, but, sorry . . . you just don't. And the style? Well, it's kind of . . . OK, I'll tell you straight. It makes you look fat.

FIRST MAN: Thanks.

SECOND MAN: Hey, what did I say? You ask me what I think, I tell you. What's the matter? You don't want me to be honest? What are friends for? [*pause*]

COMMENTATOR: Whoever said, "Honesty is the best policy," did not mean hurting other people's feelings and then, when they feel bad, hurting them again by saying they don't believe in honesty.

NUMBER 2: Helpfulness

FIRST WOMAN: [*On phone*] I really can't believe you're dating Norman. Why, he's fifteen years older than you are. Now, I'm only saying this because I care about you, but I really don't think it's a good idea for you to date someone that much older. Your interests – they'll be so different.

SECOND WOMAN: Yeah, well, thanks for your concern about my life. [*pause*]

COMMENTATOR: Of course it's nice to be helpful – but not when it means telling people how they should live their lives. Minding your own business is fine, but minding someone else's just isn't.

NUMBER 3: Health-consciousness

[*Sound of restaurant*]

WAITER: Are you ready to order?

WOMAN: I'll have the tofu salad – no salad dressing – and a bottle of mineral water.

MAN: And I'll have the steak, a baked potato, and let's see . . . chocolate ice cream for dessert.

WOMAN: Steak? Baked potato? Ice cream? Think about your health. You know red meat isn't good for you. It has too much fat and cholesterol. And potatoes – all carbohydrates. You need vitamins.

And ice cream? Why, that meal is a heart attack on a plate. It will kill you.

MAN: Um . . . well . . .

WAITER: Perhaps you'd like more time to look at the menu.

MAN: Yeah, I guess I would. [*pause*]

COMMENTATOR: It's good to think about your own health, but that's no reason to spoil other people's dinner by telling them that they're eating poison.

NUMBER 4: Idealism

[*Sound of elevator door closing*]

WOMAN: Twelfth floor, please.

[*Sound of dog barking*]

WOMAN: Shhhh, Prince. We'll be home in a minute.

MAN: Excuse me, ma'am. I know it's none of my business, but do you really keep a dog in the apartment building?

WOMAN: Yes. Pets are allowed.

MAN: I'm not talking about the rules, ma'am. I'm thinking about nature. Animals need to be outside. They need to run and play. They need space and freedom. I can't believe you keep an animal locked inside an apartment all day. It's really cruel.

[*Sound of elevator door opening; dog growling*]

WOMAN: I don't think Prince agrees. [*pause*]

COMMENTATOR: But *I* agree . . . with the first thing the man said: It *is* none of his business. His ideas – what he believes – are fine . . . for him. But he has no reason to criticize someone for something that is neither unusual nor his concern.

NUMBER 5: Being true to your own feelings

[*Telephone rings; picks up*]

JAN: Hello?

RICK: Hi, Jan. How are you doing?

JAN: OK.

RICK: I'm really looking forward to going to the theater tonight. They say it's a really good play. Anyway, I was just calling to check on the time we should meet.

JAN: Gee, Rick, I meant to call you. I was planning on going to the play with you, but . . . you know, I'm really tired today.

RICK: Oh, no. I bought these tickets two months ago. You know how hard it was to get them.

JAN: Yeah, I know, but . . . I just don't feel like it. I wouldn't be very good company. Maybe – I don't know – I'm sure one of your other friends would love to go.

RICK: Yeah, I guess so. [*pause*]

COMMENTATOR: Some things – like doing what we've promised, even if we don't feel like it at the moment – just need to be done. It's part of being "a civilized person."

Now listen to some questions. Follow the instructions.

COMMENTATOR: Have you ever done any of these things? Circle the things you've done. [*pause*] Did you have a good reason for doing them? If you had a good reason, write it next to the item.

Unit 11 Tales from the past

Page 37, Listening Task 1: Are you still carrying her?

This is a very old story from Japan. It's about two monks (holy men). Years ago, monks weren't allowed any contact with women.

Listen. Where should the woman be in each picture? Write this symbol in the correct place.

WOMAN: Long ago, in a certain village, it rained. It rained very hard every day for a month. The rain was so hard, no one could go outside. Finally, the rain stopped. Two monks decided to go for a walk.

FIRST MAN: Ah, it feels so good to be outside again.

SECOND MAN: Yes, it does.

FIRST MAN: But look, the rain has turned the road to mud. People are getting covered with dirt and mud.

SECOND MAN: Yes, they are.

WOMAN: On a corner, the monks saw a woman. She was wearing very beautiful and expensive clothes. She was standing on the corner. She couldn't cross the road. It was too dirty. The mud would have ruined her clothing. [*pause*]

The older monk walked up to the woman. Silently he looked at her. He picked up the woman and carried her across the street. The other monk followed. [*pause*]

When they got to the other side, the monk set the woman down. He bowed. She bowed too and thanked him. The monk didn't say a word. He and his friend walked on. [*pause*]

That night, the two monks talked.

FIRST MAN: I can't understand it. You know we are not allowed to have contact with women. Yet you picked her up. You carried her all the way across the road.

SECOND MAN: Oh, my son. Are you still carrying that woman? You *are* still carrying her. I put her down many hours ago. I put her down . . . on the other side of the road. [*pause*]

What does this story mean? What is the moral? Check your answer. [*pause*] Now work with a partner. Do you agree with the moral of the story? Why or why not? Compare answers.

Page 38, Listening Task 2: The story in your mind

You will hear part of a story. It's about traveling through time. In your mind, you'll imagine the rest of the story.
Close your eyes. Listen. Don't write anything. Just imagine.

MAN: You are going to take a trip – a trip through time. Close your eyes. Relax. Breathe deeply and slowly. Sit comfortably in your chair – your time chair.
  You are now floating back through time: 1990 . . . 1970 . . . back . . . back – as far back in time as you'd like to go.
[*Music*]
  Go back in time . . . back in time – as far as you'd like to go. And now, your time chair has stopped. You're there. In your mind, look around. Keep your eyes closed, but notice everything around you. Do you see people? How are they dressed? What do their clothes look like? Are there buildings? What kind? Are they large or small? What do they look like? Where are you? In the city? In the country? What country is it? Is it your own country or somewhere else?
  And now, someone is coming toward you. It's a messenger. The messenger smiles and takes your hand. You stand and follow the messenger. You don't know where you're going, but you feel safe.
  The messenger takes you to a small building. Look closely at the building. What color is it? What's it made of? Wood? Brick? Glass? Something else? What does the building look like?
  You go inside the building. Someone is there. The person has been waiting for you. Look closely. What kind of clothes is the person wearing? Look at the person's face. Look closely at the face. Now look at the hands. They're holding a present. It's a present for you. Take the present. It's for you.

Now the story's ending. Take a deep breath. You are back in the time chair. You're coming back . . . coming home. Relax. You feel happy to be coming home. When you're home, slowly open your eyes. Open your eyes. Think about your story. [*pause*]

Now listen to these questions. Write your answers.

NUMBER 1
MAN: You went back in time. How far? What was the year? Write your answer. When did your story happen? Write the year or time.

NUMBER 2
MAN: Where did you go? The country? A town? Another country? Where did your story take place? Write your answer.

NUMBER 3
MAN: The messenger took you to a building. What did it look like? What was the building like? Write your answer or draw a picture.

NUMBER 4
MAN: Who did you meet in the building? What did the person look like?

NUMBER 5
MAN: You were given a present. What was it? What was the present you were given?

NUMBER 6
MAN: Would you like to go back to that place? Would you like to meet those people again? Check "yes" or "no." Why or why not? [*pause*]
  You can meet them again, you know. They're as close as . . . closing your eyes.

Unit 12 Decisions, decisions

Page 40, Listening Task 1: Choosing a school

Hyung Jin is thinking about studying English in a foreign country. He's talking to his teacher.

Listen. What things are important to Hyung Jin? Write the information.

HYUNG JIN: Did I tell you I'm thinking of studying in an English-speaking country next year? Probably for about three or four months. I think I want to go to the United States or Australia.
TEACHER: That's wonderful. What kind of school are you looking for?

HYUNG JIN: I'm not sure exactly. I want small classes. I think they're better for learning spoken English.

TEACHER: Small classes? Yes, you're probably right. What kind of place do you want to live in, a city or a small town?

HYUNG JIN: Oh, location's important. I want to study in a city. I don't like small towns much. And I'm also not sure if I want to live in a dormitory or an apartment.

TEACHER: You can decide on the type of housing later. What else is important to you?

HYUNG JIN: Since I'm not going to be there very long, I want to use English as much as I can – out of class as well as during class – so I want to spend as much time with English speakers as possible. Maybe it would be best if I went to a school where I can meet students from other countries.

TEACHER: That might be a good idea. How do you evaluate your English level?

HYUNG JIN: I'd say "high-intermediate." At least the high-intermediate level here at this language institute feels about right.

TEACHER: You know, there's a "Study Abroad Fair" next month. There will be people from lots of different schools. You should try to go.

HYUNG JIN: That's a good idea. [pause]

Hyung Jin is at the "Study Abroad Fair." Representatives are talking about their schools.

Listen. Take notes. Write two important points about each school.

NUMBER 1

FIRST RECRUITER: Hi. Thinking about studying in the United States?

HYUNG JIN: Well, yes. I'm not sure where. I just want to go to an English-speaking country to improve my English.

FIRST RECRUITER: Then let me tell you about the English Language Institute. We're part of the University of Pittsburgh. We're located in the cultural heart of Pittsburgh near several other universities plus museums, libraries, concert halls, restaurants . . . you name it. There's always something to do. And we're only ten minutes by bus from downtown.

HYUNG JIN: That sounds good. I really prefer to live in a city.

FIRST RECRUITER: Then you'd like Pittsburgh.

HYUNG JIN: What kind of classes do you have? And how big are they?

FIRST RECRUITER: There are about 140 students each term. Our classes are medium-sized – between 16 and 20 students in every class. Our program is mainly for students planning to do university studies in the States. But actually, you know, classes are also general enough that they're good for people who simply want to improve their English. About one-third of our students are here for that reason.

HYUNG JIN: I see. Are there many Korean students?

FIRST RECRUITER: About fifteen percent of our students are from Korea. We have a pretty good mix of nationalities. We typically have students from about 25 different countries each term.

HYUNG JIN: Do students live with families?

FIRST RECRUITER: No, unfortunately, we can't offer long-term homestays. Most of our students live in apartments. There are many inexpensive apartments near the campus.

HYUNG JIN: Is it easy to meet Americans?

FIRST RECRUITER: Well, sometimes it's difficult to meet American students. So we have an activities director who plans parties, picnics, and tours, and finds students American conversation partners. And, of course, ELI students always become good friends with each other – they spend a lot of time speaking English with students from other countries.

HYUNG JIN: Your program sounds good. Do you have a brochure?

FIRST RECRUITER: Yes, of course. I think you'd find the ELI a good place all around.

NUMBER 2

HYUNG JIN: Australia Centre for Languages . . .

SECOND RECRUITER: That's right. The Australia Centre for Languages in Sydney.

HYUNG JIN: In Sydney? Downtown?

SECOND RECRUITER: Actually, our main campus is about fifteen minutes by train from the central business district. We're in a safe residential area.

HYUNG JIN: A residential area?

SECOND RECRUITER: Yes. Of course, there are shops and restaurants, but you'll find mostly houses and apartments. But it's easy to get to the center of Sydney by train.

HYUNG JIN: That sounds convenient. What kind of classes do you have?

SECOND RECRUITER: All kinds. We offer a full range of language programs. We've got General English, of course. We also offer English for Specific Purpose courses: English for Academic

Purposes, International Business, Australian Language and Culture . . .

HYUNG JIN: I think I'm interested in General English. How long do your courses last?

SECOND RECRUITER: It depends on your schedule. We can arrange anything from two weeks to a year.

HYUNG JIN: Two weeks to a year . . . that's very flexible. Where are the students from?

SECOND RECRUITER: All over. Mostly from the Asia-Pacific region: Korea, Japan, Taiwan, Thailand, Indonesia. But we also have some from Europe and South America.

HYUNG JIN: How big are the classes?

SECOND RECRUITER: Most are fairly small – about 12 to 14 students.

HYUNG JIN: Where do students live?

SECOND RECRUITER: There are several options. A lot of students live with Australian families.

HYUNG JIN: A homestay?

SECOND RECRUITER: That's right. Other students live in apartments with other ACL students.

HYUNG JIN: I see.

SECOND RECRUITER: Actually, many of our students like to do a homestay first – to get a bit of the culture and the family life – then get an apartment later.

HYUNG JIN: Oh, I think I like that. Do the English classes last all day?

SECOND RECRUITER: No. Classes are in the morning, Monday to Friday. In the afternoon, we offer social-program activities.

HYUNG JIN: Social-program activities?

SECOND RECRUITER: For example, sometimes we have tours: Sydney . . . the Opera House, Bondi Beach. Or we go hiking in the Blue Mountains.

HYUNG JIN: Hmm.

SECOND RECRUITER: We also have sports like tennis, golf, waterskiing, horseback riding.

HYUNG JIN: Waterskiing? Horseback riding?

SECOND RECRUITER: There's a lot to do. But the thing I should stress is the college. It's a very good school. You'll learn a lot.

HYUNG JIN: I'm thinking of six months. How much would that cost?

SECOND RECRUITER: It's pretty reasonable, really. Let's see.

NUMBER 3

HYUNG JIN: Semester at Sea . . . . Is this an English school?

THIRD RECRUITER: Yes, it is . . . but a different kind of English program! Are you interested in improving your English?

HYUNG JIN: Yes, I am, and I thought the best way to do that would be to study in a country that speaks English.

THIRD RECRUITER: Well, yes and no. Are you interested in learning about the world while you're improving your English?

HYUNG JIN: Sure.

THIRD RECRUITER: Then think about Semester at Sea. It's a unique program: a university on a ship! In a hundred days we travel around the world, stopping at ten different countries. Most of the students are American college students. They take classes while the ship is sailing and do special study trips when we're stopped at a country. But we have a new English program for international students.

HYUNG JIN: You mean I would study English while traveling on a ship?

THIRD RECRUITER: That's right. We have classes when we're traveling on the sea. That's about fifty days. You take two English classes and two academic classes. The English classes are small – between five and ten people in each class. And don't worry: there's an English teacher to help you with your academic classes. It's an excellent way to improve your English. You're with American college students all day. You'll have an American roommate, you'll eat in the cafeteria with American students and teachers. In fact, you'll have much more contact with English on the ship than you might if you studied in the United States. You know, sometimes it's difficult for foreign students to meet Americans – but on the ship, everyone is together. You don't have a choice!

HYUNG JIN: How would I talk to people in all those countries? Does the ship only stop in English-speaking countries?

THIRD RECRUITER: We stop in countries with various languages, but you'll have to use English in almost all of the ports. This trip will be excellent practice.

HYUNG JIN: This sounds really great.

THIRD RECRUITER: There is one thing, however. You have to be able to understand university classes because this program is for advanced students. You'll have to submit a TOEFL score. But I'm sure it will be the best experience of your life.

Now listen to some questions. Follow the instructions.

NUMBER 1

WOMAN: Which program is best for Hyung Jin? Circle it. [*pause*] Why do you think so? Write your answer.

NUMBER 2

MAN: Which program would be best for you? Draw a star next to it. [*pause*] Why do you think so? Write your answer.

Page 41, Listening Task 2: A place to live

Maria is studying in the United States. She has lived for four weeks with a homestay family. Now she wants to live closer to school.

Work with a partner. Look at Maria's housing choices. Write one good point and one bad point about each choice. [*pause*]

Now listen. Maria is talking to a friend about places to live. Write the good and bad points about each place. If they say an idea you already wrote, put a check next to it.

MARIA: You know, Barry, I can't decide where to live. I have to move. I want to be closer to school so I can use the library late at night. But should I live in a dorm or an apartment?

BARRY: Well, they both have advantages and disadvantages. Let's think about them one by one. First, the dormitories. Why would you want to live in the dormitories?

MARIA: They're convenient, I guess. It's easy to live in the same building where you eat your meals in the cafeteria. And somebody else cleans the bathroom.

BARRY: Right. Dorms are easy to live in. Not having to cook or clean are two good things about dorms. And don't forget: there are lots of people to talk to. There are sometimes hundreds of people in one dorm.

MARIA: Actually, that kind of bothers me. I worry that a dorm will be too noisy. It will be hard to study.

BARRY: That's true. Dorms can be noisy. But there are "quiet floors." People who live on those floors are quiet. They study a lot. They don't have parties.

MARIA: OK. Dorms are convenient, but they can be noisy. [*pause*] How about apartments?

BARRY: Of course you'd have to decide if you want to live alone or get a roommate.

MARIA: Uh . . . living alone – an apartment all to myself – is too expensive. That isn't even a choice. I'll have to get a roommate.

BARRY: So the question is what kind of roommate you want. Do you want an American roommate? That would really help your English.

MARIA: It would be very good for my English. That would be the best part about living with an American. But I wonder if it's the best thing. Could an American understand my problems? It would be nice to talk to someone who knows how it feels to be a foreigner.

BARRY: You're right. But maybe you could find a roommate who has lived in a foreign country – like someone who did a high school homestay.

MARIA: And the other thing is, well . . . values – you know, beliefs – are . . . kind of different.

BARRY: Values? They could be different with anyone from another culture. You just have to be honest with your roommate. [*pause*] How about living with another Mexican student?

MARIA: It might be a good idea. We would really understand each other's problems. We could even talk in Spanish.

BARRY: It's a good idea to be able to have a roommate who has the same experiences . . . who comes from the same culture. You'll feel more comfortable discussing your feelings. But think: already you're saying you're going to speak Spanish. I'm not sure it's a good idea to live with another Mexican. You need to speak English inside and outside school. [*pause*]

MARIA: Maybe I could live with another international student.

BARRY: That might be a good idea. You could help each other with problems. You'd understand each other . . . what you're going through.

MARIA: That would be nice. What about speaking English? Wouldn't we give each other bad English . . . you know, lots of mistakes?

BARRY: I wouldn't worry about that. English isn't like catching a cold, you know. You don't "catch mistakes." I think the main problem with living with another international student is customs and values. But again, if you can, you could try to find someone who has similar customs and values. You don't want to argue. You'll always have to negotiate things with a roommate, but you want to share some basic ideas.

MARIA: Well, I have to think some more about this. Thanks for helping me think about the different options.

T24

Unit 13 Your type of personality

Page 43, Listening Task 1: It's in my blood.

Listen. If the information on page 42 is true, what do you think these people's blood types are? What helped you guess? Write two or three things about each person.

NUMBER 1: This is Charles.

CHARLES: What's my personality like? Well, I guess I'm pretty competitive. I like sports – volleyball, soccer – and I play pretty hard. That's important to me. Let's see . . . my job? I'm a student now, but I want to be a travel agent. I think I'd like working in a travel agency, maybe even starting my own agency someday. I like the idea of being in business. I know that will be a challenge, but that's OK. I like a challenge.

NUMBER 2: This is Jenny.

JENNY: I'm definitely a leader-type. I'm good at organizing things . . . and people. That's one of the things I like about my job. I'm responsible for setting up projects. About the only thing I don't like is my boss. She's a nice person and all, but she always tells me exactly how to do everything. I don't like that at all. People work best when they have more freedom – to figure out the best way to do something by themselves. At least *I* work best that way.

NUMBER 3: This is Valeria.

VALERIA: I work for the city . . . you know, at City Hall. I enjoy it. It's busy, but I do get to help people. What I don't like is when people who have problems with the city get really angry – especially at me. I can understand why they feel that way, but getting angry doesn't help. People should . . . uh . . . control themselves. I think if you display emotions too much, that's just not good. So, what else about my personality? I guess I prefer to have a few very close friends . . . you know, the kind of friend it takes awhile to get to know. That way we really get to know each other deeply. For me, that's better than having surface-level friendships.

NUMBER 4: This is Daniel.

DANIEL: Me? I'm an office worker. I work for a large electronics company. I like the job a lot. It's very organized. I know exactly what I have to do, and that helps me do it well. That's important to me – knowing that I'm doing my job well. I like to keep my desk very neat and clean. It shows I'm organized, that I know what I'm doing.

Page 44, Listening Task 2: Personality types

This cartoon shows four basic types of people.

Look at the cartoon. Listen.

WOMAN: The glass is half full. [*pause*]
FIRST MAN: The glass is half empty. [*pause*]
SECOND MAN: Half full. No! Wait! Half empty! No, half . . . What was the question? [*pause*]
THIRD MAN: Hey! I ordered a cheeseburger! [*pause*]

Now listen to someone talking about the people in the cartoon. Who are they describing? Follow the instructions.

ONE

MAN: This person is indecisive. An indecisive person can't decide – maybe yes, maybe no. Which person can't make a decision? Write "indecisive," I-N-D-E-C-I-S-I-V-E, on the picture. I-N-D-E-C-I-S-I-V-E.

TWO

WOMAN: This person is a pessimist. A pessimist is a person who always sees the bad side of things. If something is good, a pessimist thinks it will become bad. If it's bad, a pessimist thinks it will become worse. Which person is negative? Write "pessimist," P-E-S-S-I-M-I-S-T, on the person. P-E-S-S-I-M-I-S-T.

THREE

MAN: The opposite of a pessimist is an optimist. Optimists are always positive. They look for the good side of everything. Which person is an optimist? Write it, O-P-T-I-M-I-S-T, on the person who sees the bright side of life. O-P-T-I-M-I-S-T.

FOUR

WOMAN: There's only one person left. This person is a complainer. Complainers always find problems with everything. They act as if no one does things right. Nothing ever goes right. There are problems all the time. Find the complainer. Write C-O-M-P-L-A-I-N-E-R on the person. C-O-M-P-L-A-I-N-E-R.

Now listen to some questions. Follow the instructions.

MAN: Which type of person are you? Draw a star next to the person who is most like you. Draw a star next to the person in the cartoon who seems like you. [*pause*]

WOMAN: Do you believe most people fit these personality types? Write "yes," "maybe," or "no" in the square. Are most people one of these types? In the square, write "yes," "maybe," or "no." [*pause*]

MAN: Sometimes cartoons from other cultures are difficult to understand. Do you understand this cartoon? Write "yes," "maybe," or "no" in the circle. Do you understand this cartoon? In the circle, write "yes," "maybe," or "no." [*pause*]

WOMAN: Sometimes you can understand a cartoon from another culture, but it isn't funny. Is the cartoon funny to you? Write "yes," "so-so," or "no" in the triangle. Do you think the cartoon is funny? In the triangle, write "yes," "so-so," or "no." [*pause*]

Work with a partner. Compare answers.

Unit 14 You've got to have art.

Page 46, Listening Task 1: It's surreal.

Surreal art is very unusual. This picture is surreal.

Listen. Look at the picture. Answer the questions.

NUMBER 1
WOMAN: What do you see? Is it a vase? Perhaps a vase for flowers. Do you think so? Circle "V" for "vase." [*pause*]

A man? If you think it's a man, circle "M" for "man." [*pause*]

Is it a sculpture? If you think so, circle "S" for "sculpture." [*pause*]

NUMBER 2
WOMAN: Look at the picture again. What's the most important part? What part do you notice the most? The eye? If the eye is the main thing you see, circle "E" for "eye." [*pause*]

The nose? Circle "N" if the nose is the most important thing for you. [*pause*]

How about his mustache – the hair on his face? Circle "M" if the mustache is the main thing. [*pause*]

His lips are very large. Circle "L" for lips if they're what you notice. [*pause*]

Now you're going to do an unusual activity. You'll need a piece of paper. Listen and follow the instructions. [*pause*]

MAN: Who is this? Put your piece of paper over the bottom of the picture. Put the left side on the number 4 . . . the number 4. Put the right side of your paper on the letter "M" . . . "M" as in "mad," "M" as in "mad." What do you see? His eye – the artist's eye. He's looking at you. [*pause*]

Now you're going to put your paper over the top of the page. Put the bottom of your paper on the letter "Q" . . . "Q" as in "question" . . . or "questionable." Put your paper at an angle from the letter "Q" to the number 2 . . . the number 2. You can't see the top of the page. Your paper goes from 2 to "Q," diagonally. What do you see? His mustache – the artistic, very famous, very unusual mustache. [*pause*]

Now, you're going to see the artist. Put the top of your paper on the letter "A," as in "art." Put the bottom on the number 21 . . . 21. The paper goes from A to 21, diagonally. Can you see him? Not yet. [*pause*]

Try putting your paper from "C" – as in "crazy" – "C" to 19 . . . 19. You might see him now. [*pause*]

Now, try once more. This time, put your paper vertically – up and down. It goes from "E" – "E" for "elegant" (or "E" for "elephant") to 18 . . . 18. Now you're looking at the artist, and he's looking at you. Can you see him? [*pause*]

Imagine the artist is standing behind a door, looking at you. This is what he looked like. The artist is Salvador Dalí. He was a famous surrealist artist who lived from 1904 to 1989. Salvador Dalí's art was always strange. And now, the artist is looking right at you.

Page 47, Listening Task 2: The Lovers

This painting is called *The Lovers*. It was painted by René Magritte.

Listen. Two friends are in an art museum. They're talking about *The Lovers*. What do they think the painting means? Write two details for each interpretation.

[*Sound of museum*]
MAN: Oh, look. This is by René Magritte.
WOMAN: What does the catalogue say about him?
MAN: Let's see. Magritte, who lived from 1898 to 1967, was a Belgian surrealist. He was a leader of a surrealist group in Belgium. His paintings often contained shocking and unusual, dreamlike images. They were influenced by psychology.

WOMAN: This one is strange, but I kind of like it. It's sort of a "blind love" message.

MAN: Blind love?

WOMAN: Yeah. The people – the man and the woman – can't see anything bad about each other. They can't see the other person's weaknesses or faults.

MAN: No weaknesses or faults? Maybe.

WOMAN: It's like they're holding each other, not thinking about anything else.

MAN: Funny. I get a totally different feeling.

WOMAN: Really?

MAN: To me, the painting is really cold. There's a coldness, a distance between the two people. They aren't really touching.

WOMAN: Sure they are.

MAN: No, they're separated by the cloths . . . almost like masks. They can't even see each other. They're only thinking of themselves.

WOMAN: I don't know.

MAN: Oh, and look at the catalogue. Oh, this is strange. Magritte's mother killed herself when he was 12 years old. She committed suicide by throwing herself in the water, and when they found the body . . . her face was covered by her dress.

WOMAN: His dead mother's face was covered? Just like in the painting.

MAN: Yeah. Strange, huh?

WOMAN: For sure. So we don't know if Magritte meant "Love is blind" or "People are cold and untouching."

MAN: Maybe he meant both.

WOMAN: Or . . . maybe he meant something else.

MAN: That's a real possibility.

WOMAN: Or maybe a surreal possibility. [*pause*]

Now listen to some questions. Write your answers.

NUMBER 1

WOMAN: What do you think the painting means?

NUMBER 2

MAN: How does this painting make you feel?

Unit 15 I wonder how that works.

Page 49, Listening Task 1: How does a vending machine work?

Listen. How does a vending machine know that you have put in the correct coin? Complete the chart.

WOMAN: Did you ever wonder how a vending machine knows that you've put the correct coin in? Here's how. Basically, the machine is looking for these three things: What is the coin made of? How much does it weigh? How big is it?

When you put a coin into the coin slot, it goes down a chute. First, the machine checks what the coin is made of. Coins are made of different metals. How does the machine check the type of metal? It uses electricity.

The electricity can tell what metal the coin is made of. If the coin is made of the wrong metal, the coin drops down and gets returned. If the coin is made of the right metal, it continues. [*pause*]

The next step is to find out if the coin's weight is correct. How does this happen? Well, the coin goes between two magnets. This slows down the coin. Different coins slow down at different speeds, so this step is really a speed check. If the magnets find that the coin slows down at the correct speed, the coin moves on. If the coin is too heavy or too light, it drops down and gets returned. [*pause*]

The last step is to make sure the coin is the correct size. The coin goes between two lights. The lights measure the size of the coin. They make sure that the coin is neither too big nor too small. [*pause*]

So if the content, weight, and size of your coin are correct, the machine will accept it and you'll get what you paid for. [*pause*]

Now complete the sentences.

Page 50, Listening Task 2: How do they make CDs?

STEP 1

Look at the pictures. One shows "digital" sound recording, and the other shows "analog" sound recording.

Now listen. Friends are talking about different ways of recording sound. Write "digital" or "analog" under each picture.

[*Music*]

MIKE: Wow! Nice. CDs have such good sound. Do you ever wonder how they make CDs?

KATHY: Well, they get a bunch of musicians together, and they sing and play.

MIKE: Come on. You know what I mean. Why is the sound quality so good? I mean, why do CDs sound so much clearer than cassette tapes?

KATHY: Actually, I do know that.

MIKE: Really.

KATHY: It's all based on digital sound. CDs are digital. Digital sound is like several photos, all taken one after another. It's kind of like pictures of sound. The intensity of the sound – how strong it is – is measured very quickly. Then it's measured again and again. When we hear the sound, it all sounds like one long piece of sound, but it's really lots of pieces close together. And each piece is really clear.

MIKE: So digital is like lots of short "pieces" of sound.

KATHY: Exactly. This is different from analog – that's how they used to record. Analog is more like one wave of sound. It moves up and down with volume and pitch. Anyway, analog is like a single wave. Digital is like a series of pieces.

MIKE: OK, I understand that. But how do they make the CDs?

KATHY: I told you. They get a bunch of musicians together, and they sing and play.

STEP 2

Listen. Kathy and Mike are talking about making CDs. Number the steps (1 through 5). There is one extra step.

MIKE: OK, I understand that. But how do they make the CDs?

KATHY: I told you, Mike. They get a bunch of musicians together, and they sing and play.

MIKE: Kathy!

KATHY: No. What really happens is first they do a digital recording – on videotape.

MIKE: On videotape?

KATHY: Yeah, they use videotape. [*pause*] So then the videotape is played through a computer.

MIKE: OK. What does the computer do?

KATHY: Well, the computer is used to figure out the "pieces" of sound we were talking about: how long everything is, how far apart spaces are.

MIKE: OK. So the computer is figuring out those separate "pieces" of sound. [*pause*]

KATHY: Yeah. They need to do that to make the master.

MIKE: The master?

KATHY: The master is the original that all the other CDs are copied from. It's made of glass. It's a glass disk that spins around – just like a regular CD. And the glass disk is covered with a chemical. They use a laser to burn the signal, or the song, into the glass plate. The laser burns

through the chemical, but not through the glass. [*pause*]

MIKE: So the laser cuts the sound into the plate?

KATHY: Right. What it's doing is cutting little holes into the back of the disk. Those holes are called "pits." The laser puts in the pits.

MIKE: So CDs really have little holes on the back? I didn't know that.

KATHY: Yeah. Tiny pits. They're too small to see. [*pause*] Anyway, then they've got the master, and they make copies from it. Then you buy your copy and put it in the CD player.

MIKE: Put it in the CD player . . . . That part I understand.

KATHY: There's another laser in your CD player. The light of the laser reflects off the CD. The smooth part of the CD reflects straight back, like a mirror. But the light that bounces off the pits is scattered. Anyway, the computer in your CD player reads the light that bounces off the pits. And you get the music. [*pause*]

MIKE: Reflected light, huh? . . . Uh . . . you know what I like? Just relaxing, listening to music, and not really worrying about how it gets on the disk.

KATHY: You want me to explain it again?

[*Music*]

Unit 16 *A matter of values*

Page 52, Listening Task 1: Who's right?

Radio talk shows usually present two sides of an argument.

Listen. What is the topic of the debate? Complete the sentence.
"[*Sound of bell*] is/isn't good for the island."
Which things does Ms. Selles say? Write "S" in the boxes.
Which things does Mr. Williams say? Write "W."
There are three extra sentences.

[*Music*]

HOST: Good evening. I'm Jim Langley, and welcome to "Late Night Talk Line." Our guests tonight are Ms. Joyce Selles, the mayor of Annabel Island, and Mr. Robert Williams, leader of the Save Our Island committee. Mayor, Robert, welcome.

MS. SELLES: Thank you, Jim. Good evening.

MR. WILLIAMS: Thank you for having us on the show, Jim.

HOST: Mayor Joyce Selles and Robert Williams both live on Annabel Island. I went there myself last month to visit them, and it's a lovely place –

the most beautiful beaches I've ever seen. The water is clear and clean. You can stand still and watch tropical fish swim by. There are magnificent birds. Flowers and tropical fruit grow everywhere. And the way of life is very relaxed. So what's wrong?

MR. WILLIAMS: Nothing – and that's the way we'd like to keep it. We love the beauty of our island, and we don't want it to change. My group, Save Our Island, is trying to protect Annabel from being destroyed.

HOST: Destroyed by what?

MR. WILLIAMS: Destroyed by tourism.

HOST: Mayor, do you have a response?

MS. SELLES: Yes, Jim, I do. Robert is absolutely right that we the people of Annabel love our island. But there are one thousand people living on Annabel, and 25 percent of them don't have jobs. We have a serious unemployment problem. But I have a plan. I want to develop the tourism industry. We think that many people would be interested in coming to Annabel Island for a vacation. Tourism will help our economic development. It will create jobs, and that's what we need.

MR. WILLIAMS: Yes, it will bring jobs, but what kind of jobs? In the tourism industry, the jobs are low paying: bus drivers, maids, and restaurant workers. We don't need to destroy the beauty of our island for a few low-paying jobs.

MS. SELLES: But when people have jobs, they have money to spend and that will create other jobs and new businesses. In addition, we'll be able to collect more tax money. We'll be able to improve our roads and schools.

MR. WILLIAMS: But having so many more people means problems: our beaches will be crowded, our food prices will become more expensive. Our roads will be crowded and noisy with extra cars. It will destroy our way of life – our peaceful, quiet way of life.

MS. SELLES: That's a possible problem, of course. But changes will come anyway. I want to plan the development. If we plan the number of hotels and tours, we can control the number of people so that it won't be a problem. Besides, we're very isolated on Annabel. We need to know more about the outside world. People will bring us new ideas and help us to be more progressive.

MR. WILLIAMS: I think the only new ideas will be bad ideas. It would be better for us to learn new ideas by visiting other places. When we visit other places, we can bring back the good ideas

that we want. When people come to Annabel, we have no choice about the ideas they'll bring.

MS. SELLES: You're lucky. You can travel. You have the money – because you have a job. Well, that's a narrow way of thinking.

MR. WILLIAMS: It's not narrow, Ms. Mayor. It's realistic! But there's one other problem: an environmental problem. More people means more pollution. There will be pollution from the cars and buses. There will be garbage on our beaches and our streets. So, in addition to our peace and quiet, our beauty will be destroyed as well.

MS. SELLES: As usual, you're exaggerating . . .

MR. WILLIAMS: And as usual, you're refusing to see the truth . . .

HOST: Let me interrupt you. The issue is: Is tourism good or bad for Annabel Island? We can see there is no easy solution. Now, before we open up the talk line for callers, let's hear a word . . .

Now listen and follow the instructions.

WOMAN: Do you agree with Ms. Selles or with Mr. Williams? Check your answer. [*pause*] Why do you feel that way? Write your answer.

Page 53, Listening Task 2: Tough choices

Listen. People are talking about problems. Write the problem.
Then write the important factors in each choice.

NUMBER 1

LEE: Hi, Jane. How are you?

JANE: Fine, Lee. No, I'm not fine. I don't know what to do.

LEE: What's the matter? Do you want to talk about it? I hope it's not a problem with Allen.

JANE: Well, yes and no. Our wedding is planned for next month.

LEE: Yes, I know. Allen is such a nice person.

JANE: Yes, he is. He's very good to me. He owns two sporting goods stores. He makes quite a lot of money, and he's generous with it.

LEE: But . . . ?

JANE: Do you remember my first boyfriend, Stan? He moved to Africa to teach school?

LEE: Yes, I remember him. He wanted you to marry him and go to Africa too.

JANE: Yes, but I didn't want to leave my family. Well, Stan is back from Africa, and he still wants to marry me.

LEE: Do you want to marry him?

JANE: I don't know. I still love him. I've never forgotten him. But everything is arranged for the wedding with Allen.

LEE: But it would be wrong to marry Allen if you don't love him.

JANE: It's not that I don't love him. It's just . . . I don't know. But there's something else. My mother just lost her job, and my father can't work because of his accident. Allen will help my family. Stan has no money. I love Stan, but Allen and I have already planned a wedding and a life together. I just don't know what to do.

NUMBER 2

CLARE: What's the matter, Jim? You look like you haven't slept in a week.

JIM: Oh, Clare. It's Frank.

CLARE: Frank? He's one of your best friends, isn't he?

JIM: Yeah, we've been friends since we were eight years old.

CLARE: So what's wrong?

JIM: Well, you know his uncle died. The funeral is the day of the final exam in economics, so he's going to take the exam three days after the rest of the class.

CLARE: And . . . ?

JIM: He wants me to copy the questions and give them to him.

CLARE: That's cheating.

JIM: I know. But economics is hard for him. He hasn't done very well this semester. And he's been my best friend for ten years.

CLARE: But a really good friend wouldn't ask someone to do a favor like that. Doesn't the teacher know you two are best friends?

JIM: Yes, she does. If Frank does really well, she'll know it was me who told him about the test.

CLARE: And you might get into trouble.

JIM: I guess so, but it's not only that. She's my best teacher. I respect her – and I don't want to lose her respect.

CLARE: You'll probably need a recommendation from her too.

JIM: That's right. But when your best friend asks you for a favor, what can you do? Especially since he's going to a funeral and all.

NUMBER 3

TOM: Hey, George! Congratulations! I heard about your good news.

GEORGE: Thanks, Tom. Yeah, what luck, huh? I still can't believe it.

TOM: How much did you win?

GEORGE: Ten thousand dollars.

TOM: Boy, that's great! What are you going to do with the money?

GEORGE: You know, we're not sure. Our daughter, Emily, will be ready to go to college next year. She's very smart. We're very proud of her. She was accepted at one of the best universities in the country. She'd be the first in our family to go to college. But the cost is very high – more than $10,000 a year. We had planned to use the money for that.

TOM: That sounds like a good use for your lottery money to me.

GEORGE: Well, it's more difficult than that. You see, my mother just got some bad news. Her house needs some major repairs – new electrical wiring and plumbing, and the roof is a mess! It's going to cost a lot.

TOM: Can't she just move?

GEORGE: She's lived in that house for over fifty years, Tom. And now with Dad gone, it's all she has. She really doesn't want to move. She doesn't have the money for the repairs, so she needs to borrow it from me. The problem is we can't afford to send Emily to college and help Mom at the same time.

TOM: Boy, that's a hard decision to make. Your daughter's young and has her whole life before her. If she can go to a good university, she'll probably do very well in life. But your mother has always helped you.

GEORGE: Yeah, this is tough. She's my mother. How can I say no? At the same time, my daughter's future . . . ?

TOM: This is hard . . . really hard.

NUMBER 4

LARRY: Hey, Marta. How are you doing? How's the job search going?

MARTA: It's going well . . . too well, in fact! I've had two job offers, and I don't know which one to take.

LARRY: Which one do you want?

MARTA: Well, there are parts of both of them that I'm not sure I like. One of the jobs is being a sales representative for a computer company. I would travel between two and three weeks each month, mostly in Europe and Asia.

LARRY: That sounds really exciting. I'd like that.

MARTA: Yeah, I would too. I love the idea of traveling. But my salary would depend completely on sales. So if I don't sell anything, I don't get paid.

LARRY: Ouch! That's tough.

MARTA: On the other hand, if I'm successful, I could make a lot of money.

LARRY: Hmm. What's the other job like?

MARTA: It's also working with computers. But it would be in a very small office – only two other people. There would be no outside travel.

LARRY: So it would probably be kind of dull.

MARTA: Maybe. But it would be safe. The salary is pretty good – not great, but enough to live on. I wouldn't be able to travel, but I'd know that I'd always have a paycheck.

LARRY: Hmm . . . sounds like a tough choice to me.

Unit 17 Food for thought

Page 55, Listening Task 1: Food trends

Charts and graphs help explain information.

Listen. You will hear information about food. Number the graphs and charts (1 through 4). Then write the names of the foods on the lines. There is one extra graph or chart.

NUMBER 1

FIRST NEWSREADER: Although some people worry about how much fat they eat, others are not very concerned about their health. In fact, in many cases, people are eating more fatty foods now than they did in the past. For example, the consumption of beef has gone up fifteen percent since last year. People ate fifteen percent more hamburgers and steaks than they did a year ago.

Visits to steak houses increased twenty-four percent during the same period. People visited restaurants that serve steak almost twenty-five percent more often than they did last year. That's a lot of beef!

MAN: Honey, maybe we should turn off the TV till we're done eating.

WOMAN: This will be over soon.

NUMBER 2

SECOND NEWSREADER: Butter sales rose over ten percent in the last year. They had been falling ever since the early 1960s. People had been eating margarine instead of butter. Now people eat the same amount of butter that they did thirty-five to forty years ago. Despite these figures, about fifty percent of people surveyed said that they are very cautious about fat in their foods. It looks as if the other fifty percent don't care very much. They're saying, "If it tastes good, that's all that's important."

MAN: Could you pass the bread, please?

NUMBER 3

FIRST NEWSREADER: There's a lot of fat in some milk products. Sales of super-premium ice cream rose eight percent one year. Super-premium ice cream is ice cream with lots of fat in it. It's very expensive – much more expensive than regular ice cream – and very delicious. Eight percent more people thought its taste was worth the price. Other figures show that the growth of super-premium ice cream may be slowing down. The year after sales rose eight percent, they dropped again – from eleven percent of all ice cream sold to three percent. So that was an eight percent drop in popularity.

WOMAN: So what do you want for dessert?

MAN: Maybe we should skip dessert.

WOMAN: You're kidding.

NUMBER 4

SECOND NEWSREADER: Salsa – the hot sauce made from tomatoes, peppers, onions, and spices and served on Mexican food like tacos and tortilla chips.

Salsa has recently replaced ketchup in popularity. In the mid-1980s, salsa was a 300 million-dollar business. Ketchup made 600 million dollars in sales, twice as much as salsa. So there was a large gap between ketchup and salsa: 300 million dollars to 600 million dollars. Two years later, sales of ketchup had not gone up at all. Sales of salsa, however, went from 300 to 400 million dollars. Around 1990, more salsa than ketchup was sold. Salsa passed the 600-million mark, and ketchup stayed about the same. Salsa is expected to keep climbing – and soon reach over a billion dollars in sales – while ketchup may only reach 800 million (200 less).

[*Sound of TV being turned off*]

Page 56, Listening Task 2: What's on the menu?

Some foods are popular in some places and avoided in other places.

Listen. Do people in the places listed eat or avoid these foods? If people eat the food, check the place. If people don't (or didn't) eat it, put an X. Then write one extra fact about each food.

NUMBER 1: Milk and milk products

WOMAN: Foods that are "normal" to eat depend on where you live. They differ from place to place, from culture to culture. For example, North Americans and Europeans eat a lot of cheese and drink milk. In the United States, for example, most children drink milk every day. Some people in parts of Africa and China find this strange. Milk products just aren't part of their regular diet.

NUMBER 2: Beef

MAN: One important factor in determining what people eat is religion. Thousands of years ago, early Egyptians and Greeks didn't eat beef – even though today they do. Bulls were very important to their religion. In fact, many ancient people thought that bulls were gods. It was illegal to kill cattle. Today, in India, many Hindus don't eat beef: cattle are sacred. Throughout the world, many other religions have rules about what food should and shouldn't be eaten.

NUMBER 3: Horse

WOMAN: In some parts of the world, people don't eat horse meat, but it's a favorite among many people in northern European countries like Sweden and Finland. In fact, in Sweden, more horse meat than lamb is sold. France and Italy are two other places where horse is a popular food. In France, there are special stores that sell horse meat.

Why horse meat? It has to do with the people's history. More than a thousand years ago, people in northern Europe worshiped the horse. They thought it was a god. People sometimes ate horses in special religious ceremonies.

NUMBER 4: Fish

MAN: Fish is popular in many places, but like any other food, not everyone thinks about it in the same way. For some Africans and for some Native American groups in the southwestern United States, water is given by God, so everything that lives in water must be protected. Fish are God's creatures, so many people may not eat them. In parts of Southeast Asia, children may not eat fish. Parents think that fish will make their children sick. In most places, fish are dead when they're sold. However, in some countries, like Switzerland and Iraq, fish must be alive. Most people wouldn't buy a dead fish.

NUMBER 5: Chicken

WOMAN: Just as people feel differently about fish, attitudes about eating poultry – chicken and other birds – vary from place to place. Chicken is a very popular food in the United States and Canada. People enjoy it fried, baked, broiled, roasted – prepared in many different ways. But different cultures have different ideas about chicken. In the Philippines and in Vietnam, for example, most women don't eat chicken. They think it will make them sick. And people in many parts of the Middle East simply do not eat chicken. [pause]

What you eat really does have a lot to do with where you live.

Unit 18 We mean business.

Page 58, Listening Task 1: Billions sold!

Business Today is a radio program. Today they're talking about McDonald's restaurants.

Listen. What happened in each of these years? Write the missing information.

[Music]
HOST: And we're back with Business Today. Our next guest is Jane Taylor, author of McBusiness, The Building of a Hamburger Empire. Welcome, Jane.

JANE: Thank you for inviting me.

HOST: Your book, McBusiness, is of course a history of the world's largest restaurant chain, McDonald's.

JANE: That's right.

HOST: The name everyone associates with McDonald's is Ray Kroc.

JANE: Well, Ray Kroc was certainly a genius. There's no question about that. But I think we should start with two other people: the McDonald brothers, Mac and Dick. In 1940, the McDonald brothers opened their first hamburger stand in San Bernardino, California. It was just a regular drive-in hamburger stand. People would eat in their car. The waiters – called car hops – came out and took orders and then brought you your food. It was small and simple, but the brothers did all right. What's important is what they did eight years later. They totally changed their restaurant. They developed the idea of self-service. Customers came to a window to order. But what's really important is that they limited the menu. In 1948, they cut the menu to only seven items: hamburgers, cheeseburgers, potato chips, pie, coffee, milk, and soda. And everything was standard. The customers no longer said what they wanted on a hamburger. It came with ketchup, mustard, onion, and pickles.

HOST: And this was revolutionary?

JANE: Yes. For two reasons. Speed: the burgers were standard – fast food was born. And also price: the burgers cost only 15 cents. That was about half the regular price in those days.

HOST: I see.

JANE: Now, at first, people weren't sure. Business dropped by 80 percent. Teenagers stopped coming. But because the prices were low, families started coming.

HOST: And the business took off from there.

JANE: It sure did. That was in 1948. Just two years later, they put up a sign that said, "Over 1,000,000 sold."

HOST: One million hamburgers in just two years.

JANE: Yes. They had started opening more restaurants during that time.

HOST: So McDonald's was already successful when Ray Kroc arrived.

JANE: Oh, yes. The brothers had several franchises; that is, they had sold other people the right to open McDonald's restaurants. But they also had a problem. Mac and Dick didn't like to fly. They hated airplanes, so it was hard for them to expand their chain.

HOST: Really?

JANE: Yes. So, in 1954, Ray Kroc became the franchising agent. There were twelve McDonald's restaurants at the time.

HOST: Twelve.

JANE: Yes, but Ray was a brilliant businessman.

HOST: He increased the number of restaurants?

JANE: Remember, it took the McDonald brothers seven years to go from their first fast-food outlet to twelve. By 1959, just five years after their agreement with Ray Kroc, there were one hundred McDonald's restaurants. And only one year later, Kroc had doubled the number – to 200. The year after that, Kroc bought out the McDonald brothers' part of the company. McDonald's was an idea that America was ready for.

HOST: You know, it's interesting that the menu back then really wasn't so different from the menu today.

JANE: That, again, is something McDonald's has always done right. They've kept the menu small, which keeps prices down and makes fast food fast! There have been some changes, of course – for example, the Filet-O-Fish™ sandwich. Now, in those days . . . this is 1963 . . . members of the Catholic religion couldn't eat meat on Fridays. In Cincinnati, Ohio, there was a McDonald's restaurant in a part of the city where many Catholics lived. The restaurant needed something to sell on Fridays, so the Filet-O-Fish™ was born. This was important because it was an example of a local restaurant's meeting the needs of its own customers. Another important invention – from a business point of view – was the Egg McMuffin™. That came in 1973. The significance of the Egg McMuffin™ is that it created the market for fast-food breakfast. Before then, most fast-food restaurants opened in time for lunch. With the introduction of the breakfast, McDonald's added four hours to their business day.

HOST: It made the business day longer – a smart business move.

JANE: It was. And the company continues to make smart business moves . . . and to grow.

HOST: And it's the largest chain in the world.

JANE: The size of the company is truly amazing. McDonald's has over 18,000 restaurants . . . 18,000 restaurants in 90 countries around the world. This one company feeds twenty-five million people every day.

HOST: Twenty-five million people!

JANE: In the U.S., 20 percent of all restaurant meals – that's 1 in 5 – come from McDonald's. It's so large that 96 percent of all Americans will eat there at least once this year.

HOST: Ninety-six out of one hundred people! McDonald's is an amazing company. And I'm getting hungry. We'll be right back after this commercial message.

[*Music*]

Page 59, Listening Task 2: The richest man in America

Sam Walton was the richest person in America. His chain of WAL-MART stores has sold more products than any other group of stores in the world.

Listen. These are Sam Walton's ten rules for business. What does each rule mean? Check your answers. Then write the extra rule on the line at the bottom.

MAN: Number one: Commit to your business. You've got to believe in your own business and work. Work as hard as you can on it. If you love what you're doing and really believe in it, it will show. Then everyone will want to work hard. They'll catch the feeling. [*pause*]

MAN: Number two: Share your profits with everyone you work with. They're your partners . . . and partners work hard. If your company does well, the people who work there should, too. They should get a bonus of some kind. Owning stock in the company is a good way to share profits. [*pause*]

MAN: Number three: Motivate your workers. Just giving money isn't enough. Think of new ways to do things. Challenge them. Encourage people to compete – with one another as well as with other businesses. Competition brings out the best in people. [*pause*]

MAN: Number four: Communicate everything you can. Information is everything. The more you tell people, the more they'll know. Knowing things makes people care. And the more they care, why . . . they can do anything! [*pause*]

MAN: Number five: Appreciate everything people do. Now, profit sharing – giving everyone a piece of the company – is important, but there are some things that money just can't do. But a word of praise – telling people when they're doing well – that will do wonders. Everyone likes to know they're appreciated. [*pause*]

MAN: Number six: Celebrate your success. Don't be like a big, serious company with no emotions. When you're successful, celebrate! Why, Sam Walton did a hula dance on Wall Street. Have fun. Be original. And when you make mistakes or have failures, don't take those too seriously either. Learn to laugh at yourself. [*pause*]

MAN: Number seven: Listen to everyone in the company. You know, if you have a store, it's the clerks operating the cash registers who really talk to the customers. They know what the people who come to your store are thinking. The people in your company are a wonderful source of information. But you've got to really listen to them, or you're going to miss the message. [*pause*]

MAN: Number eight: Exceed your customers' expectations. It isn't enough to serve your customers. You need to do more than they expect. If there's a problem, apologize and fix it. Make absolutely sure they're satisfied. Do more than you need to, and your customers will keep on coming back. [*pause*]

MAN: Number nine: Control your expenses. Don't waste money. Every time you spend more than you need to – on a first-class airplane ticket or a first-class hotel room, by paying more for products than you need to – your customer has to pay more. If you keep your costs down, that means lower prices for your customer. That's what makes your business grow. [*pause*]

MAN: Number ten: Swim upstream – just like a fish swimming against the current of a river. Figure out the way everyone else is going and go in the opposite direction. If everyone is doing things one way, run your business the other way. [*pause*]

Now, it's not like these are the ten things you absolutely have to do. They're just ten things Sam Walton believed in. And if I could add one more . . . or maybe this is just a different way of saying, "Swim upstream." Anyway, if I could add one more, it would be "Break all the rules." That's right! Break all the rules. Be original.

Unit 19 Everything we know is wrong.

Page 61, Listening Task 1: Of course that's true . . . isn't it?

Read the statements. What do you think? Are they true or false? Check your answers. [*pause*]

Now listen. What's really true? Correct your answers. Then write one more piece of information about each item.

NUMBER 1
FIRST WOMAN: OK, here's a question for you. True or false? Thomas Edison invented the light bulb.
MAN: That's true.
FIRST WOMAN: No, it's not. Edison didn't invent the light bulb. Sir Joseph William Swan, an Englishman, did. That was in 1860, eighteen years before Edison's light bulb. Edison improved on the electric light, but he didn't invent it.
MAN: You're kidding.

NUMBER 2
MAN: OK. Here's a good one. Bulls hate the color red.

SECOND WOMAN: I think that's right.
MAN: Not really. You see, bulls are colorblind. All colors look the same to them.
SECOND WOMAN: But in bullfights – like in Spain or Mexico – the bullfighter has a red cape.
MAN: It says here that what the bulls hate is the motion. In a bullfight, the matador moves the cape. It's the movement that makes the bull run at the matador, not the color.

NUMBER 3

SECOND WOMAN: My turn. Um . . . Big Ben is a clock.
FIRST WOMAN: That has to be true.
SECOND WOMAN: Sorry, but it isn't. And Big Ben isn't the tower either. Big Ben is the bell – the bell in the clock tower.
FIRST WOMAN: I'm not sure I like this game.

NUMBER 4

FIRST WOMAN: The next question: Brown eggs are healthier than white eggs.
MAN: I've always heard that. But everything else I've heard has been wrong, so I'm going to say, "False."
FIRST WOMAN: You're right! A lot of people think so, but – no – color doesn't have anything to do with how healthy an egg is. There just isn't any difference.
MAN: What I can't believe is that I actually got a point.

NUMBER 5

MAN: Ready? The fastest animal in the world is the cheetah.
SECOND WOMAN: Yeah, everyone knows that.
MAN: Let's see . . . well, it looks like everyone is wrong. The cheetah is the fastest land animal, but it's not the fastest animal. The fastest animal is a bird: the Peregrine falcon. It's like a hawk. It can fly 350 kilometers an hour – that's over 200 miles an hour – when it's finding food. The cheetah is fast – about 100 kilometers (60 miles) an hour – but not as fast as the falcon.

NUMBER 6

SECOND WOMAN: OK, let's see. True or false? Hot water freezes faster than cold water.
FIRST WOMAN: That's got to be false.
SECOND WOMAN: Actually, this one is true. Hot water does freeze faster than cold water.
FIRST WOMAN: That's crazy. How could hot water freeze faster? It's got to cool off.
SECOND WOMAN: It says here that there's a reason. Hot water evaporates – bits of steam go

into the air. They carry heat with them. So hot water cools faster, and it freezes faster.
FIRST WOMAN: That's hard to believe.
SECOND WOMAN: Try it. They say it's true.
FIRST WOMAN: Amazing!

NUMBER 7

FIRST WOMAN: Here's the next question: Mosquitoes are more dangerous than tigers.
MAN: Again, I'm going to guess against common sense. I'll say, "True."
FIRST WOMAN: You're right. Tigers kill only about a hundred people a year. Mosquitoes kill more than a million and a half people every year. That's because they carry diseases like malaria. Mosquitoes are the most dangerous animals on earth.
MAN: Still, would you rather go camping in a place with mosquitoes or with tigers?
FIRST WOMAN: Neither, thanks.

NUMBER 8

MAN: This is a literature question. Frankenstein, the monster, was invented by a crazy doctor.
SECOND WOMAN: Yeah. I saw the movie.
MAN: I guess the movie was wrong. There are two mistakes here. First of all, in Mary Shelley's book, Frankenstein is not the name of the monster. Frankenstein is the inventor: Baron von Frankenstein. And Frankenstein wasn't a doctor. He was a student. He studied science and math.
SECOND WOMAN: This game is a monster.

Page 62, Listening Task 2: The flat earth

Most people know the earth is round. However, some say it's flat.

Listen. A "flat earther" is trying to prove the earth is flat. Try the experiments he suggests. Circle your answers.

WOMAN: Dr. Teirson, you're a member of your university's Flat Earth Group.
DR. TEIRSON: That is correct.
WOMAN: And you really believe the earth is flat?
DR. TEIRSON: Of course.
WOMAN: Isn't that silly, doctor? Everyone knows the earth is round.
DR. TEIRSON: Most people think so. But the earth is flat. Let me prove it to you. Why do you think the earth is round?
WOMAN: Well, look at the stars. They look as if they move – but we know they don't. The earth is moving.

DR. TEIRSON: Of course it is. But the earth moves slowly. Why does it move so slowly? Because we're on the back of a giant turtle. So of course it's slow.

WOMAN: A giant turtle?

DR. TEIRSON: It's easy to prove. Put your ear on the table. That's right. Put your ear right on the table. Listen carefully. Do you hear the sound? It's like a low "grrrrrr." That's the turtle. It couldn't be cars driving by or other things moving. The sound is too even.

WOMAN: I'm not sure what to say, but let's move on. [*pause*] You say the earth is only about ten kilometers – six miles – thick. Yet earthquakes come from the center of the earth. How do you explain that?

DR. TEIRSON: Well, the earth is sitting on the back of giant elephants. The elephants, of course, are on top of the turtle. Sometimes the elephants just can't hold the weight. Try this experiment: Pick up something heavy . . . anything. A dictionary would be good, even a textbook. Hold out your right hand, fingers up. Put the book on the tops of your fingers. Try to hold it without moving. . . . Hold it very still. You can't! No one can hold an object still for very long. And your book isn't even that heavy. The earth is heavy, though! So the elephants move. That's why we have earthquakes: the elephants move, and then the earth moves. [*pause*]

WOMAN: Let's try something else. You say the earth is flat. If I look across a large lake, I can't see the other side.

DR. TEIRSON: Of course not. That's because of reflection. Try this. We'll use this desk as an example. Get out of your chair, kneel down, and put your face next to the desk. Now move your eyes along the desk.

WOMAN: Put my eyes at the level of the desk?

DR. TEIRSON: Right. Put the middle of your eyes at the edge of your desk.

WOMAN: OK. I'm doing that.

DR. TEIRSON: Can you see the full top of the desk?

WOMAN: Actually, no. It's kind of . . . well, you can see *some* of it.

DR. TEIRSON: Right, but it's distorted. The view isn't clear at all.

WOMAN: Yeah.

DR. TEIRSON: The same holds true for lakes . . . and oceans. Large, flat areas look distorted. You can't see everything. [*pause*]

WOMAN: Doctor, that's interesting, but let's be serious. There are hundreds of photos from space that show the earth is round.

DR. TEIRSON: Those photos? Don't trust them. They don't prove anything. Try this: Look at a spot in the front of this room. Focus on that spot. As you can see, the middle area is very clear.

WOMAN: Yes.

DR. TEIRSON: Now, don't move your eyes. Just notice everything you see. Don't move your eyes, but notice the edges of what you can see. The picture isn't very clear, but basically you see a circle on the outside. Am I right?

WOMAN: Yes, but . . . [*pause*] Doctor, you've given some very interesting answers, but I have to ask: Do you honestly think the world is flat, or is this a joke?

DR. TEIRSON: Do you really need to ask that?

WOMAN: Professor Teirson, you're a doctor, right? You have a Ph.D.

DR. TEIRSON: Yes.

WOMAN: May I ask what your Ph.D. is in?

DR. TEIRSON: Eighth-century science. Why do you ask?

Now work with a partner. Do you think the flat earther *really* believes the earth is flat? Why?

Unit 20 Poetry

Page 64, Listening Task 1: Four poems

Listen to these poems.

WOMAN: The Boy from Baghdad
There once was a boy from Baghdad,
A curious sort of a lad.
He said, "I will see
if the sting has a bee."
And soon he found out that it had. [*pause*]

MAN: Rivers
Rivers,
beautiful, clear
gurgling, rushing, chasing
swift or slow they're fun to play in
creeks, streams. [*pause*]

WOMAN: Across the calm path
Branches snake, telling people,
"Do not come in here." [*pause*]

MAN: White
White is
a soft breeze

or a snowflake on my nose.
White is
a wedding
a shower of love.
White is
soft, not too rough,
white is a beautiful color. [*pause*]

Now listen to someone describing three of the poems. Write the numbers (1. quintet, 2. limerick, 3. fugue) in the boxes above. Then write one more thing about each poem.

NUMBER 1: A quintet

MAN: This is called a quintet, which means "something with five parts." That is, this poem has five lines. In this poem, the title is also the first line. It has two syllables, or beats. Listen: Rivers.
[*Tones*]
The next line has four syllables: beautiful, clear.
[*Tones*]
Then come lines with six and eight syllables.
[*Tones*]
Finally, the poem ends with a line of two syllables.
[*Tones*]
These poems can be about anything. The important thing is to follow the number of syllables in each line: 2, 4, 6, 8, then 2 again. This one is about nature.

NUMBER 2: A limerick

MAN: This is a limerick. A limerick is a humorous poem that has a very special rhyme. The first, second, and fifth lines must rhyme, or sound the same. The third and fourth lines also rhyme. Usually, these poems also begin with "There once was . . . ." They tell a story, usually about something funny or silly that happens to the person in the poem. In this one, an inquisitive boy – someone who is curious – tries to find out why things happen. He gets hurt instead.

NUMBER 3: A fugue

MAN: This poem is a fugue. That means it uses the same word over and over again. That word is the theme of the poem. Just like in music, when the theme is repeated or changed throughout a piece, in poetry the use of a word changes. In this poem, one word is defined in many ways. The poet gives us different ways of looking at "white."

Now listen and answer the question.

MAN: Which poem do you like the best? Why?

Page 65, Listening Task 2: Talking blues

The words in blues songs are one form of African-American poetry. There are many styles of blues. One style is called "talking blues."

Read the words. [*pause*]

Now listen. Follow the instructions.

WOMAN: You're going to write a talking blues poem/song. The blues talk about everyday life. Often, the stories are sad, but yours can be whatever you want it to be.
MAN: My talking blues
Woke up this morning
Feeling so . . .
WOMAN: How were you feeling when you woke up? How did you feel? Write an adjective – a feeling – on the line. Write an adjective that describes your feeling. When I woke up this morning, I was feeling so . . . [*pause*]

MAN: Yes, I woke up this morning
I was feeling so . . .
WOMAN: This part is typical of the blues. The first line is quite long. Then that line gets repeated. You say it again, so write the same word you wrote in the first space. Write the same word – the word that describes your feeling. [*pause*]

MAN: Went . . .
Started feeling so . . .
WOMAN: You were feeling so . . . so strongly that you went someplace. Where did you go? Write a place. It can be a specific place, like the name of a restaurant or a friend's house or even a different town. Or it can be any other kind of place. Where did you go? Write the place. [*pause*]

WOMAN: Then your feeling changed. How did you start to feel? Write it on the line. How did you feel? Write your emotion. [*pause*]

MAN: I saw somebody walking.
I had to say . . .
WOMAN: Now, you saw someone. Who? Who was it? Imagine who you saw. What did you say to this person? [*pause*]

MAN: Well, I saw somebody walking.
I just had to say . . .

WOMAN: What did you say? Write it again.
  [*pause*]

MAN: And you know that somebody
  Acted . . .
WOMAN: How did the person act? Was it warm?
  Was it cold? Was it love? Was it hate? How did
  the person act? [*pause*]

WOMAN: How are you feeling? Happy? Sad?
MAN: Are you feeling sad, child? Well, you've got
  the blues.

Now listen again. Read along with the tape.

MAN: Woke up this morning
  Feeling so . . . .
  Yes, I woke up this morning
  I was feeling so . . . .
  Went . . . ,
  Started feeling so . . . .
  I saw somebody walking,
  I had to say . . . .
  Well, I saw somebody walking,
  I just had to say . . . .
  And you know that somebody
  Acted . . . .

Work with a partner. Read your "talking blues."
Then listen to your partner's poem.

A Listening and Speaking Game

Activation is a review game. The questions and tasks are designed to encourage students to use the forms, functions, and topics they've heard throughout *Active Listening*.

1. Divide the class into groups of four.
T: *Work in groups of four.*

2. Hold your book so that students can see the game on pages 66 and 67. T: *Each group uses one book. Open the book to pages 66 and 67. Put the book on the table.*

3. T: *Each person needs a place marker – a coin, an eraser, or any small object. Put the marker on the "Start here" square.*

4. Point to the "How many spaces?" box on page 67. T: *One person, close your eyes. Touch the "How many spaces?" box with a pencil.*

5. T: *Move that many spaces. Read the sentence or sentences. Answer with at least three things.*

6. T: *Now each partner asks one question about what the first player said.*

7. T: *Continue playing. Take turns.*

8. Allow adequate time for students to play.

NOTES

• Although *Activation* reviews language from the entire syllabus, you may wish to have students play it before they have finished the book.

• With activities that have several steps, sometimes giving instructions can be difficult, particularly in large classes. It is usually better to demonstrate. Divide the class into groups. Direct one group through the game as one member from each of the other groups watches. Those members then return to their own groups and teach the other players what to do.

• Many students often enjoy playing the game more than once. If they change partners each time they play, the information will remain new.

• As students play, encourage partners to ask questions about each other's answers. The questions can be either to clarify things not understood or to expand on interesting information.

• If there is a question someone doesn't want to answer, allow any other player to ask a different question.

• *Activation* is best used as a cooperative game. It isn't necessary to give points. However, if you feel your students need the extra support of competition, you can give one point for each sentence a student says while answering each item.

• Because this is a fluency game, corrections are usually not appropriate while the students play.

Could you repeat that?

Pardon?

I'm sorry?

Excuse me?

Could you play the tape again?

How do you say _____ in English?

How do you spell _____?

Once more, please?

I don't understand.

I don't know.

ACTIVITY SHEET *It's a match.*

	Your answer	*Who agrees?*

1. What's your favorite music to relax to?

2. What's your favorite dance music?

3. Who's your favorite singer?

4. What's your favorite sport to watch?

5. What's your favorite sport to play?

6. What's your favorite food?

7. Who's your favorite movie star?

8. What's a very difficult word in English to pronounce?

9. What's your favorite English expression or word?

10. If you could have any job in the world, what would it be?

What's your experience?

a baby	a bakery	a summer day
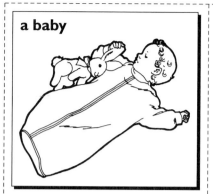		

early morning in the country	a winter day	early morning in the city

your home	the beach	a great restaurant

your idea:	your idea:	your idea:

You are **A**. Work with a partner. Read your sentences.
Listen to your partner. Write the missing words. Then answer these questions:
• What magazine reported pirate attacks?
• Where are pirate attacks taking place?
• What do some pirates look like?

Pirates Today

A: When people talk about pirates, they usually mean from several hundred years ago.

B: But there are still _____ _____. And they are _____.

A: *Yachting World,* a magazine for people who like boats, reported on recent pirate activity.

B: It said that there has been an _____ in pirate _____.

A: Most attacks have taken place in the South China Sea, off the east coast of Africa, and off the northeast coast of South America.

B: Most pirates carry _____, and some people have been _____.

A: Pirates in some areas are disguised as government officials.

B: Boat _____ should be very _____ when _____ boats approach them.

You are **B**. Work with a partner. Read your sentences.
Listen to your partner. Write the missing words. Then answer these questions:
• What magazine reported pirate attacks?
• Where are pirate attacks taking place?
• What do some pirates look like?

Pirates Today

A: When people talk about _____, they usually mean from several _____ years ago.

B: But there are still pirates today. And they are dangerous.

A: *Yachting* _____, a _____ for people who like boats, _____ on recent pirate activity.

B: It said that there has been an increase in pirate attacks.

A: Most attacks have taken place in the _____ _____ Sea, off the east coast of _____, and off the northeast coast of _____ _____.

B: Most pirates carry guns, and some people have been killed.

A: Pirates in some areas are disguised as _____ _____.

B: Boat owners should be very careful when government boats approach them.

T47

Name	Age	When did they meet?	How did they meet?
1.			
2.			
3.			
4.			
5.			

Take care of yourself.

1. If you have a cold, you should _____.

2. If you have a headache, _____.

3. If you have a toothache, _____.

4. If your legs hurt, _____.

5. If you cut your hand, _____.

6. If you have a sore back, _____.

7. If you burn your hand, _____.

8. If you feel too much stress, _____.

9. If your eyes hurt, _____.

10. If you _____, _____.

Your points: [   ]

running shoes 	**this school** 	**the teacher of this class** 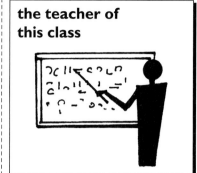
a pen 	**a new car** 	**vitamins** 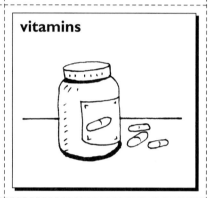
a soft drink 	**broccoli** 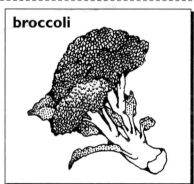	**a hamburger** 
a diamond necklace 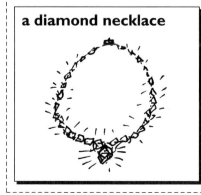	**this book** 	**a flamingo** 

Superstition Concentration

If you break a mirror,	If you stand a broom upside-down behind a door,	so they will have good luck.	you will have 7 years' bad luck.
Throw salt over your left shoulder	If you step on a crack on the sidewalk,	to keep away bad luck.	you will have good luck.
If you walk under a ladder,	When the sky is red at night,	tomorrow's weather will be good.	you will have bad luck.
If you find a penny and pick it up,	Throw rice at the couple after their wedding ceremony	you will break your mother's back.	your visitors will go away.

2. I'm listening.

10. Go away.

3. No.

11. I'm confused.

4. Say that again.

12. Come here.

5. I don't understand.

13. I really like this.

6. I don't know.

14. How tall is it?

7. I don't like this.

15. That person is crazy.

8. Who, me?

16. How much does it cost?

9. I'm bored.

17. I love you.

E

E

D

D

C

C

B

B

A

A

A SHEET

B SHEET

a man	a woman	a wizard or witch

gold	a magic mirror	strange music
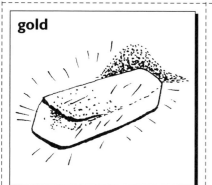		

a forest	a mountain	a storm
		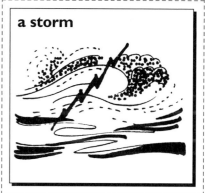

a white horse	a dragon	a castle
		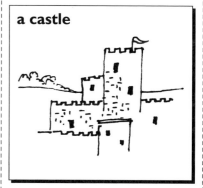

ACTIVITY SHEET

A. Find someone who . . .

Find someone who . . .

names

. . . would like to take an English course this summer.

. . . likes to speak English but doesn't like to write it.

. . . would like to study English on a ship.

. . . prefers learning British English.

. . . would prefer a roommate from his/her own country.

. . . would like a roommate from another country.

. . . would like to live alone.

. . . wishes English classes were longer.

. . . uses movies to study English.

. . . would like to study English in a smaller class.

ACTIVITY SHEET

B. Roleplay

A You really like nature. You go hiking every weekend. You like small classes because you think you can get more help from the teacher. You want to work for an international airline.

C You love to meet people from other countries. You would like to study in a place where there are lots of different nationalities. You would also like to take something besides English at the school, maybe a psychology class.

B You love cities because they have museums and art galleries. You want to enter an American university after you study English. You want to study business. You want to meet people from as many countries as you can.

D You want to have a vacation in an English-speaking country. You want to learn English, but you also want to have time for recreation. You just finished university, and you start a job in four months.

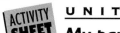

My partner's personality

1. If you play a game, do you "just have to" win? ☐ yes ☐ no

    extra information: _____

2. When you get angry, do you show it to other people? ☐ yes ☐ no

    extra information: _____

3. Is your room neat? ☐ yes ☐ no

    extra information: _____

4. How many really close friends do you have? ☐ 1 ☐ 2–4 ☐ 5 or more

    extra information: _____

5. Would you rather go hiking or to an art museum? ☐ hiking ☐ art museum

    extra information: _____

6. Would you rather read a new book or read a favorite book again? ☐ new ☐ favorite

    extra information: _____

7. Are you often late? ☐ yes ☐ no

    extra information: _____

8. Do you like to be the leader of your group? ☐ yes ☐ no

    extra information: _____

9. Would you rather work in an office or outdoors? ☐ office ☐ outdoors

    extra information: _____

10. Can you make decisions quickly? ☐ yes ☐ no

    extra information: _____

Topics	Examples	Points			
		Partner 1	Partner 2	Partner 3	Partner 4
Famous paintings and sculptures	*Mona Lisa, Venus de Milo*				
Names of artists	Picasso, van Gogh				
Types of art	oil painting, film				
Art that is typical of their country (or countries)	(answers will vary)				
Places in your area to see art	a museum, a bank lobby				

1. I think the world _____

2. The thing that makes me _____

3. The most important thing I could _____

4. I would like to _____

5. If I could, I would _____

6. The hardest _____

1. What does the world need more of? What don't we have enough of? Write something you would like to see more of in the world today. It can be something important or something not so important.

3. What do you want to do with your life? What's the best or most important thing you could do? It might be a job, or it might be an action you could take.

5. What would you like to change about yourself? It can be something small, or it can be something big. If you could, what would you like to change about yourself?

1. I think the world _____

2. The thing that makes me _____

3. The most important thing I could _____

4. I would like to _____

5. If I could, I would _____

6. The hardest _____

2. What makes you really angry? You see this in the city or on TV, and you get angry right away.

4. What would you ask if you could ask the leader of this country any question – just one question?

6. What's the most difficult decision you've ever had to make? Maybe it was about a school. Maybe it was about a friend.

The "Big-Mac™ Index" is used to compare different countries' money. It was invented by *The Economist*, a _____ magazine. The idea is simple: A Big Mac™ sandwich is the _____ anywhere in the world. It should cost about the same, too. If it doesn't, it means the local money's value is _____ _____ or too low. The "Big-Mac™ Index" is a way to _____ long-term exchange rates. If a Big Mac™ is too _____, the value of that country's money will probably drop soon.

A SHEET

		country	cost (U.S. dollars)
Canada	$2.10		
France	$3.41		
Japan	$2.70	U.S.A.	$2.36
Malaysia	$1.51		
Thailand	$1.90		

The "Big-Mac™ Index" is used to compare different countries' _____. It was invented by *The Economist*, a British magazine. The idea is simple: A Big Mac™ sandwich is the same anywhere in the world. It should _____ about the same, too. If it doesn't, it means the local money's value is too high or _____ _____. The "Big-Mac™ Index" is a way to predict long-term exchange _____. If a Big Mac™ is too expensive, the value of that country's money will probably _____ soon.

B SHEET

		country	cost (U.S. dollars)
Australia	$1.97		
Germany	$3.22		
Hong Kong	$1.28	U.S.A.	$2.36
Korea	$2.95		
Taiwan	$2.39		

Questions

1. **What two countries are mentioned?**

(Answer: Iceland and Greenland)

2. **What color is most of Greenland?**

(Answer: white – from the ice)

3. **How much of Iceland is covered with ice?**

(Answer: 13 percent)

4. **How much of Greenland is covered with ice?**

(Answer: 95 percent)

5. **Who gave the countries their names?**

(Answer: Vikings)

6. **Why did they give the countries those names?**

(Answer: to confuse people)

A. Newspaper poem

for peace Me too.

independence
Me too.

Work hard Me too?

New government vows self-control Not me.

President hopeful Me too!

B. A poem of your own

POETRY TYPES

Limerick
(*There once was a boy . . .*)
- humorous
- five lines
- rhyme scheme: a-a-b-b-a
- often begin: *There once was a ____ from ____*

Haiku
(This was not explained on tape, but *Across the calm path* . . . is a haiku.)
- three lines
- syllable count: 5-7-5
- present tense
- often mention nature or seasons

Quintet
(*Rivers, . . .*)
- five lines
- syllable count: 2-4-6-8-2
- Any topic is OK. The important thing is the rhythm.

Fugue
(*White is . . .*)
- One word is the theme.
- That word is used many times.
- That word is used or defined in different ways.